Sea Power 2000

Sea

▲
Sleeker than the LAMPS I Seasprite, the SH-60B Seahawk
LAMPS III belies her extra size.
It is shown above the frigate
Crommelin (FFG-37) which has
the modified raked after end
which gives an extra three
metres of flightpad. Class serials
FFG-7 to 35 (less FFG-8) will
retain their original LAMPS I
capability. (United Technologies
Sikorsky Aircraft)

Power 2000

BERNARD IRELAND

ARMS AND
ARMOUR

First published in Great Britain in 1990 by Arms and Armour Press, Artillery House, Artillery Row, London SW1P 1RT.

Distributed in the USA by Sterling Publishing Co. Inc., 387 Park Avenue South, New York, NY 10016–8810.

Distributed in Australia by Capricorn Link (Australia) Pty. Ltd, P.O. Box 665, Lane Cove, New South Wales 2066, Australia.

British Library Cataloguing in Publication Data
Ireland, Bernard
Sea power 2000.
1. Warships
I. Title
623.8'25
ISBN 0-85368-979-2

Designed and edited by DAG Publications Ltd. Designed by David Gibbons; edited by Michael Boxall; layout by Anthony A. Evans; typeset by Typesetters (Birmingham) Ltd, Warley; camerawork by M&E Reproductions, North Fambridge, Essex; printed and bound in Great Britain by The Bath Press, Avon.

▶
Despite the wider use of sub-surface launched anti-ship missiles, the heavyweight torpedo will be around for the foreseeable future. Here, the frigate *Lowestoft* is expended as a target during Spearfish development trials. The convulsive whip caused by the under-keel explosion breaks the target's back. (Marconi Underwater Systems)

CONTENTS

INTRODUCTION

Few students of naval affairs will not be familiar with a certain artist's impression, painted shortly after the First World War. It depicts a line of capital ships steaming imperiously, but, by implication, blindly and to ultimate destruction, through swirling clouds of poison gas, dropped by a handful of frail biplanes circling, unmolested, above. Mature technology is shown to be powerless against the latest high-tech combination.

With the benefit of hindsight we can look at such portrayals with amusement, but there is certainly a lesson to be learned in that it is unsound to portray the mortal threat of the near future in terms of today's state-of-the-art technology. Furthermore, despite the occasional revolutionary breakthrough, periods of protracted peace produce, on the whole, slow and measured evolution. Charged, therefore, with making an assessment of the shape of Seapower in the year 2000, just a decade ahead, the Author has found it prudent to temper more optimistic evaluations by looking back occasionally by a similar space of time. What he has attempted to do, therefore, is first to review the current situation in those areas most significant to any definition of 'Seapower'. Secondly, he has identified lines of current development most likely to affect those areas and, lastly, has highlighted possible points at which breakthroughs could occur. As in the case of the poison gas, however, he is aware that he who would be a prophet runs a considerable risk of developing clay feet!

Even the first objective was not simple. During the period of writing there has been considerable technological change, East–West rapprochement and a recovery from a decade of general recession. Each was a major factor in the progress of military projects, which could be summarily abandoned, not on grounds of impracticability, but because of new techniques or a change in the political scene. For instance, since the announcement of Canada's bold intention to acquire up to a dozen nuclear attack submarines, there has been a general election, an overall consequent belt-tightening, and a cancelled project. A change of administration in the United States has precipitated a similar spate of cancellations and deferments by a leadership concerned with budget deficits. Among the casualties look to be the revolutionary Tilt-Rotor V-22 Osprey, the long-term future of the airship and the 600-ship 'Reaganavy'. It is also a fact that, when cuts are to be made, unproven technologies are the first to go.

Despite such major changes, however, the text and assessment have not been altered because the original military case was sound, the need still exists and there is an excellent chance that, during the period under consideration, political rethink will take place. Evaluation of the current scene and trends for the near future demand up-to-the-minute data. Technical journals provide the greater part of this and the Author would like to acknowledge their value, together with that of the standard reference works, in the lists of references attached to each chapter.

The Author would like to thank also a wide spectrum of organizations, both official and commercial, who have supplied data and assistance along the way. Where they have provided illustrations in the text, these are credited. Lastly, as ever, he would again record his indebtedness to his wife in her roles of typist, secretary, researcher and supporter.

Bernard Ireland
Fareham, 1989

Fixed Wing

With its unique blend of potency and versatility, the American nuclear-propelled aircraft carrier (CVN) represents, today, the quintessence of seapower. It can respond as appropriately to a civil disaster as to total nuclear war. The US Navy employs a forward strategy, including power projection, and requires its ships to be capable of operations world-wide. Because of a lack of suitable land bases for associated air power, the carrier enjoyed an early prominence in American Pacific fleet plans of the inter-war years. Subsequent events bore out the correctness of this approach and, as little but political geography has changed, a powerful carrier force still attracts esteem and funding.

Because carrier aircraft are expected to meet an adversary's shore-based aircraft on equal terms, it is axiomatic that they should have comparable performance. This dictates large aircraft which, in turn, demand large decks. All arguments, and they surface frequently, for reversion to smaller and more numerous carriers, fall at the same hurdle – smaller ships are simply insufficiently capable. Big decks, unfortunately, mean big price tags, but, while the 600-ship 'Reaganavy' has been shelved on economy grounds, the target of fifteen carrier battle groups still holds. This number depends currently on the retention of the *Midway* (CV41) and *Coral Sea* (CV43) to a considerable age. The earlier hull has already seen 44 years afloat, while successive improvements have added so much extra displacement and draught that bulging was attempted to reduce wetness. That it was not successful through inducing heavy rolling can only hasten a decision on retirement.

There exists a five-year gap between the completion of CVN73 (*Washington*) in December 1991 and that of the next hull, CVN74 (*Stinnis*) in 1996.[1] Assuming the retirement of the *Coral Sea*s, CVN74 will be able to replace the *Forrestal* (CV59), the first of the supercarriers and then 41 years of age, and still maintain the fifteen-deck total. Of crucial importance is the Service Life Extension Program (SLEP), whereby each carrier is given a three-year upgrading to extend her useful career by 10–15 years. SLEP began as a rolling programme of about 28 months per ship, but this proved over-ambitious, so that hulls are already some 30 years old before being SLEP-ed, and this average age is increasing. American carriers are built to a basically standard design, which can accommodate about 86 aircraft, an impressive number whose strength is somewhat reduced by the range of types that this covers.

▶ Maritime Patrol Aircraft are fitted with comprehensive ESM suites to detect, locate, identify and track electronic transmissions from submarines, or surface ships. As important is surveillance, or electronic intelligence (ELINT), yielding data for the design of the next generation of countermeasures. The picture shows the ESM outfit of the Atlantique 2 (ATL2). (Thomson – CSF (Aerospace Group))

◄ The variable-geometry F-14 Tomcat has provided a formidable carrier fighter component since 1972. This pre-production model of the F-14D heralds a new variant with improved avionics and weapons systems, together with more powerful General Electric F-110-400 engines. (Grumman Corporation)

A typical air wing includes twenty F-14 Tomcats (all-weather fighters, able to undertake photo-reconnaissance), eighteen F/A-18 Hornets (multi-role fighters), twenty A-6E Intruders (all-weather attack aircraft, to be superseded by the A-12 Advanced Tactical Aircraft in the mid-nineties), ten S-3A Vikings (ASW aircraft), five EA-6B Prowlers (electronics warfare aircraft), five E-2C Hawkeyes (AEW/air control aircraft) and eight SH-3D Sea Kings (ASW helicopters, soon to be superseded).[2] Should the mission demand it, the attack element may be eroded further by the embarkation of KA-6D tanker variants of the Intruder, while a further indispensable link between ship and shore is the C-3A Greyhound carrier-on-board delivery (COD) logistics aircraft.

Until 1972, larger decks had been categorized 'attack carriers' (CVA), but, in that year, the last of the warbuilt *Essex* class that had been modified as dedicated ASW carriers (CVS) made a final deployment in the role.[3] This necessitated a large carrier assuming responsibility for the aerial element of the AS protection of her group. For general ASW operations a new class of austere single-screw, light carriers was, therefore, proposed, to be termed Sea Control Ships (SCS). Though this course appeared reasonable, it was unfortunate for the navy that, despite its big carriers losing some 20 per cent of their strike capacity by 1978 in the interests of ASW, Congress saw fit to veto the SCS, following intense lobbying that ignored the obviously complementary role for the smaller ship, portraying it instead as a 'less-capable' and 'non-nuclear' threat to the continued development of the CVN. This gap in general-purpose ASW has now

existed for a decade and a half, and its continued existence can only diminish the validity of the concept of vital transatlantic re-supply convoys being run in the event of an extended conventional war on European soil.

The scale of initial ship movement is considerable. NATO plans call for 300,000 men and their equipment, together with 100 air squadrons, to be shipped over the Atlantic within 30 days of the decision to reinforce Europe. At the same time, 100,000 men, 25,000 tons of *matériel* and 20,000 vehicles must be moved from the United Kingdom to the European mainland. In addition to airlift, this calls for 400 transatlantic shiploads for each of the first two months, followed by a further 400 shiploads of re-supply *matériel*.[4]

Remorseless increases in capital and running costs of CVs guarantees a periodic call for smaller and cheaper decks, available in large numbers. The most thorough review,[5] conducted in the seventies, narrowed the choices down from 'limitless' to just four:

(a) A *Nimitz*-type CV; 90,000 tons and 1,100 feet (335m) in length. Able to undertake simultaneous launch/recovery with a maximum four catapults;

(b) A *Midway*-sized CVV; 40,000–60,000 tons and 900 feet (274m). Able to undertake simultaneous launch/recovery of conventional aircraft;

(c) A new-style VSS; 20,000–35,000 tons and 800 feet (244m). Able to undertake simultaneous launch/recovery of VSTOL aircraft, and

(d) VSTOL-only ships, of less than 20,000 tons and capable of safe operation of VSTOL aircraft with effective combat loads.

Comparing (a) and (b) it was noted that useful volume

varies as the cube of the dimensions, whereas size and wetted area vary only as the square; increasing a flightdeck to the scale of that of the *Nimitz* thus created a larger bonus in terms of aircraft stowed. Larger hulls are more easily driven and, having a more moderate motion, can operate effectively in a wider range of sea states. Accident rates aboard the larger have proved to be only half that of the smaller, an important consideration for forward deployments, where replenishment could prove difficult. Survivability is also directly related to size.

A hypothetical 60,000-ton CVV with a 912-foot (278-metre) flightdeck was calculated to be able to support an air wing of 48–54 aircraft, assuming no reduction in the quality of aircraft in either the attack (2D) or attack/ASW (3D) configurations. Flightdeck length was that required by an F-14; by substituting the F-18 (and surrendering some capacity in long-range interception), the ship could be reduced to 813 feet (*c.*248 metres) and displace only 35,000–40,000 tons. As volume decreases rapidly with length, however, only 30 aircraft could then be stowed, a number considered inadequate for an efficient mix. A CVV of this size would, therefore, have to be configured either for a general-purpose wing of 28 aircraft, or an ASW wing

of 30 aircraft. For supporters of an AS carrier, the latter is interesting in comprising a dozen S-3s in either AS or tanker versions, eight SH-3D (or equivalent) helicopters, four E-2Cs and a flight of six F-18s for fighter cover or limited attack.

Everything below 40,000 tons was considered insufficient to support other than VSTOL, while a 20,000-tonner of some 650 feet (198m) – approximating to a British *Invincible* – was considered the smallest able to operate a 'useful' number of aircraft. An interesting finding was that, by doubling displacement from 20,000 to 40,000 tons, the air wing nearly quadrupled, from eight to thirty aircraft. Such a ship still has neither aircraft nor armament to defend herself adequately, and requires dedicated escorts.

The conclusion of the review, still valid, was essentially that a '2D' all-attack configured CVV would offer a better strike capacity than a '3D' air wing if required.

More decks would be required (an advantage in itself, both for peacetime activities and as being more difficult to destroy by pre-emptive warfare) but these could be built to keener prices. This was because eight yards could compete for CVV orders whereas only one yard could build a CVN. Nevertheless, the nuclear propulsion/big-deck lobbies won the day and limited

▶
The giant nuclear-propelled carrier, typified by this trials picture of the USS *Theodore Roosevelt* (CVN71) will, for the foreseeable future, represent the ultimate expression of offensive seapower. Any arguments for the construction of smaller and cheaper decks were extinguished with the knowledge that the Soviets were also building large carriers. (Newport News Shipbuilding)

numbers of CVNs continue to be built. In view of the fact that the Soviets have commenced construction of a carrier of about 75,000 tons, some 10,000 tons larger than the current *Tbilisis*, this may well have been the wisest policy, yet, at the same time, may have contributed in turn to the Soviet decision to build.[6]

Four *Kiev*s were completed at 3–4-yearly intervals from 1975 and, at some 40,000-ton displacement, would lie at the low end of the American scale, except that the Soviets have never considered them as 'carriers', but as 'Large Anti-submarine Cruisers'. This, quite accurate, categorization shows again how misleading it is to apply Western stereotypes to Soviet vessels. The *Kiev*s' role appears to be to act as the core of a group exercising AS control at strategic locations; for this, their mainly helicopter air wing is consistent. Both function and location, however, are likely to be briskly contested, accounting for the VSTOL strike element and the anti-surface ship armament, centred on eight 300-mile SS-N-12 (Sandbox) missiles with, it is reported, sixteen reloads.[7] As some of a *Kiev*'s helicopters are fitted for the purposes of targeting and mid-course correction, the missiles' full range can be utilized.

Coupled with a *Kirov* or a *Slava*, a *Kiev* AS battle group would prove a difficult problem for a surface force and the planned American counter would probably be a carrier battlegroup (CVBG) co-ordinated with operations by land-based B-52s, each armed with eight or more Tomahawk cruise missiles.

American carrier construction programmes would have been little influenced by the *Kiev*s, but, immediately following the 1982 launch of the last, *Baku*, the building dock (the only one in the Soviet Union suitable for the task) was extended and the first section of a larger ship laid down.[8] This vessel, the estimated 65,000-ton *Tbilisi*, would seem to be the Soviets' first true carrier although, at the time of her working-up in the Black Sea during 1989, her official category remained unannounced. She has an unencumbered through deck, American in plan, with two deck-edge elevators. A ski-jump forward supports VSTOL operations, but, while there could be arrestors, no catapult seems to have been fitted initially.

For some years a test site in the Crimea has been used to evaluate naval aircraft. Among these is believed to be a multi-mission STOL variant of the Su-27 ('Flanker') fighter and a new strike aircraft, possibly based on the Su-24 ('Fencer').[9] If, as is thought, about two-thirds of a *Tbilisi*'s 65–75 aircraft will be CTOL, a catapult will certainly be required, as deck size is not generous. If the carrier's propulsion system is a 'double *Kirov*' (combined nuclear and steam turbine), powering the catapult should present no problem. A 'Flanker' may be considered a poor match for an F-14, but its inclusion would mark a significant step forward.

◄

Unlike the British at present, the West German Navy uses Tornado fighter-bombers in the maritime strike role. The aircraft shown is carrying four Kormoran anti-ship missiles, due to be replaced by a combination of Kormoran II and American HARM (High Speed Anti-Radiation Missile). (German Navy)

As planning must have consumed considerable time, the fact that the *Tbilisi* was laid down shortly after the Falklands War must be coincidental. Nevertheless, it will not have gone unnoticed that:

(a) the British could not have responded to the situation on the islands without possessing naval aviation;

(b) the British never really established air superiority, being fortunate that enemy aircraft were obliged to operate near the limits of their endurance;

(c) once stung by the loss of *Sheffield*, the British task force lost much of its freedom of manoeuvre for fear of losing a major unit such as a carrier, and

(d) VSTOL aircraft, through operating in combat for the first time with certain advantages, may well have become over-rated.

What is certain is that any naval aviation is better than no naval aviation, but VSTOL can never be better than complementary to high-performance aircraft. The latter require large decks, and any fleet charged seriously with out-of-area activities must acquire them.

At a time when the Soviet Union is emphasizing preliminary force reductions to demonstrate a more pronounced defensive posture, it is ironic that the first of the new carriers underscores actual capability that implies the opposite. This alone will guarantee an uncontested flow of American defence dollars for the funding of CVNs.

Some authorities[10] estimate the *Tbilisi* air wing strength at no more than fifty aircraft while a further analysis, taking into account hanger size and assuming no deck park, arrives at a possible total of twelve Su-27s, twelve Yak-41 ('Forger' VSTOL derivatives, experiencing delays on entry into service) and 15–18 Ka-27 ('Helix-A') AS helicopters.[11] As an F-14 sized 'Flanker' demands as much space as two VSTOLS or three helicopters, the actual mission of the ship at any time will determine numbers of aircraft aboard. The incorporation of an all-defensive armament and a through flightdeck demonstrates a clear change of philosophy; a *Tbilisi* operates at the centre of a CVBG.

At current rates of construction, the end of the century will see two 65,000- and one 75,000-tonner completed, and a second of the larger type nearly so. While the Soviets have never overtly sought to exercise 'power projection' after the American style, they are approaching the point where this could be an option.

With Great Britain, as is traditional, ignoring experience and declaring CTOL carriers unnecessary as her fleet is 'fringe NATO', only the French, otherwise, are still actively building though, as is their manner, at a pace varying between the leisurely and the moribund. Their bold project for a nuclear-powered helicopter carrier was first announced in 1974, but passed through many phases before emerging as the current plan to replace the existing pair of conventionally

▶

Aircraft, with their superior speed and mobility, can be valuable in the defence of surface ships. By interposing themselves between an incoming strike and the ships to be protected, aircraft can use ESM to analyze the threat and ECM to assist in countering it. Countermeasures can take the form of expendible offboard decoys such as this French example. (Thomson – CSF (Aerospace Group))

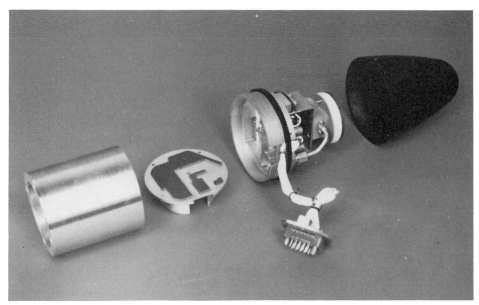

▲
As no naval air arm exists in Norway, the airforce has responsibilities for reconnaissance, ASW and anti-surface ship strike. Here, a Norwegian F-16 'Fighting Falcon' is seen over terrain which would suit admirably the possibilities of in direct attack offered by the Penguin Mk 3 that it carries. (Norsk Forsvarsteknologi as)

propelled carriers with new-construction nuclear carriers. Recently refitted, *Clemenceau* is planned to serve until 1996 and *Foch* until 2001, each in turn being replaced by 32,000-tonners of much the same physical size.[12] Of these, the first (provisionally named *Richelieu*, but later *Charles de Gaulle*) was ordered early in 1986 for completion at the time of *Clemenceau*'s retirement. While the timescale for the second unit is probably tied to plans for *Foch*, it has not yet been announced.

While air wings of 35–40 aircraft are planned, half will need to be accommodated in American-style deck-parks.[13] The fighter element will, initially, comprise Super Etendards. The French Navy's current all-weather F-8E Crusader interceptors are elderly, and due to be withdrawn in 1993,[14] but carrier evaluation of the proposed F/A-18 Hornet replacements has stimulated domestic opposition, about which the French Government is still (spring 1989) prevaricating. It is possible that the planned Avion de Combat Maritime (ACM), the order for whose prototype has yet to be placed, may well require in time to replace both Super Etendard and F-8E. It appears unlikely that the ACM could be operational by 1996.

Although nuclear-powered, *de Gaulle* will be slower than her predecessors. This will not detract from air operations by virtue of her longer and more powerful catapults. It should, however, be noted that, while nuclear power confers effectively unlimited high-speed steaming, it does not imply unlimited endurance. Non-nuclear escorts need regular replenishment, as do all manner of aviation- and crew-related stores for the carrier. During high-level activities, this could mean RAS every 48–72 hours.

A noteworthy absentee from announced French plans is a dedicated AEW aircraft. A possible solution would lie in the acquisition of the ubiquitous E-2C Hawkeye, already serving under five flags.

Carrier fighters/interceptors are tasked with winning the so-called outer air battle. This is best decided at the maximum possible range, but this range will depend on such factors as the number, speed and endurance of available interceptors, the degree of early warning received, and the range and effectiveness of the air-to-air missiles (AAM) carried.

The US Navy's F-14 Tomcat, first introduced in 1972, has reached its 'D' variant, whose deliveries commence in 1990. Its new power plant will almost certainly improve on the earlier speed of Mach 2.34, although combat radius is dependent on speed employed. References suggest that its margin over the carrier variant of the Su-27 ('Flanker') will hardly be overwhelming.[15]

Much of the F-14's size is dictated by the need to accommodate its AWG-9 weapon control system, capable of simultaneously engaging six targets while tracking eighteen more. For dog-fighting, the F-14 carries two/four AIM-9 Sidewinders, currently being produced in the 'M' version with improved infra-red counter-countermeasures (IRCCM) and reduced smoke emission.[16] A further updated ('R') variant is expected during 1990. An F-14 flight will, however, seek to avoid the unpredictable outcome of close-order combat by deciding the issue at long range, using the AIM-54C Phoenix missile, of which up to six can be carried. Their quoted range of 'about 120km' (say, 75 miles) is boosted by the speed of the aircraft and the likelihood that an attacking target will be closing.[17] Phoenix is expensive and, being paired with the AWG-9 outfit, not found outside the US Navy. A new missile is, therefore, being developed in the AAM (Advanced Air-to-Air-Missile), compatible also with Air Force requirements for use against cruise missiles, high-speed bombers and AWACS aircraft at stand-off ranges.[18] While the AAM will improve fleet air defences, its planned operational date has yet to be announced.

In terms of capability, the Sparrow lies between the Sidewinder and the Phoenix, its semi-active radar homing complementing the IR-seeking Sidewinder, but over the longer range of 26km (about 17 miles). Continuously developed over 40 years, the Sparrow is entering its 'P' variant to counter more effectively the low-flying SSM.[19]

Also under development is the AIM-120A AMRAAM (Advanced Medium Range Air-to-Air Missile). Though said to be a Sparrow replacement, its 74km (46-mile) range suggests that it will require more advanced supporting electronics. Sparrow itself is used so widely that its employment is assured yet well into the future. AMRAAM should enter the American operational inventory during FY89 and be acquired by the British during the 1990s. The latter who, together with Germans, lack high-performance, carrier-based strike fighters, will need to rely on land-based Tornado squadrons. About 100 such aircraft are already available to the West German Navy, but will not be used similarly by the British until the phasing out of the Buccaneers 'in or around 1996'.[20] Such Tornados will have a stretched airframe to house extra fuel. The likely missile load will include the anti-ship Sea Eagle, and either AMRAAM, or the Sparrow-derived Sky Flash for self-defence. Where the French currently employ the 10km (6-mile) range R530 in either IR or radar-homing versions, together with the short-ranged R550 (Magic), both are likely to be replaced by the 50km (31-mile) MICA, still under development for the French carrier-borne fighter of the nineties.

Vertical/Short Take-off and Landing (VSTOL)

Ten years ago it would have been difficult not to predict a glowing future prospect for VSTOL at sea yet, despite the fillip that it received from combat experience in the course of the 1982 Falklands War, progress has been slow. Only a short while before those hostilities, the US Navy had declared a general policy of moving toward VSTOL-only aircraft and ships by the turn of the century. In 1976 it was thought that there would be insufficient real growth in the Defense Budget to support the then twelve carrier battlegroups (CVBG) with fully modernized conventional air wings.[21] The Chief of Naval Operations (CNO) observed that one range of aircraft was developed for carriers and another, entirely different, for deployment by other ships; VSTOL offered a commonality, applicable across the board. An essential and obvious condition however, was performance: '. . . . if the successor of the A-6 is to be a VSTOL aircraft, its military performance has got to be superior to [that of] the A-6'.

Logical progression was to be achieved by the replacement of each aircraft type, at its normal retirement age, with a VSTOL successor. VSTOL would thus be proven on existing carriers, whose air wings would become all-VSTOL by stages. Finally, new-construction decks would be VSTOL-only by design. Three basic aircraft types were defined as necessary. Type A was to be sub-sonic and tasked with ASW, AEW, COD (Carrier On-board Delivery), SAR (Search and Rescue) and Marine Medium Assault. Type B would be super-sonic and applicable to both fighter and attack roles. Finally, Type C would be the eventual replacement for LAMPS II helicopters. The programme was given impetus by the declared Marine policy of going all-VSTOL by the mid-eighties.

Given the eventual target, other ideas began to flow. Typical of the new concepts was the Litton/Ingall 'Flight Deck DD963', a basic *Spruance* hull re-designed to support a mixed VSTOL/helicopter group. On a 12,300-ton deep displacement, the ship would have hangared 8–14 Type A VSTOLs or up to 12 helicopters.[22] It is not fully clear how, if or when the eventual all-VSTOL goal for US naval aviation was dropped, but it is quite obvious now that, with the Soviets in the course of building 75,000-ton carriers capable of operating high-performance fighters, the United States is little likely to embark on new development when proven technology is to hand.

Were a period of heightening international tension to demonstrate a class of complementary, lower-performance carriers to be necessary for ASW, and the screening of convoys and surface groups in lower-risk areas, VSTOL would certainly come into its own. As it is thought that there exist no insuperable difficulties in designing a supersonic version of the AV-8B, a candidate for the Type B appears already available.[23] Indeed, the only reason that this project has not already been undertaken appears to be its unwarrantable expense when the US Navy requires no replacement for the F-14 or F/A-18 before 2005–2010.

In any decision to embark on a smaller type of carrier, its chosen size would be crucial to the development of a supersonic Harrier. A CVV of about 40,000 tons, with an 813-foot (248-metre) flightdeck, could still operate F/A-18s,[24] but would appear to be an unlikely choice in its being so large as to make a full-size *Nimitz* a more cost-effective alternative. The Americans dislike the 20,000-ton sized *Invincible*-type carrier as carrying too few aircraft to be of practical use, while being itself a liability in being too lightly armed to defend itself adequately. Thus, the most likely size for the 'alternative' carrier would appear to be a 35,000-tonner, accommodating 25–30 aircraft. While, for such a ship, supersonic VSTOL would be viable, it is still difficult to see how it could then be developed sufficiently to make the big CTOL carrier unattractive. At best, the high-performance conventional fighter and supersonic VSTOL would seem complementary, the latter supportable only to enhance the value of a 'second-line' carrier.

Although, perhaps, not what was originally in mind as 'VSTOL', the V-22 (Osprey) would make an interesting candidate for Type A. As the MV-22, Bell-Boeing's revolutionary tiltrotor was configured initially to Marine requirements, but it is proposed, too, in the SV-22 ASW version. For use on carrier or escort, its strength is in the way in which the wing and the two, enormous 38-foot (11.6-metre) diameter airscrew/rotors ingeniously fold and pivot to stow in line with the fuselage. Thus configured, the SV-22 is only 7¼

inches (0.18 metres) longer then F-14, while being only half as wide. At 55,000 pounds (25,000kg) her STOL weight is identical. At 17 feet 10 inches (5.4m) folded, the SV-22 is only 8½ inches (0.22m) higher than a CH-53. While thought of generally as a large aircraft, therefore, the Osprey can be handled by any elevators that could accommodate an F-14, while, in terms of space, it could be flown from a pad on an escort the size of a DD-963.[25]

Like the AV-8B, the SV-22 benefits from a rolling take-off; compared with a vertical start, its rating is thus increased by 1,500 pounds (682kg). In its AS role, it couples a UYS-2 Acoustic Processor with the capacity to lay the larger active sonobuoys that will become increasingly necessary as submarines' noise levels reduce toward those encountered in the oceans as ambient conditions. Such sensors may be too expensive to be viewed as universally expendable and Bell-Boeing point out that the SV-22's capability allows not only for gentle placement but also the option of recovery after use should circumstances permit.[26] Flying high, it can use its APS-137 Inverse Synthetic Aperture Radar (ISAR); working low, it can deploy a dipping sonar in a 'dash and loiter' mode. The combination of ISAR and Harpoon missiles give the SV-22 its secondary anti-surface ship capacity, but it can also lay mines or work in COD, SAR or tanker roles. In short, it can fulfil the requirements stipulated for VSTOL Type A.

Where it could be assumed that so useful an innovation as the Osprey would be hastened into service, there actually seems to be a risk that it will be axed under US Defense Budget cuts.[27] To assist in cutting ten billion dollars from a proposed 305.6 billion dollar budget, the Defense Secretary is reported to favour a 'large capacity conventional helicopter', probably because these already exist in abundance. As the Osprey is all about speed of reaction, the measure would appear as ill-advised as that of the British Government in originally failing to champion the Harrier. Like the Harrier, the Osprey marks a turning-point in aviation technology, a first stage in a new and significant area of flying. Interestingly, the same report mentions British Aerospace as being in the course of a two-year feasibility study, assessing the validity of the Osprey to European needs.

There is also reported a multi-national European interest in the development of a 30-seater civilian tiltrotor aircraft with a range of about 1,000km (625

◄

British Sea Harrier VSTOL fighters 'cross-decking' with the Italian *Giuseppi Garibaldi*. With the Italian parliament finally passing the necessary legislation to enable the navy to operate fixed wing aircraft, ten will eventually be carried. It will be noted that the flight deck compromises with a gentle sheer rather than a 'ski jump'. (Italian Navy)

miles) at a speed of 500km/hr (c.313mph).[28] The project is termed Eurofar (European Future Advanced Rotorcraft). It would be ironic if European interest were to save the Osprey in the same manner that the US Marine Corps proved to be the salvation of the Harrier.

At least one American service voice has pointed out that the V-22 could supersede both the SH-60F helicopter for inner-zone ASW and the S-3A (Viking) aircraft in the vast mid- and outer-zone roles.[29] With SH-3Hs now anything up to 25 years old and many S-3As of like vintage, the possibilities of replacing them both with a single aircraft must be worth exploring.[30] Emphasizing that VSTOL does not rigidly imply jet propulsion, there is a further contender in the 'X-wing' vehicle.[31] This concept utilizes a four-element rotor with very broad blades of necessarily symmetrical cross-section. The lift generated by this rotor is enhanced by the blowing of air through slots in the leading and trailing edges of each blade. As the engine also drives a propeller for forward motion, there comes

a point where the rotor can be declutched, stopped and locked symmetrical with the aircraft's axis, thereafter acting as a novel wing in conventional forward flight. As each operates from ships designed around it, both the AV-8B and the Yak 38/41 would seem assured of a steady, if unspectacular, future. A major difference is in the attitude to export sales for, while the Soviets appear to have no interest in this area, the Harriers are gaining a steadily widening market. Operators of older 'Light Fleet' carriers are limited by their size, speed and equipment to the use of small conventional aircraft. Harrier operation has not proved difficult, however, and may well encourage some fleets to build simple carriers to mercantile class.

India, with two small, ex-British decks, seeks to build indigenous carriers, but reportedly[32] of a more ambitious size than that of the modified SCS constructed by Spain to American plans, with the French bureau DCN carrying out a project-definition study for two, possibly three, 30,000-tonners. Argentina is desperately trying to upgrade the performance of her single venerable

▶ The Spanish Navy adopted VSTOL at an early date, due largely to the limited size of their sole carrier, the *Dedalo*, of Second World War vintage. AV-8As (known as Matadors) proved viable, allowing the eventual replacement deck in *Principe de Asturias*, to be only some seven metres longer. (British Aerospace (Military Aircraft Division))

carrier sufficiently to permit all-weather operation of at least the Super Etendard, but the prospects for success must be marginal at best.

Having finally repealed the law limiting fixed-wing operation to only the Air Force, the Italian parliament has freed its navy to commence the evaluation of VSTOL aircraft for the new carrier *Garibaldi*. It is reported that evaluation will commence 'shortly', though it is understood that the Anglo-American AV-8B is favoured, with an acquisition of up to 18 aircraft, expected to commence in 1992.[33] As the Italian fleet's three helicopter cruisers are expected to be deleted during the nineties, a second carrier is a distinct possibility, with the possible name of *Mazzini* or *Conte di Cavour* already being suggested.

Difficult to assess in terms of carriers are the plans of either China or Japan. Where the former could build an unsophisticated example, the provision of suitable aircraft would be another matter. Japan is seeking to assume a greater role in her own area defence, and one or more decks would greatly enhance her ability to do

this. Both in the home country and in the United States, however, there remain too many memories of the previous generation of Japanese carriers, and sheer weight of public opinion may well block any such new construction.

Helicopters

It is now nearly 30 years since the British *Tribal*-class frigates began to commission as the first ASW ships designed to maintain and operate a helicopter. Intended initially to give a frigate a rapid, stand-off response, the aircraft has progressed to the status of a weapons-system in itself, offering also an anti-surface ship strike capacity, over-the-horizon (OTH) identification and targeting, and remote electronic support, besides acting as a general-purpose utility. In the process, it has made a major impact on the design of the ships that carry it, while their limitations, together with the demanding marine environment, have, in

◄

Lynx helicopters of the Royal Navy will have to wait for a desperately needed update, including a 360-degree radar, MAD and new EW gear. The example shown has FLIR and a 180-degree radar; as, to track its target, it has to keep it on a forward bearing, the indirect attack pattern of its Penguin Mk 3 is beneficial. (Norsk Forsvarsteknologi as)

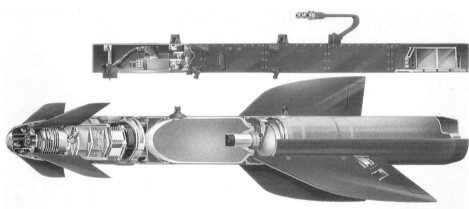

◄

Described as a high sub-sonic missile with canard control, the Penguin Mk 3 packs a 120kg warhead in its centre section. Right forward is the IR seeker, altimeter control unit and inertial navigation unit. The sustainer motor can be complemented by a booster if required. A folding-wing version will be carried by **US LAMPS III** helicopters. (Norsk Forsvarsteknologi as)

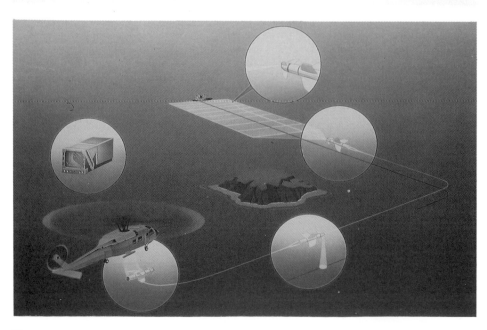

◄

The flight-profile of the helicopter-launched Penguin Mk 3 allows the aircraft exposure time to be reduced to a minimum, vulnerability being reduced further by the weapon's ability to incorporate a radical change of course at a preselected waypoint. (Norsk Forsvarsteknologi as)

▶ A demonstrator model of the SH-2G Super Seasprite, of the type to be operated by all LAMPS I frigates not upgraded to LAMPS III. Only two-thirds the weight of a LMPS III, the SH-2G is fitted with the same T700 engines. Operational versions are now painted in the grey, low-visibility tactical paint scheme. Note MAD and external fuel tank. (Kaman Aerospace)

turn, influenced the helicopter. Cost constraints, however, demand usually that basic helicopter airframes be adaptable to multi-service roles, sometimes creating unsatisfactory compromises.

Larger helicopters have been operated from such as carriers, assault ships and auxiliaries for even longer and these, too, have moved from the original, usually assault or vertical replenishment functions to roles such as mine countermeasures (MCM), airborne early warning (AEW) and search and rescue (SAR). Helicopters have become so essential at sea that it is time to consider seriously a move away from the idea of the conventionally configured warship, grudgingly yielding its after end to the operation of one or two aircraft, to a miniature carrier whose design is optimized for their purposes. With respect to this, the single most important parameter affecting operational efficiency is seakeeping. This rather ill-defined quality embraces such ingredients as ship motion and wetness, the ship being able to keep the sea far beyond the point at which helicopters have to cease operations. Neither the aircraft nor its ship tend to be robust, and high relative velocity at contact can damage both undercarriage and deck.[34] A rolling deck may cause the aircraft to touch down first on one side, possibly initiating a cross-deck slide. High transverse relative velocities can encourage a topple or see part of the undercarriage set down beyond the deck edge. Wet decks encourage sliding while spray is ingested into engines and, blasted into

joints, causing corrosion, particularly in aluminium alloys. Hauldown and transfer systems alleviate problems for both pilot and handling crew, but the true answer must lie in changing the ship's design to one promoting maximum helicopter flexibility allied to minimum ship motion. Such a concept exists already in the SWATH (Small Waterplane Area, Twin Hull), discussed further in this book's final chapter.

The SWATH's inherent steadiness and rectangular topside plan promise optimum helicopter operating envelopes together with the qualities necessary for the low-speed deployment of towed arrays. Conventional frigates have not the space for the latter gear, and are uncomfortable, even dangerous, while steaming at low speeds in quartering seas. A SWATH's deep draught is also a distinct advantage for the hull-mounted sonars. A SWATH with a displacement akin to that of a medium-sized frigate could be optimized to support four large helicopters and a defensive armament. Its improved seakindliness may even allow for a relaxation in aircraft specification and the lack, so far, of an evaluation hull being built can be explained only in that budgets are so tight that only the well-tried and cheapest has a hope of being considered.

Shipborne helicopters have tended, understandably, to be 'marinized' versions of multi-purpose airframes, but there is evidence now of less compromise. Unfortunately 'better' usually means 'bigger', the Anglo-Italian EH101 (Merlin) for instance, being some 30 per

cent heavier at take off than the Sea King that it will shortly replace. Two ASW helicopters are, undeniably, more than twice as effective as one, but pairs of Merlin-sized aircraft force up the size of a conventional frigate to the point where it becomes unaffordable. This suggests the concept of integrating ASW operations between Merlin-equipped SWATHs and frigates with aircraft no larger than the still-capable Lynx.

Merlin itself is due to go operational from 1993 with the fleets of Canada, Great Britain and Italy.[35] Its size bestows the twin merits of useful range and generous payload, qualities that are always desirable but always conflicting. Range is becoming more important than ever, it being vital to detect increasingly stealthy submarines out to better than 100 miles (160km), from which distance they are now able to threaten a surface ship with submerge-launched stand-off missiles. As a direct consequence of this, the US Navy is developing the so-called ALFS (Airborne Low Frequency Sonar) which, it is claimed, will extend a helicopter's sonar range by a factor of ten.[36] Lower frequencies mean not only longer potential ranges but also larger equipment. The EH101's margin can cater not only for this but also on-board data processing, which makes the always vulnerable data-link with the mother-ship a tactical option rather than a necessity.

For use in so-called 'bistatic' operation, dipping sonars could grow even larger. In this mode, the aircraft's active source generates the energy from which the component reflected by a target is received covertly by the mother ship's towed array. Detection range is thus increased by the benefits of active equipment without the ship directly betraying its position. The target will, of course, be alerted but, in ASW, a target alerted is better than one undetected or even unsuspected. The ship's towed array will give bearing to target; this is signalled to the aircraft, which flies along it, finally localizing a contact with sono-buoys.

Agusta, Westland's Italian partner in European Helicopters (the 'EH' in EH101), is hedging its bets through its links with the Dutch, French and Germans in the NH90 (NATO Helicopter for the nineties).[37] This aircraft is being kept to take-off weight and dimensions inside those of a Sea King or LAMPS III, making it compatible with a wide range of frigates, but particularly the NATO frigate (NFR 90). An estimated 59 of these ships will be required (USA, 18; UK, 12; Italy, 8; Canada, 6; Spain, 5; France, 4; West Germany, 4; Netherlands, 2), but the helicopter already looks a compromise.[38] Designed as a joint army/navy machine, the French Army requires it to carry a two-ton 'air-mobile combat vehicle', dictating dimensions and layout for all aircraft alike. European co-operation must be beneficial to cost if satisfactory compromise can be reached, for it is thought that the total demand will be for 220 naval versions and 360 land-based. Production runs of this magnitude eclipse even the American LAMPS III programme, where the eventual 204 SH-60Bs will be joined by 175 SH-60Fs, the 'CV Helo', of which deliveries commence in 1989.[39]

The SH-60F will operate from carrier decks against submarines that have infiltrated to the group's 'inner zone'. For this role, it carries a dipping sonar optimized for use in the high ambient noise level likely to be found there.

The basic SH-60B LAMPS III is already being upgraded to carry the Mk 50 AS torpedo when it belatedly replaces the Mk 46 in the early nineties. Faster and deeper-diving, the Mk 50 has also a considerable weight penalty of 362kg against 232kg. The aircraft will also be fitted for the Norwegian Penguin ASM. This is the Mk 3 version of a well-tried weapon, with a launch weight near identical with that of the Mk 50 torpedo. With the advantage of air launch, the Penguin can engage a surface target at ranges of better than 40km, carrying an armour-piercing 50kg warhead (large enough to disable a frigate) at high subsonic speed. Carrier aircraft could deploy the missile at speeds up to Mach 1.2. A pilot can control a Penguin directly on his head-up display or programme it through his onboard avionics. A useful feature is the ability to incorporate a waypoint in the weapon's course, enabling it to approach its target from an unexpected direction. Only target position and waypoint need to be set before launch, the missile flying under inertial control to the point of acquisition, at which an IR seeker takes over.[40]

Both naval variants of the H-60 benefit by commonality of spares with the US Army's UH-60A (Black Hawk), the 60H Helicopter Combat Support (HCS) and 60J Medium Range Recovery (MRR), together with the 'international' 70B version sold to Australia, Japan and Spain. Of these, the Australians incorporate the MEL Super Searcher surveillance and targeting radar. This equipment is fitted also in Sea Kings built in the United Kingdom for the Indian Navy, enabling them to deploy the Sea Eagle anti-ship missile, whose launch weight is half as much again as that of the Penguin. As the Royal Navy still operates a fair number of Sea Kings, this is a useful precedent.

Another function, currently unique to the British Sea King, is AEW. Following the well-documented problems inflicted on the Royal Navy in the Falklands by a lack of AEW, eight aircraft were refitted for the role. This included the tacking-on of an ungainly but effective retractable enclosure for the Searchwater radar antenna. The AEW Sea King is not in the same league as, say, an E-2C Hawkeye, whose radar is 250 nautical miles compared with only 130, giving a fourfold area coverage.[41] Nevertheless, with the growing interest in smaller carriers, a market for the AEW helicopter certainly exists, it having been sold to the Spaniards and, probably, the Indians. It is claimed that three such aircraft, with five crews, can maintain a round-the-clock coverage, but it remains to be seen whether the radar-equipped airship, or even tethered aerostat, could offer a viable alternative.

The Sea King still attracts updates, the Mk 6 entering Royal Navy service from mid-1989. Its size permits deployment of sonobuoys and dipping sonar in addition to an on-board acoustic processor, a combination beyond the scope of the smaller Lynx, itself the subject of a stop-go improvement programme. This upgrading is urgently needed, as many frigates can accommodate neither Sea King nor Merlin. Included would be a GEC Avionics Sea Owl thermal imager, a Mk 3 Ferranti Seaspray radar and a Canadian-developed MAD outfit, the trends for which are to site an antenna within an aircraft structure rather than trailed or housed in a projecting 'sting'.[42] The new radar has a 360-degree coverage, compared with the 180-degree forward sector-only of the present Mk 1. Its fitting would obviate the requirement for a helicopter to be headed in the general direction of the target either to track it or attack it with Sea Skua ASMs.

Faced with, say, a flotilla of SSM-armed Fast Attack Craft (FAC) rather than a larger surface combatant, a larger number of smaller ASMs would be more appropriate. In this respect the light French Dauphin 2 helicopter has offered a neat small-ship solution since 1983, carrying a Thomson-CSF Agrion radar and four AS 15 TT missiles from Aerospatiale.[43] These each pack a 30kg warhead on a 100kg launch weight, but, while having a 15km range sufficient to engage a target beyond the reach of its point-defences, they are optically-guided with no homing, and good visibility is thus essential. Twenty have been sold to Saudi Arabia.[44]

Where LAMPS III has entered service on recent US frigates, LAMPS I will thrive on earlier ships until beyond the turn of the century. The extensive FF-1052 (*Knox*) class will not receive the LAMPS III upgrade, yet are still scheduled to serve beyond 2015. As it costs 45 million dollars to make a single FFG-7 (Perry) LAMPS III-capable, even more will find themselves with LAMPS I (itself 10 million dollars cheaper).[45]

Kaman are upgrading the LAMPS I SH-2 Seasprite to the 'G'-variant Super Seasprite, whose YSH-2G prototype has paved the way for the first production module roll-out in mid-1989. Operating at 13,900 pounds (6,318kg), compared with the SH-60B's 21,700 pounds (9,864kg), the SH-2G has identical engines. In the words of the firm, it is a 'hot little number'. Currently, 42 new SH-2Gs have been ordered, while the navy is negotiating to update the whole 2F fleet.

With no new heavy helicopters known to be in the pipeline, the H-53 series continues in production. The latest is the MH-53E Sea Dragon Airborne Mine Countermeasures (AMCM) version, fitted with a 30,000-pound (13,640kg) tension towing boom for hauling mechanical, acoustic and magnetic sweep gear. Endurance is sufficient for a four-hour tow of one of the sleds on which the MCM gear is mounted, although this period can be extended by in-flight refuelling.[46] The MH-53E is usually deployed by sea, but its only known imitator, the Soviet Mi-14 ('Haze-B'), even at only one-third the weight, is land based. For ASW, the well-tried Ka-25 ('Hormone-A') soldiers on, though it is being superseded in larger ships by the 12,600kg Ka-27 ('Helix-A'), introduced in 1980.[47]

Advances in material technology is benefiting the helicopter as well as orthodox aircraft. Fibre-in-epoxy composites and fibre-reinforced alloys which, themselves, contain exotic trace elements, offer both increased strength and the opportunity to reduce weight by as much as 25 per cent in certain areas though, currently, at considerable extra cost.[48] Besides the more obvious options that reduced structural weight confers – greater range/endurance, lower-power engines, larger payloads, etc., – there are more subtle advantages. Composites can have a much lower radar signature than metal, a factor of growing importance as the range of responsibilities of an embarked helicopter grow ever wider. Composites dampen the effects of vibration far better than metal, greatly reducing fatigue damage. The 'lay' of fibre reinforcement and local thickness can be controlled at points of high stress level to extend life expectancy. Properties of composites are of particular importance in rotor blades, which can be designed better to cope with the complex cyclic stresses to which they are subjected.

▶ A Sikorsky SH-60B LAMPS III in the tactical paint scheme. Visible are the 25 slots of the sonobuoy dispenser, above the unoccupied support point for a Mk 50 AS torpedo, and the large shallow dish below the cockpit that accommodates the APS-124 surveillance radar. It carries ALE-49 chaff and flare dispensers and an ALQ-144 IR jamming system. (United Technologies Sikorsky Aircraft)

As shipboard and submarine sensors and stand-off weapons increase in effective range, helicopters need to fly both farther and faster. Conventional rotors, before pitch correction, give an asymmetric lift, due to the blades on one side 'advancing' with respect to the helicopter, while those on the other side 'retreat'. There is a limit to pitch correction that can be applied, so helicopters tend to have a theoretical maximum speed of about 375km/hour (c.235mph).[49] This is well above the 240km/hour (150mph) of the average AS helicopter, but research such as the British Experimental Rotor Programme (BERP), utilizing advanced design and materials, promises to push speeds towards the maximum and will likely trigger a wider application of paired contra-rotating rotors.[50] Beyond this point, development will probably depart from the true helicopter to the hybrid helicopter/aircraft, of which the first example to go operational will be Bell-Boeing's V-22 (Osprey), already dealt with above. Without a radical change in ship design, however, the deployment of such 'helicraft' will be limited to larger hulls, guaranteeing a market for the more orthodox helicopter for at least the duration of the period considered by this book.

Little attempt has been made so far to develop an anti-helicopter weapon for submarines, which still seek to evade rather than counter-attack. Improved airborne sensors and weapons are likely soon to render evasion a more difficult and risky process than attacking the platform itself. While this will give the helicopter new opportunities for attack, it will also oblige it to carry a new range of defensive countermeasures. The form of the weapon in question is not yet defined, but will probably not be of the British SLAM type or the reported Soviet fin-mounted launchers, both of which compromise the submarine's position. One approach is that of the Franco-German Polyphem programme, which includes a buoyant launch canister towed a kilometre or more astern of a submarine.[51] The towing line includes a fibre-optic control cable and, in the nature of developing off-board submarine sensors, the canister could, itself, be a helicopter detection and classification platform.

Airships and Remotely Piloted Vehicles (RPV)

American forward strategy in time of war would see their major carrier battle groups (CVBG) deployed in areas remote from operations supporting the vital Atlantic sea lines of communication (SLOC). In the continued absence of auxiliary or smaller, second-line carriers, high-value groups and convoys would depend greatly on such organic aviation as was available. One limitation, all-too-obviously exposed by British experience in the South Atlantic in 1982, is lack of AEW (Airborne Early Warning).

On 9 April 1979, the British *Daily Telegraph* reported that the Royal Navy was to test its 'first airship in 60 years'.[52] This craft, an AD-500, was to be equipped 'with powerful search radars and the latest electronic aids'. In March 1982 the same columnist was writing that it was 'certainly in the AEW rather than the ASW role that the (now re-named) SKYSHIP 500 attracted most interest in the Ministry of Defence (Navy) since this is a particularly serious gap in defences at sea at present while the threat from air-, surface- and sub-surface-launched anti-ship surface-skimming missiles is growing almost daily'.[53] Within a month the Falk-

lands War was a reality. Within two the air-defence destroyer *Sheffield*, positioned well forward as a radar picket, had, herself, been destroyed by an air-launched ASM due to the total lack of Task Force AEW. Following this event, which shook even Government complacency, British naval deployment was influenced greatly by the operational aerial envelopes of the enemy.

Fixed-wing AEW in the Royal Navy had, of course, died along with its carriers. The stopgap solution of fitting eight Sea Kings with Searchwater surveillance radar is looking, seven years later, disturbingly permanent. To exacerbate the situation, the originally planned eleven AWACS Nimrods have been replaced by just six Boeing E-3As which, however excellent, cannot hope to give an equivalent degree of coverage. Following a thorough review in 1983, which highlighted the fact that an airship's endurance is such that fewer might be needed as AEW/ASW platforms than conventional aircraft, the US Navy awarded Airship Industries/Westinghouse a contract in June 1987 for an Operational Development Model (ODM) with options on a further five.[54] Fitted with the radar of an E-2C Hawkeye, the ODM is scheduled for delivery at the end of 1990. Completion of the evaluation is due in 1993.

A modern airship combines the helicopter's ability to hover with an endurance that can, if required, be measured in days. It can be fitted with precise navigation systems, a communications and avionics package to suit a wide range of missions. (Airship Industries (UK) Ltd)

Airship Industry/Westinghouse's Sentinel 5000, under evaluation by the US Navy, can exceed 80 knots at a height of 14,000 feet (4,250m). Its mission payload of 11,500 pounds (5,200kg) and low signatures make it particularly suitable for battle management, AEW, ASW and surface ship surveillance and control. (Airship Industries (UK) Ltd)

It is worthy of note that, at the time of placement of the ODM contract, the British Minister of Defence Procurement went on record as saying that British forces had no staff requirements for airships.[55]

The chosen design is the Sentinel 5000 (known to the Americans as the YEZ-2A), the largest non-rigid airship ever to be constructed. Nearly twice the length of a Boeing 747, it has a gross volume of 2.5 million cubic feet (nearly 71,000 cubic metres) and a payload capacity of 50,000 pounds (22,700kg). While its 86-knot top speed would cause no lack of sleep to the helicopter lobby, its primary asset is its endurance of 60 hours at 40 knots.[56] Refuelling, re-provisioning and even crew change can be effected, while on the hover, from any ship with basic fittings. In fact, refuelling at sea every 48 hours, the YEZ-2A is reckoned by the Americans to be capable of remaining on station for up to 30 days.[57] The Sentinel 5000 is far from being a vulnerable, slow-speed gasbag. Its envelope is virtually invisible to radar, which means that, while an enemy may not detect it, its skin causes only low loss of energy to its own antennae, housed within, atop the gondola structure. Itself shaped for minimum radar reflectivity, the gondola can also be coated in radar-absorbent material (RAM). Airship engines, unlike those of aircraft, are low powered, their propellers being ducted. Audible noise and IR signatures are, therefore, low. Even if damaged, the craft contains its non-inflammable helium at such a low pressure (only 0.1psi, or about $680N/m^2$ above atmosphere) that any escape is unlikely to result in catastrophic failure.

By the mid-nineties the US Navy hopes to be able to replace the initial radar fit with a purpose-built phased array set. Deployed from a normal maximum ceiling of 10,000 feet (c.3,000m) such a radar would command a considerable horizon, the navy being interested particularly in its ability to detect new types of SSM employing stealth features. To achieve a possible 'forever on station' overhead surveillance, an investment of between 40 and 50 airships, together with their infrastructure, would be required. Impetus for such a 'force multiplier', however, is given by the recent introduction by the Soviet IL-76 ('Mainstay') AWACS aircraft, whose capabilities are significantly greater than those of the Tu-126 ('Moss') that it is replacing.[58] The sheer versatility of the airship, once in service, would be an added bonus. In an ASW role, it can deploy a towed array with no self-noise. It can lay and retrieve sonobuoys and accommodate signal processing equipment and the data link essential to close

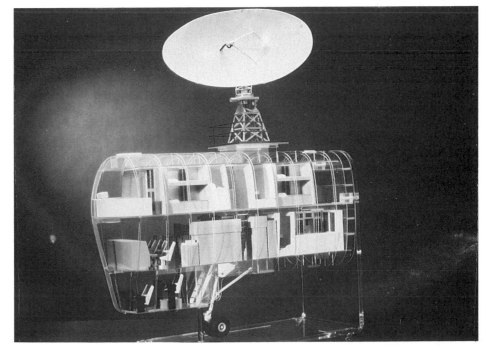

The Sentinel 5000's enormous lifting power enables it to accommodate a crew of 15 in considerable comfort during long patrols. Atop the three-storey gondola is the large AWACS antenna, operating inside the low-loss envelope which, in turn, is nearly invisible to enemy radar. (Airship Industries (UK) Ltd)

co-operation with AS surface ships. Its characteristics favour sprint and loiter operation. It is reported also that the Americans are interested in the airship's potential as a mine countermeasures (MCM) platform.[59] Whether it has the power to tow sleds in the manner of helicopters has yet to be seen, but, in the deployment of remotely operated MCM vehicles it could hover virtually at surface level with signatures unlikely to be detected by any practical mine.

Maritime-related aviation could show possibly no greater contrast than that exhibited between lighter-than-air (LTA) platforms, such as airships, and unmanned aircraft. These fall into several categories, which it may be well to summarize.[60] An unmanned aircraft (UMA) is an airborne system capable of autonomous operation. A remotely piloted vehicle (RPV) is a UMA which transmits mission-related data to an external operator and accepts commands issued in response to this or other information. A drone is a UMA that is not an RPV, capable of undertaking only a pre-programmed mission. Unmanned aircraft, as defined, would be a highly likely development at sea, but would necessarily follow the experience of over-land operation. Once shown to be feasible, they would have many attractions. The lack of pilot allows for associated gear to be dispensed with, an estimated saving of 2,300kg (more than 5,000 pounds) on a combat aircraft.[61] Because safety factors could also be relaxed, a lighter and simpler construction would reduce weight even further. British Aerospace estimate that the resulting vehicle could cost only one-third that of a manned aircraft. Recovery, always a more difficult problem than launch, could be solved, according to British Aerospace, by capitalizing on the UMA's ability to make fairly simple transition from wing-borne to jet-borne flight, hovering briefly before being secured by an overhead 'Skyhook' recovery and strikedown system, already proposed for use with the Harrier.

Although unsuccessful by virtue of being ahead of the technology of its time, the drone AS helicopter (DASH) is now perfectly feasible, as evinced by its deployment with the Japanese fleet. It is a good example of an RPV, and a class of vehicle having the most immediate prospects at sea. An essential pre-requisite for a practical shipborne RPV would seem to be the ability to hover, in order to simplify recovery. With this ability, small RPVs would have applications on just about any surface ship or submarine. It is reported that serious American interest in RPVs dated from their 1983 operations off the Lebanon, where valuable aircraft were lost while spotting for bombarding warships.[62] Under consideration for Harpoon OTH targeting, an indigenous RPV, the Sea Ferret, was abandoned in favour of the established Israeli Pioneer.

◄ Working on the periphery of a carrier's 200-mile operating zone, the Grumman E-2C Hawkeye, accompanied by a brace of F-14s, extends her horizon by a further 200 miles or more. Hawkeyes have been flying for 30 years, and are adaptable enough to extend their service for a considerable time to come. (Grumman Corporation)

▶ Hovering above a Canadian task group, a CL-227 Sentinel RPV acts to decoy an incoming SSM. For use in surveillance or spotting, its signatures can be made very low. Its small size, knock-down construction and ability to hover means that it can be deployed by even a submarine for a variety of tasks. (Bombadier Inc/Canadair Defence Group)

Able to carry a 45kg payload on a nine hour mission, 72 of these vehicles will be acquired by 1991; these will be organized into nine flights, each with its own support organization. Pioneer is rocket-assisted at launch and recovered, somewhat precariously, by net capture. While small, it meets the US Navy's requirements for a short-ranged RPV, and can carry television and forward-looking infra-red (FLIR) gear or, alternatively, payloads such as laser designators, electronic support equipment or a communications relay. American specifications for medium- and long-ranged RPVs call for 250 and 750nm (460/1,380km) ranges and a 40,000-feet (c.12,200-metre) ceiling. Two existing target drones are being evaluated as interim vehicles. These can deploy a variety of payloads, interchangeable in underwing pods and extending options to early warning, decoy, electronic intelligence or weather reporting. The weak area is again in recovery, the vehicle descending by parachute, following which the parent ship needs to run a degree of risk in steaming to its position and recovering it. This may well prove unacceptable so, for the long term, unobtrusive high-altitude vehicles are being purpose-designed. The High Altitude, Long Endurance (HALE) programme, for instance, is looking at a jet-propelled VTOL aircraft able to work from escort-sized ships on missions of up to 14 hours' duration. With a useful payload of 1,500

pounds (c.682kg) and a radar conformal with its wing structure, the HALE will be valuable particularly in giving early warning or SSM detection for groups not enjoying conventional air cover. As HALE's designed speed is only some 160 knots (c.294km/hour) it would seem to have a competitor in Bell-Boeing's Pointer, essentially a miniature version of the V-22 Osprey. Simple in concept, Pointer can be assembled from space-saving kits and, because of its tilt-rotor design, poses no launch or recovery problems.[63] Inevitably, the RPV, which can be made almost radar-transparent, will evolve into a weapons carrier or even a weapon itself, a sort of infinitely flexible, medium-speed cruise missile. There is no doubting the RPV's future, but publicity surrounding its development is generally kept low-key. Any navy, however, that ignores its progress does so at its peril.

Long-Range Maritime Patrol Aircraft

Although not specifically 'naval aviation', Maritime Patrol Aircraft (MPA) exert such an influence as to demand consideration. Developed directly from the wide variety of flying-boats and bombers that had materially contributed to the defeat of the U-boat during the Second World War, the MPA went on to

▲
The McDonnell Douglas F/A-18 Hornet was designed to simplify onboard logistics by combining the fighter functions of the F-4 Phantom with the attack role of the A-7 Corsair, replacing both. While regarded as something of a lightweight, the aircraft can carry 7,700kg externally and its adoption must improve carrier efficiency. (McDonnell Douglas)

▼
A Grumman EA-6B Prowler is catapulted from USS *America*. The aircraft's task is to accompany strike aircraft, confusing hostile defence systems with the electronics countermeasures gear accommodated in five pods. Prowlers can also support their group by passive surveillance or jamming of enemy transmissions. (Grumman Corporation)

▲
Model-like on a calm Atlantic, the Spanish carrier *Principe de Asturias* awaits her airgroup. She enables the navy to form a credible carrier task group. Her design is basically that of the austere Sea Control Ship (SCS) cancelled by the US Navy despite a requirement in lower-threat areas. (Empresa Nacional BACAN)

▼
As defences become ever more sophisticated, few attack formations can afford operations without the accompaniment of specialist-fitted aircraft. Here, a Mirage 2000 is shown with a pair of Remora underwing podded jammers, configured for noise and deception jamming to deflect incoming missiles and to confuse targeting data. (Thomson – CSF (Aerospace Group))

occupy an essential billet in the sophisticated ASW tapestry that evolved steadily in post-war years to meet the increasing threat from more technically-advanced submarines. With the ability continuously to monitor submarine comings and goings, through the likes of seabed sensor chains, the MPA automatically became the primary means of fast response in the localizing and classifying of a specific contact. From this role stemmed the need to be fitted for close co-operation with other ASW assets.

On the general adoption of exclusive economic zones (EEZ), usually continental shelf areas extending out to 200 miles (320km) from a shoreline, came the requirement for policing, particularly once a state had committed capital investment to seabed resource exploitation. The MPA here assumed a natural and cost-effective peacetime role.

Finally there arrived the long-range, air-launched anti-surface missile (ASM), which advanced the MPA from a dedicated surveillance and ASW platform to one able also to find, classify and attack both surface ships and targets ashore. Deploying such weapons courted new dangers, and the MPA assumed also air-to-air missiles (AAM) to resist the attentions of marauding fighter aircraft.

NATO, other west European and Warsaw Pact states use MPAs in large numbers, in designs whose robust airframes seem to be capable of undergoing almost limitless updates. Thus, for instance, the P2V Neptune served from 1947 to 1962, being phased out in favour of the commercially based P-3 Orion which has been in service for more than a quarter-century since.[64] Similar records of longevity attend the French Atlantique and British Nimrod. The capabilities of sensors, signal processing and weapons are now, however, advancing at a rate greater than that at which some of the older airframes can be stretched to accommodate them. Not only will competition produce new 'state of-the-art' production designs, but will also release for disposal a large number of still highly capable but superseded aircraft. Availability of these should well cause several smaller powers, which seek a viable naval air arm, to re-assess their position.

Of Third World powers, only Argentina, Brazil and India have maintained the means, namely the aircraft carrier, by which naval air power could assist a fleet as an instrument of policy at any distance from home waters. Doubtless, several states could construct simple, austere carriers to mercantile class and deploy

from them limited-capability aircraft such as modified Hawks or Alpha Jets. This, however, has yet to be attempted, the only 'simple' carrier yet built in recent times being the modified SCS by Spain. Smaller states, however, do not need fleets fashioned for world-wide deployment; disputes are likely to be over offshore assets or boundaries. Acquisition of MPAs, even lacking the latest of equipment, would confer the ability to identify and strike from beyond the defensive range of any surface ship likely to cause a nuisance in the normal course of events. With the stamina to remain on a 1,550-mile (c.2,500km) distant station for three hours and the speed to get there in under four, an Orion equipped with ASMs would allow a fair measure of sea control to be established over a considerable area against any hostile force devoid of maritime air and beyond the radius of shore-based fighter support.[65] Should a Third World state be permitted to purchase MPAs there would seem little point, other than for reasons of prestige, of it going to the expense of acquiring and maintaining carriers in addition.

Following competition, the US Navy has decided against a new-style MPA, based on the Boeing 757 or McDonnell Douglas MD-80, opting instead for a 'highly modified P-3' defined, somewhat tautologically, as an LRAACA (Long-Range Air ASW-Capable Aircraft).[66] Lockheed are to build 125 for the US Navy, with deliveries commencing in 1994. Avionics stem from Boeing, who are also up-grading eighty of the more recent P-3Cs to the same standard, known as Update IV, which is compatible with most P-3s operated by friendly fleets. Lockheed have proposed also an ASW conversion of the ubiquitous C-130 (Hercules), aimed at being a cheaper alternative for smaller budgets. The LRAACA's specification, comfortably exceeded by Lockheed, called for a four-hour endurance on a 1,875-mile (3,000km) distant station, with a 10,730kg (23,600-pound) payload.[67] An ability to stow up to 300 sonobuoys is, perhaps, a reflection on the difficulties encountered by a shore-based conventional aircraft in pursuing a submerged contact. Interrogation and signal analysis are carried out aboard by a well-tried acoustic processor. In addition to Mk 50 torpedoes, for use against localized submarine contacts, the LRAACA can deploy up to a dozen extended-range Harpoon anti-ship missiles. Coupled with on-board Inverted Synthetic-Aperture Radar (ISAR) and comprehensive ESM, to facilitate positive target identification in

▶
Although long-range maritime patrol aircraft can lay mines, their capacity can nowhere near match that of the ubiquitous C-130 Hercules transport, whose builders, Lockheed, have co-operated with Babcock to devise a simple. high-volume delivery system for rapid deployment in emergency. (Babcock Energy Ltd)

adverse conditions, the ASMs give the aircraft a formidable sea control capacity to a considerable distance offshore. In the absence of carrier support, surface groups so threatened would find VSTOL their only practical defence. It is possible that the growing potency of the MPA will prove a spur to the wider acceptance of VSTOL, in the same way that the depredations of the FW200 (Kondor) of the Second World War proved a powerful stimulus to the rapid development of the auxiliary escort carrier.

Another long-serving workhorse due for retirement is the French-built Atlantique Mk 1, being superseded from 1989 by the Mk 2 version. West Germany appears to be planning to convert its Mk 1s for electronic warfare during the lead-up to a replacement programme, not due to commence before 1997. The Germans apparently favour the LRAACA, not only from political expediency but also because, by 1997, the Atlantique Mk 2s will already require a first update.[68]

Seventeen Italian Mk 1s are being brought up to Mk 2 standard with new radar, inertial navigation, acoustic processor and sonobuoy dispensers.[69] British Nimrods have state-of-the-art equipment in a roomy but dated airframe, the latest of which was delivered as recently as 1985. Proposals for limited-capacity

MPAs proliferate, and the would-be purchaser can choose between such as the market leader, the Fokker F27 variant, or others from France, Italy or Canada, all of which are based on proven airliner or transport airframes.

With limited assets, most Western operators are tending to multi-function MPAs, with a degree of dilution in their effectiveness. Not so the Soviets who, with an estimated 1,375 operational first-line naval aircraft, can afford to specialize.[70] Thus Backfire 'B' and 'C's are dedicated to long-range reconnaissance; Badger 'D', 'E', 'F' and 'J' to medium-range reconnaissance and electronic warfare; Badger 'C' and 'G' for medium-range surface ship attack; May and Mail for long- and medium-range ASW respectively, and Moss and Mainstay for AWACS overview and control. Except for those of Backfire and Mainstay, designs are as vintage as those prevalent in the West, but, being special-to-task, may well be more effective as well as being more numerous. While the West believes generally that it enjoys an offsetting qualitative edge, there is little in published sources to substantiate such optimism.

Recent encounters with Soviet AWACS aircraft highlight the great influence such assets can exert on an operational theatre, as demonstrated by the Americans in the recent Gulf War. With round-the-clock AWACS coverage, they were able to deploy economically as the situation developed. Incidents, such as the frigate *Stark* convincing herself that hostile manoeuvrings were friendly and virtually allowing herself to be hit by a pair of SSMs, leading to the cruiser *Vincennes* convincing herself that the intentions of an airliner were hostile rather than neutral, and shooting it down with SAMs, were local aberrations and not due to AWACS failure.

Granted adequate funds, the line taken by both the Americans and the Soviets would seem correct; develop the AWACS aircraft for direction without participation, freeing MPAs for their primary role of investigation and prosecution. Ultimately the satellite must assume the AWACS commitment, but this would seem unlikely before the turn of the century, as universal coverage would require an uneconomic number of short-lived vehicles with very high-quality sensors and signal conditioning.

References and Notes

1. Figures from Jean Lebayle Couhat. *Combat Fleets of the World, 1988/9* (hereinafter *Combat Fleets*), p.697.
2. See *Combat Fleets*, p.698.
3. Norman Friedman. *US Aircraft Carriers*. Arms & Armour Press, London, 1983, p.351.
4. 'UK Shipbuilding - do we have a basic capacity left?', *Shipping World & Shipbuilder*, March 1989, p.84.
5. See Lehman. 'Aircraft Carriers: The Real Choices', in *The Washington Papers*, No.52, Beverley Hills, 1978, p.54.
6. Elliott/Starr 'Soviets "building third carrier" ', in *Jane's Defence Weekly*, 25 March 1989, p.495.
7. *Combat Fleets*, p.573.
8. Schulz-Torge 'Tbilisi - Only a Super Kiev', in *RUSI Journal*, Autumn 1988, p.30.
9. 'Future Soviet carrier aircraft', in *Jane's Defence Weekly*, 25 March 1989, p.524.
10. e.g., Schulz-Torge, op.cit., p.31.
11. 'New Soviet aircraft carrier in detail', in *Jane's Defence Weekly*, 5 November 1988, p.1147.
12. *Combat Fleets*, p.130.
13. 'French Naval Exhibition' feature in *Navy International*, January 1989, p.44.
14. Isnard. 'France delays F/A-18 aircraft carriers tests', in *Jane's Defence Weekly*, February 1989.
15. *Combat Fleets*, p.710, and Taylor. *Naval Air Power*, Hamlyn, London, 1986, p.57.
16. Walters. 'Top Cover for Tomorrow's Fleets', in *Navy International*, April 1988, p.175.
17. *Combat Fleets*, p.693.
18. 'US Navy Advanced AAM Project', in *Navy International*, April, 1988, p.177.
19. 'Next Generation Sparrow', in *Navy International*, April, 1988, p.176.
20. Cook. 'Tornado set for RAF maritime role', in *Jane's Defence Weekly*, 11 March 1989, p.382.
21. Lehman. op.cit., p.72.
22. Rains and Adams. 'The Flight Deck DD 963', in (US) *Naval Engineers' Journal*, April, 1978, p.149.
23. Taylor. *Naval Air Power*, Hamlyn, London, 1986, p.147.
24. Lehman. op.cit., p.60.
25. Data from 'The V-22 Osprey',

Bell-Boeing Publication No.4-87/20M/HER.
26. Letter to Author from Bell-Boeing, Arlington, VA dated 5 August 1988.
27. Fox. 'Defence Cut in US may hit British firms', in London *Daily Telegraph*, 20 April 1989.
28. Hobbs. 'New Technology and Naval Helicopters', in *Naval Forces*, 1988.
29. Toombs. 'HS to VS: Leave the Hovering to Us', in *US Naval Institute Proceedings*, October, 1987, p.145.
30. Galdoris. 'The SH-60F: New Capabilities for the Battle Group', in *US Naval Institute Proceedings*, February, 1987, p.88.
31. *Hobbs*. ibid.
32. 'More on India's indigenous carrier', in *International Defence Review* (hereinafter, *IDR*), March, 1989, p.248.
33. Ciampi. 'Italians to evaluate carrier aircraft', in *Jane's Defence Weekly*, 1 April 1988, p.555.
34. Lloyd. *Seakeeping. Ship behaviour in rough weather*. Horwood, Chichester, 1989, p.437.
35. Hewish. 'EH101 adopted by three navies', in *IDR*, February, 1989, p.185.
36. Hewish. ibid., p.186.
37. Salvy. 'HF90: Crucial decisions due this year', in *IDR*, February, 1989, p.184.
38. Elliott. 'NFR 90 frigate requirement likely to reach 59 hulls', in *Jane's Defence Weekly*, 15 April 1989, p.631.
39. 'Sea Services Benefit from growing Sikorsky Programmes', Sikorsky Press Release, 88-No.87.
40. 'The Penguin Anti-Ship Missile System', in Forsvarsteknologi: A/S Publication.
41. Hewish, Salvy and Sweetman. 'Naval Helicopters', in *IDR*, March, 1987, p.296.
42. Hewish, Salvy and Sweetman. ibid., p.297.
43. Bussiere, 'AS 15 TT Lightweight Anti-Ship Search and Attack System', in *NATO's 16 Nations*, June/July, 1983, p.108.
44. Hewish and Turbe. 'French and British (helicopter) programmes', in *IDR*, February, 1989, p.187.
45. Letter to Author from Kaman Aerospace International Corporation dated 5 January 1989.
46. 'US Navy MH-53E Sea Dragon', United Technologies/Sikorsky Aircraft Factsheet

Rev. 3–87.
47. *Combat Fleets*, p.577.
48. Hobbs. 'New Technology and Naval Helicopters', in *Naval Forces*, 1/1989, p.18.
49. Hobbs. ibid., p.20.
50. Sweetman. 'New Technology for the Military Helicopter', in *IDR*, February, 1986, p.183.
51. Steven Zaloga. 'Soviets place high priority on submarine modernization program', in (US) *Armed Forces Journal International*, April, 1989, p.26.
52. Wettern. 'Navy Pilots to test Airship', in London *Daily Telegraph*, 9 April 1979, p.21.
53. Wettern. 'The Airship in ASW and AEW', in *Naval International*, March 1982, p.932.
54. Wettern. 'US Plans for Airships', in *Jane's Defence Weekly*, 4 July 1987, p.1447.
55. Wettern. ibid., p.1449.
56. Data from *Sentinel Series Skyships*, Westinghouse - Airship Industries Publication.
57. 'Anti-stealth airship review success', in *Jane's Defence Weekly*, 11 March 1989, p.395.
58. 'New developments in (Soviet) naval C^{3}I', in *Jane's Defence Weekly*, 8 October 1988, p.889.
59. Cook, 'US Navy wants ASW airship details', in *Jane's Defence Weekly*, 3 December 1988, p.1394.
60. As quoted by Cunningham. 'Unmanned Offensive Aircraft - Have they a Future?' in *RUSI Journal*, Summer, 1988, p.27.
61. Cunningham. ibid.
62. 'RPV at Sea', in *Defence Update/90*, August, 1988, p.16.
63. *Pointer*, Bell-Boeing Publication, 1988.
64. Swanborough and Bowers. *US Navy Aircraft since 1941*, Putnam, London, 1983, pp.264–5.
65. Swanborough and Bowers. ibid., p.280.
66. Hewish. 'Airborne anti-submarine warfare', in *IDR*, December, 1988, p.1597.
67. Sweetman. 'P-3 Update IV and LRAACA US airborne ASW assets for the 1990s', in *IDR*, February, 1989, p.215.
68. 'P-3Gs to replace W(est) German Atlantics', in *Jane's Defence Weekly*, 26 November 1988, p.1327.
69. *Combat Fleets*, p.298.
70. *Combat Fleets*, p.576.

NUCLEAR SUBMARINES

Attack Submarines (SSN)

Known alternatively as a 'fleet' submarine in the Royal Navy, the SSN has progressed steadily from her introduction, three and a half decades ago, to a point where, today, she is vulnerable really only to another of her own kind. Her primary asset, the virtually unlimited endurance conferred by nuclear power, has been combined with a 'high speed hull', stealth features and long-ranged sonars and weapons to create a formidable fighting platform. The cost of the SSN and her infrastructure have, so far, guaranteed exclusiveness to a small 'nuclear club', thus further enhancing the type's superiority over other fleets not so equipped. Expenditure is spoken of in terms of 'billions' rather than 'millions', e.g., even after having constructed more than eighty SSN-688 (*Los Angeles*) SSNs, the Americans' unit cost for the pair funded for FY89 is stated to be 0.84 billion dollars, while appropriations for the first-of-class SSN-21 (Sea Wolf) follow-on is equal to the two 688s combined.[1] It is an irony that, while the SSN is a machine supreme in its field, it needs continual improvement because 'the club' has members on each side of the great East/West political divide.

Only France, the Soviet Union, the United States and the United Kingdom produce original SSN designs (and even the UK uses so much American technology that export to a third party is usually only by permission). Communist China is slowly feeling its way to 'go solo' following dependence upon Soviet knowhow.

A notable 'first' during 1988 was the transfer of a Soviet Charlie I on charter to the Indian Navy. Although non-aligned and lacking a true maritime enemy in its theatre, the Indian Navy is making a determined bid for pre-eminence, but SSNs can be seen mainly as prestige units. In this case, the policy may backfire. With the boat's charter complete, the Indian Navy will not willingly revert to an all-conventional submarine force, however modern. The state will then either be saddled with a crippling bill for a permanent force and infrastructure or, worse, accept further boats on 'friendship' terms with concomitant Soviet demands for concessions as a price for technological support. When selecting one's supper mates, one should take into account the length of one's spoon.

The supremacy of the SSN over the 'conventional' (SSK) rests on her higher performance, effectively unlimited endurance and her lower indiscretion rate. Unlike the SSK, the SSN can hunt down a specific

▶ Not the Grand Canyon but a perspective mosaic of about 125km of the Mississippi and the Florida Escarpment at a depth of 3,000 metres. This 'picture' was constructed by Marconi using the British-developed 'Gloria' side-scan sonar. Sub-surface warfare will be greatly influenced by such detailed topographical knowledge. (Marconi Underwater Systems)

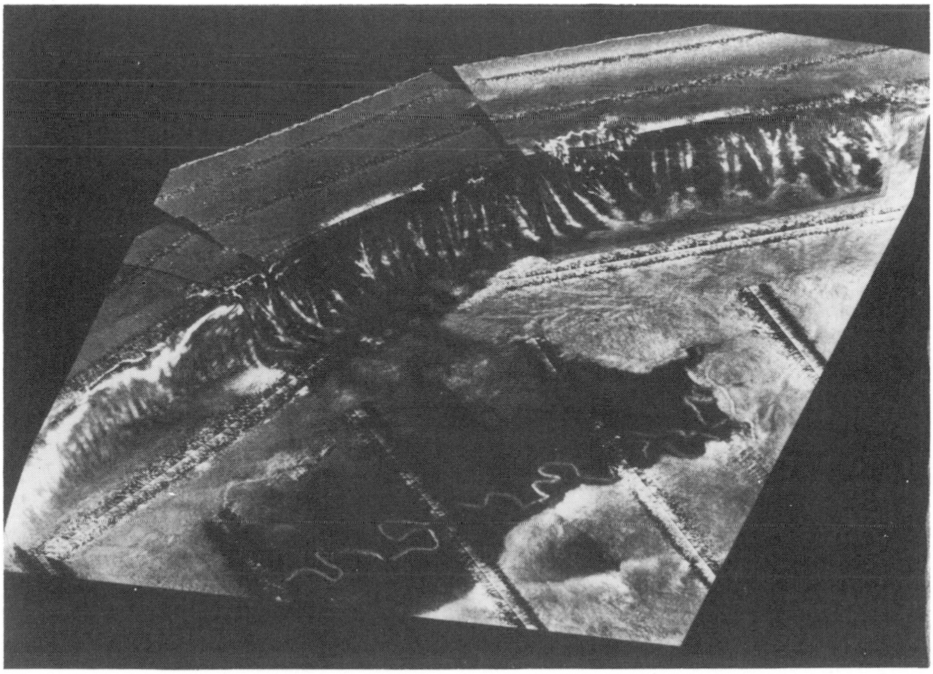

◄ Despite the entry into service of several submerge-launched anti-ship missiles, the heavyweight torpedo is likely to remain the most cost-effective weapon in the submarine's arsenal. A suitably jacketed Tigerfish is shown being loaded, tail-first, into a British C-class SSN. The acoustic cladding on the submarine's hull is shown to advantage. (Marconi Underwater Systems)

► Scheduled to enter service in the 'late eighties', the heavyweight Spearfish is due to replace the Tigerfish torpedo. Reputed to have attained 70 knots during trials, this two-tonner relies on good targeting and sheer speed rather than stealth, a logical development when targets are becoming quieter. (Marconi Underwater Systems)

quarry, assume an ideal attack position and disengage rapidly. Her much-vaunted high speed is used sparingly as it generates noise which both advertises her presence and degrades her sonar reception.

In the classic East/West hot war scenario, an embattled Europe survives a conventional war only by a constant stream of re-supply convoys successfully crossing the Atlantic from the United States. Soviet SSNs seeking to interdict this vital SLOC (Sea Line of Communication) must be frustrated by their Western counterparts, acting as an element of a barrier applied at strategic chokepoints.

Much of the Soviet surface fleet is dedicated to friendly submarine support through ASW and this, too, will have to be countered. Opinions differ on whether the strategic missile submarines (SSBN) of each side should be left alone at the outset of war, or neutralized immediately. This decision could well depend upon the manner of their employment. Successive improvements in the range and accuracy of ICBMs have seen

the SSBNs carrying them being able to deploy ever farther afield. The support of these distant forces has been a major factor in the Soviet surface fleet's transition from coastal to 'blue water' capability.

Inevitably, strategic missiles have reached the stage where SSBNs no longer require to leave home water. This has produced the 'bastion' concept, where the boats lie back in a protected area, covered by supporting forces with the advantage of working close to their home bases. Enemy SSNs tasked with penetrating such a zone would find themselves heavily out-numbered, and would be fortunate to inflict a one-for-one loss rate. With the West's current slim superiority in numbers, such a campaign of attrition would be unsustainable. Fortunately, the defences have caught up somewhat. Likely targets are supported against multiple re-entry vehicles by anti-missile missile systems, while such as the Strategic Defence Initiative (SDI, or 'StarWars'), however much bluff rather than reality, seek to intercept the missile in ballistic flight.

The longer the range, the longer the defences have time to react, and evidence is mounting that Soviet SSBN patrols are again being undertaken closer to the US coast. Although such patrols are probably supported by friendly SSNs, it does simplify the job of the defence.

It is in the support of surface groups that SSNs have problems. Such formations will attract submarine attack and the concept of an attached SSN is logical. Indeed, it is reported that the American SSN-688 (*Los Angeles*) class was procured 'mainly to defend the battle group in direct support operations'.[2] While the sheer numbers of these boats suggest that other tasks are of equal importance, they have been difficult to integrate into an AS defence. To operate closely enough to a group to be of use causes sensor performance to be degraded due to the group's radiated noise, while for the submarine to keep pace with the group the problem is exacerbated. A listening submarine requires to proceed slowly and independently. Integrated operation with the defence is complicated further by com-

munications, real-time exchange of data requiring shallow submergence. Such a limitation will demand a high-priority solution, yet even this will not amount to a full answer. Soviet doctrine embraces a co-ordinated, multi-directional assault on a high-value surface group, using a variety of platforms. In the case of a carrier battle group (CVBG), this would be mounted from at least 250 miles distance, resulting in a 1,500-plus mile perimeter, which no friendly submarine could control.

The generous size of the SSN-688s, will allow for progressive improvement. From SSN-719 (USS *Providence*) on, each will have twelve vertical-launch Tomahawk cruise missiles sited in the free-flooding space between the forward end of the pressure hull and the spherical containment of the BQQ-5 active/passive sonar array. While this arrangement could release internal space for more torpedoes, reports indicate that eight Tomahawks will continue to be carried internally.[3] Space forward will be under even greater

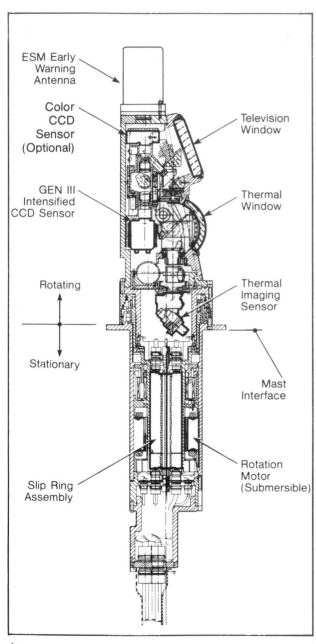

ESM Early
Warning
Antenna

**Color
CCD
Sensor
(Optional)**

Television
Window

GEN III
Intensified
CCD Sensor

Thermal
Window

Rotating

Thermal
Imaging
Sensor

Stationary

Mast
Interface

Rotation
Motor
(Submersible)

Slip Ring
Assembly

▲
Kollmorgen's Model 86 Optronic Mast not only provides several
means of imaging, but is non hull-penetrating, with only the head
rotatable. The next stage will be off-board sensing by towed devices,
the reconstituted 'pictures' and target data being displayed on
screens in a control room sited more conveniently in the submarine.
(Kollmorgen Corporation)

pressure from SSN-751 (USS *San Juan*) on because of
the shift of the diving planes from the fin ('sail') to the
bows. This measure is part of the 'Arcticization' of the
class, reducing the likelihood of damage when surfacing through ice. The low fin, now strengthened, does
not permit planes to be tuned into the vertical, while
hydrodynamic considerations militate against its being
heightened.

The SSN-688 programme will, by its termination,
have occupied two decades and, though the US Navy
considers later units to be twice as capable as those of
the initial design, the hull has reached the limits of its
potential.[4] In 1994, therefore, the first of the new Sea
Wolf (SSN-21) class will enter service. The reason for
what looks to be a radically different submarine is
simply that Soviet designers, having for years concentrated on rugged survivability and numbers, have
achieved experience and fleet strength sufficient to
allow indulgence in greater refinement and innovation,
reducing the qualitative lead on which the West
depended. Thus the Sea Wolf will be 'several times'
quieter than a 688, with silenced auxiliary machinery
and the adoption of the 'pump jet' propulsor permitting
silent steaming at up to 20 knots.[5] Considerably larger
in submerged displacement (9,150 against 6,927 tons),
the SSN-21 will be shorter and beamier to improve
agility, an important factor in the 'dog-fighting' thought
likely to result from attempts to penetrate bastion
areas. With this emphasis on ease of manoeuvre, the
after control surfaces have been subject to several
reported variations. While a conventional cruciform
layout appears in some artists' impressions, neither the
'X' nor 'inverted Y' (as favoured by Dutch and Swedish
SSK designers) is ruled out. An advantage of these
configurations is that each surface is part-rudder, part-
hydroplane, obviating the classic 'jammed-planes'
emergency. The drawback is the complexity of control,
particularly at high speed. The Sea Wolf's speed is
quoted[6] as '6 per cent' higher than that of the 688
which, itself a high-speed surface group escort, is
credited with 'over 32 knots' submerged.[7] Considering
the size of a 688, its four-tube armament appear
meagre, sited near-amidships to allow the sonars
pride-of-place right forward.

Although the best of weapons are of little use without
adequate sensors, the layout allowed only 26 weapons
to be loaded, four of which were in the tubes. While
this is believed to have been improved in later units,
the Sea Wolf will revert to bow-mounted tubes,

doubled in number and increased in diameter, probably to 24-inch (610mm). Better termed 'discharge' rather than 'torpedo' tubes, they have an increase of more than 30 per cent in cross-section, to facilitate handling the now wide range of submarine weaponry, including Sea Lance, Tomahawk, Harpoon, mines and heavyweight torpedoes. Both Sea Lance and Harpoon require encapsulation for launch, a factor that limits weapon diameter. A larger tube will relax this restriction though, in turn, requiring that standard 21-inch (533mm) rounds be sleeved. Oversize tubes will also allow a 21-inch Mk 48 torpedo to be 'swum-out' rather than ejected, the annular gap allowing water to flow in to fill the vacated volume of the torpedo. Swim-out tubes are simpler, a factor in permitting the SSN-21 to accommodate eight. The British prefer torpedo ejection by a positive water pulse, marginally noisier but obviating the need for the weapon to expend some if its limited energy in initial acceleration.

The trend to fewer tubes followed logically on the greater accuracy of modern weapons, but has proved limiting. The variety of current weapons may require more than one type to be loaded at one time. Improved weapon control systems allow several targets to be engaged simultaneously, while a wire-guided Mk 48 may run for a quarter-hour, during which time the tube cannot be reloaded.

While the pattern of American SSN procurement is characterized by substantial numbers of a standard design, the Soviets experiment widely. It is estimated that they have a lead in hull materials and design, operational depth, maximum speed, reactor power density, automation (surprisingly) and survivability.[8] Obviously the sum of these qualities cannot be applied to every submarine class, while some may be deliberate American over-emphasis to alarm Congress into the release of more funds. Nevertheless, Soviet SSNs are undeniably improving in every respect, including what is no longer seen as an out-of-date concept, the double hull.

Because large quantities of oil fuel no longer needed to be carried in external tanks, Western SSN designers adopted the single hull to minimize weight and wetted area for a given internal volume. The Soviets remained with the double hull (i.e., the pressure hull completely or partially surrounded by a free-flooding casing), accepting a smaller diameter pressure hull for, while the useful volume of this could be maximized by siting deep frames between the hulls, it could also resist

greater pressures. Further fittings, which necessarily occupy space within Western boats, can, when suitably strengthened, be fitted externally in Soviet types, increasing their internal usable space even further. The Russians are also ready to exploit novel constructional materials, with a massive investment having been made, for instance, in the production and fabrication of titanium. Due to the characteristics of this material, the Soviet Alfa reportedly is able to dive to 700 metres or better, against the SSN-688's 450 metres.[9] While all such released figures should be treated with caution, they suggest that Soviet boats with smaller-diameter hulls in high-yield steel could achieve 500–600 metres, with titanium-hulled boats moving towards 1,000 metres.[10] Alternatively, such stronger materials would allow for lighter hulls at more moderate depths, with benefits in increased payload. Also reported is Soviet interest in hulls constructed of composite materials.[11] If feasible, these would be cheaper and have reduced acoustic and magnetic signatures.

Compared with the bulk of a 688, the Alfa's appears to confound hydrodynamic laws in being able to develop power for 40 knots on a submerged displacement of only 3,700 tons. Its secret appears to lie in compact systems, using liquid metals rather than pressurized water for reactor cooling. Western experiments in this area indicated corrosion rates incompatible with safety, lower Soviet standards being evidenced by their higher accident rate.[12]

Double hulls have advantages in addition to those discussed above. While a water-filled space would appear to offer little protection from the shock wave produced by a torpedo exploding against the outer hull, a submarine is more likely to survive in a shock-damaged condition than with a breached pressure hull. This obliges torpedoes to be fitted with larger and more complex explosive charges which, for a given size of weapon, has to be at the expense of something else. It is further possible that an outer hull, as on a fighting vehicle, could be fitted with reactive armour.

Given sufficient inter-hull spacing, it is possible to install pressure-tight missile silo/launchers, as the Soviets have long done and towards which the Americans are moving with their vertical-launch Tomahawk-armed 688s. The consequent ability to ship larger numbers of cruise missiles erodes the earlier distinction between the SSN and SSGN.

Of the remaining two SSN operators, France and the United Kingdom, current interest is directed primarily

The raw power of the nuclear attack submarine, exemplified by the USS *Helena* (SSN 725). While yielding nothing in terms of capability, the SSN 21 successor to such boats will place more emphasis on stealth, particularly in under-ice operation, an area of increasing importance. (General Dynamics. Electric Boat Division)

not only at technical development but also at the successful sale of a flotilla to Canada. Repeated and uninvited incursions by American submarines beneath the ice covering Canada's vast northern offshore zone have demonstrated the nation's total inability to enforce sovereign rights. The Americans seem to have behaved with arrogant heavyhandedness that smacks of British attitudes prior to the War of 1812, convincing the normally passive Canadians that they, too, need nuclear submarines – but not American nuclear submarines. Ten or twelve hulls have been mentioned and the choice would appear to be a straight one between British or French, although political considerations may prove as significant as technical excellence.

The British contender is the new 'W' (SSN 20) design, derived directly from the currently completing septet of *Trafalgars*, themselves the latest in a steady quarter-century of evolution. Top-quality boats, they are immensely quiet and effective, their under-ice capability demonstrated in numerous exercises. The French are marketing the *Amethyste* derivative of the four-boat *Rubis* class, which were not only the first French SSNs but which began to enter service as recently as 1983. They are cheaper than the British boats, smaller and probably more agile, but slower. Under-ice capability, not required for French deployments, was hastily added. The British Ts have a reported endurance of 85 days, the *Rubis* only 45.[13] Strangely the *Amethyste*, with virtually the same displacement as a *Rubis*, and with a larger crew, has an official endurance of 90 days.

A drawback to the British design is its requirement for 100 crew, compared with the French 66, making for a vastly greater recruitment, training and retention problem. This, coupled with the lower French-unit price and the specification for the British entry being possibly over-high for Canadian requirements, must favour the French. The French-Canadian lobby is vociferous and the Ottawa government is clearly having difficulty in reaching a decision, gratefully deferring an announcement until the dust of a general election has settled. It may well prove that a shift in the political centre of gravity results in the abandonment of the entire programme.

A possible surprise could result from Brazil's announced policy of building an indigenously designed SSN by the turn of the century. This may be no more than sabre-rattling to upset the neighbours, Brazil only now obtaining her first submarine-building experience through technology transfer from the Germans. This is by the usual route of contracting for a specific number of boats, only the first one or two of which are constructed in the country of origin, which then provides an appropriate degree of technical expertise and parts to complete the remainder in the customer's own yards. Even with such assistance, construction times tend to be protracted and extrapolation from SSK to SSN appears unrealistic.

Cruise Missile Submarines (SSGN)

The Soviets early introduced the large, submarine-launched cruise missile for use against Western carrier groups. For targeting and mid-course correction, the SSGNs carrying them were supported by long-range maritime patrol aircraft (MPA), themselves useful platforms for complementary air-launched weapons. Juliett and Echo II-class boats of the sixties had the tactical limitation of needing to surface to launch, accepted only through the approximately 300-mile range of their SS-N-3 and -12 missiles. The Charlie I and IIs, that succeeded them in the seventies and eighties, deployed SS-N-7 and -9s which, while having a range estimated at only 30–40 miles, were infinitely more dangerous in being launched submerged. Both are credited with a choice of 500kg conventional or nuclear payload.[14] Needing to penetrate a surface group's outer screen, the Charlies were given clean lines attuned to silence rather than speed, the hull itself being quite portly to accommodate silo/launchers between their double hulls. It is reported[15] that their construction was abandoned in turn due to the introduction of a new heavyweight, wake-homing torpedo, launched from a 650mm (25.6-inch) tube and capable of a range of 100 kilometres (54 nautical miles) at 30 knots,[16] superior to that of an SS-N-9 and deployable by faster submarines from outside the screen.

The next stage was to develop a cruise missile deliverable from a safe distance and in numbers that would saturate a defence. This was the SS-N-19, able reportedly to reach '239' nautical miles (nearly 450km).[17] As with the SS-N-3 before it, the weapon was deployed by a submarine/surface ship combination, in this case the large Kirov cruisers with 20 each and the purpose-designed Oscar II SSGNs with 24. On paper, the SS-N-19 (appropriately code-named 'Shipwreck') is

the equivalent of Tomahawk at sea, but, where all but the very latest Americans have to launch the latter singly, from torpedo tubes, even a single Oscar II could rapidly disorganize a group's defences with a ripple-fired salvo, though it is not certain how evasive a course the missiles could follow. A further new targeting element is the Punch Bowl antenna for receiving satellite information.

The Oscar II's two dozen missiles are housed in paired launchers, sited along each side between a smallish-diameter pressure hull and an enormous, slab-sided casing, the apertures at the top closed off with flush-fitting doors. Her bulk militates against high speed and she would need to reach and maintain an undetected position in order to ambush a target. Only four Oscars were built before the design was stretched by ten metres to the Oscar II variant, possibly a means to improve her lines, marginally increasing speed while also making the flow over the propeller disc more uniform as a quieting measure. Oscar II is also credited with four standard (533mm/21-inch) tubes and four oversize (650mm/25.6-inch).[18] This would enable her to deploy stand-off anti-submarine missiles, the 19nm (35km) SS-N-15 and/or the 54nm (100km) SS-N-16.

It is apparent that the dedicated SSGN is likely to survive in only small numbers for specialist tasks, while the SSN will acquire something of the versatility of the surface ship's VLS in the ability to match missile loadout with mission. This raises the interesting point that, even if continuing rapprochement between East and West succeeds in abolishing the submarine-launched ICBM, the cruise missile will merely develop to replace it. In the beginning, there was Polaris, a 1,250-odd mile weapon shipped aboard an SSBN of ad hoc design. Similar weapons of opposing camps (including that of the French, who are paying dearly for a truly independent system) have steadily kept pace with successive hikes in range and potential. For all the vast expenditure, strategic missile submarine forces represent a stalemate; enormous missiles locked in enormous hulls, protected in secure bastions. With stalemate there exists a sort of guarantee, a guarantee challenged by the American Strategic Defence Initiative, which triggered a flurry of negotiation and compromise.

The Tomahawk cruise missile is, meanwhile, already capable of being SSN-launched for a 1,500-mile precision overland flight, equivalent roughly to the A-1

▶ An encapsulated Tomahawk missile blasts from the water under boost motor power following launch from the tube of an SSN. The anti-ship version has 250-mile range, the conventionally armed land attack versions up to 700 miles and the nuclear-armed land attack version up to 1,350 miles, the latter giving an SSN strategic firepower. (General Dynamics Corporation)

Polaris. It will, of course, be improved; it may or may not be deployed on any particular SSN mission; if it is, it may or may not be nuclear-tipped. Uncertainty would abound and international monitoring be near impossible.

While the future of the SSN in its various forms is assured, that of the SSBN is less so. East/West *détente* has made great progress in the Gorbachev era, but, at the time of writing, changes wrought in the Soviet Union are by no means irreversible. Conservative elements may yet emerge triumphant to set back the clock again. The simple truth is that strategic nuclear weapons cannot be abolished without major parallel adjustments in conventional forces. In these, the Warsaw Pact currently enjoys such a superiority that

western Europe has to rely on nuclear deterrence to guarantee to the East that any major military adventure could be successful only at unacceptable cost. To accept a 'Zero Option' without conditions would leave the West open to defeat by conventional means. The alternative, of building the West's conventional forces to match those of the East, is beyond any democratic nation's pocket.

There are other aspects. As long, for instance, as Typhoons and Delta IVs deploy SS-N-20s and -23s, with steadily increasing re-entry vehicle size and warhead yield, so must the Americans lavish defence dollars on developing the means to keep them out.[19] The immense American strength in SSBNs is a counterstrike force, a deterrence. Yet, after Pearl

Harbor, it is unthinkable to Americans ever again to be hostage to pre-emptive attack so, as the initiative is with the aggressor, funds are directed to such as SDI. Resources directed to either support or to counter the strategic missile cannot be used for conventional means, so surface fleets are the less capable because of this.

It is interesting to speculate on the direction that Soviet fleet development would take once released from the heavy influence of the SSBN. In most respects it has evolved, post-Second World War, in response to Western initiatives. Western superiority in carrier and amphibious forces saw the introduction of large anti-ship missiles by the Russians, together with the surface and aerial platforms for their delivery. The West's continuing dependence upon mercantile shipping to wage a war of any magnitude attracted the Soviet response of larger numbers of submarine and cruisers to destroy it. As the 'threat' from carrier and amphibious forces diminished with the progressive retirement of war-built tonnage, a new bogey made its appearance in the submarine-launched ballistic missile. This provoked the new response of Soviet ASW ships; at first, low-endurance vessels capable of being covered by land-based air, but gradually developing more all-round capability as the need to operate farther offshore was addressed. With the introduction of the Russians' own submarine-based systems came the requirement for surface support, the submarines requiring access to the deep oceans in order to close

the enemy's coast to within a few hundred miles. Strategic missiles of both camps advanced in stages from the 1,250-mile A-1 Polaris to the near 7,000-mile D-5 Trident, planned to go to sea for the first time in the USS *Tennessee* (SSBN-734) early in 1989.[20] If not operating from protected bastions, such craft may need support on a world-wide basis, not least to counter enemy SSNs that would be seeking them out. Soviet 'anti-submarine ships' thus progressed steadily through cruisers to ·aviation carriers, lacking fixed-wing (CTOL) capability. Ships of this value themselves required support, resulting in the formation of a 'balanced fleet' closely akin to the ideals of the recent past.

Although large, however, this Soviet fleet differs significantly from the US fleet in that it is not structured for 'power projection'; its amphibious and carrier elements are comparatively modest while its Fleet Train would need to be drawn from the ranks of the, admittedly technically advanced, Merchant Marine. Despite being the carrier of the nation's major nuclear deterrence, the fleet still finds itself a service junior to the army. Nevertheless, its rapid evolution under the late Admiral Gorshkov saw it gain true 'blue water' status with attendant benefits that a world-wide 'presence' can bring. If it is argued, therefore, that the Soviet fleet has been shaped by the demands of strategic submarine warfare, what would be the effect of the removal of those submarines? It is unlikely that the army would benefit significantly for, having be-

◄
A simulated 'soft' target saturated by a deadly rain of sub-munitions released by a Tomahawk cruise missile hundreds of miles inland from the point of launch. (General

►
ESM antennae are the first to be extended above the surface by any submarine. They are for the purposes of threat warning, assessment of the tactical situation, or target designation. (Thomson – CSF)

▼
Before the commander can make a fully considered decision, the ESM operator has to construct a display such as that illustrated. Sources of emissions are numbered and, however transient, need to be identified by analysis. (Thomson – CSF)

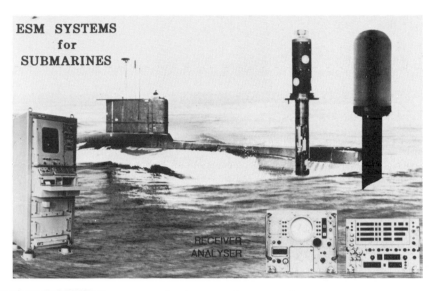

ESM SYSTEMS for SUBMARINES

RECEIVER ANALYSER

come a leading naval power, the Russians would not easily relinquish it, particularly as the Americans would not. Without SSBN-orientated strictures, it is probable that 'power projection' in the Western sense would be expanded. If Soviet Russia aims eventually to enter a free world market and if it is accepted that the Asian Pacific rim is the site of the next 'super-economy', the influence of a capable fleet would bring benefits in the classical mould of sea power.

In the real world, the cynical view may well prevail – that the SSBNs with their giant burden will be progressively negotiated away at a rate directly proportional to the growing capability of the terrain-following, SSN-launched cruise missile. Such a policy would show politicians working in a 'statesmanlike' manner, saving large defence budgets through the high-profile dismantling of universally unpopular weapons while, simultaneously, covering their rear by alternative means.

Until, however, the SSBN slips into history, it is well worth exploiting a major weakness – communications. To remain covert, it would wherever possible avoid approaching the surface for orthodox radio communication while ever-improving enemy sensors make trailing wire antennae or towed communications buoys unpopular.[21] Very-Low and Extra-Low Frequency (VLF at 3-30kHz and ELF at 3Hz-3kHz) transmissions are, however, little attenuated by water and can travel immense distances. Unfortunately, the transmitting antennae need to be of similar order of length to the wavelength of their signal. Thus, for the 16kHz reportedly used by the Royal Navy, a theoretical antenna length of nearly 6 miles would be required, while the US Navy's 76Hz would need more than 1,200 miles.[22]

The method adopted is to string a straight cable antenna above ground for a distance of several miles and, by earthing it at either end, create a return signal path through a suitable deep geological formation. In power terms the system is inefficient and, with a low bandwidth, it is able to transmit only at a low data rate. Even for VLF reception, trailing antennae of up to 640 metres are required, inhibiting the boat's freedom of movement while still obliging it to surface.[23] Worse, the boat can only receive, not transmit. For these reasons, the Americans use three-letter groups, each with a discrete meaning (yet still requiring several minutes to transmit), or use an ELF signal as a 'bell-ringer', an instruction to close the surface to receive a longer transmission at higher frequency. By the adoption of ELF the Americans have achieved their aim of being in contact with all SSBNs for 99.9 per cent of the time, transmissions even penetrating ice cover with little loss. As, however, the transmitting stations are vulnerable to attack, they duplicate the link with so-called TACAMO (Take Charge and Move Out) airborne command posts, one of which is continually in flight over the Atlantic and the Pacific.[24] The Hercules EC-130 Qs modified originally for the task are being replaced by Boeing 707 airframes modified to the E-6A (Hermes) variant.[25] For the Soviets the venerable Bear J appears to perform the same function.

The American aircraft reportedly deploy a pair of trailing antennae, one 30,000 feet (more than 9,000 metres) in length, the other 4,000 feet (c.1,200m), to transmit a signal capable of penetrating only '30–40 feet' (c.9–12m) of sea water.[26] This compared with ELF's '300 or more feet' (c.90m) or, according to another source, '120–180 metres' (c.390–590 feet).[27] Not only are such aircraft difficult to protect adequately, with their destruction having potentially crippling effects on SSBN capability, but the boats themselves need at times to cruise at depths shallower than would appear desirable.

During the early eighties, blue-green lasers, able to penetrate '100–200 feet' (c.30–60 metres) of sea water, were being suggested for communications purposes.[28] In 1987, however, this possibly vital principle, embodied in a system called SLCSAT, was not being seriously pursued by the US Navy for which the service was criticized within Congress, whose committee thought the navy to be over-influenced by ELF and TACAMO manufacturer lobbying.[29] While SLCSAT has been under development since 1978, it is undoubtedly technically difficult to scan a laser pencil-beam from a satellite with sufficient precision to allow its unambiguous reception by a particular submarine. In addition, another source suggests that the oceans' naturally occurring bioluminescence could well mask a weak laser signal at the submarine end.[30]

Currently, it is planned to decommission two Poseidon boats for every Trident *Ohio* beyond USS *Nevada* (SSBN-733). At this rate Poseidon carriers will have been phased out in favour of twenty Trident boats by about 1998. While the fleet will have diminished from a peak of about 36 boats, utilization will rise from 55 to 66 per cent, with yet more dependence upon secure and reliable communications.

References and Notes

1. US Navy Appropriation Account Figures, quoted by O'Rourke, 'US Submarines. SS-21. New Design for the 21st Century', in *Navy International*, October, 1987, p.603.
2. Frigge. 'Winning Battle Group ASW', in *US Naval Institute Proceedings*, October, 1987, p.136.
3. *Combat Fleets*, p.718.
4. O'Rourke. op cit., p.607.
5. *Combat Fleets*, pp.716–7.
6. O'Rourke. op. cit., p.601.
7. Morison and Rowe. *Warships of the US Navy*. Jane's, London, 1983, p.16.
8. Norman Polmar. *Guide to the Soviet Navy*. Naval Institute Press, Annapolis, 1986, p.1.
9. *Combat Fleets*, p.718.
10. Engelhardt. 'Soviet Sub Design Philosophy', in *US Naval Institute Proceedings*, October, 1987, p.198.
11. Engelhardt. ibid., p.198.
12. Norman Friedman. *Submarine Design and Development*. Conway, 1984, p.134.
13. *Combat Fleets*, p.208.
14. *Combat Fleets*, pp.563–4.
15. Jordan. '"Oscar" – a change in Soviet Naval Policy', in *Jane's Defence Weekly*, 24 May 1986, p.943.
16. *Combat Fleets*, p.570.
17. 'Oscar II', in *Jane's Defence Weekly*, 24 September 1988, p.733.
18. Ibid.
19. e.g., see 'Developments in (Soviet) submarine forces', in *Jane's Defence Weekly*, 12 November 1988, p.1233.
20. *Combat Fleets*, p.690.
21. e.g., see Norman Friedman. *Submarine Design and Development*. Conway, 1984, p.152.
22. Spaven. 'Communicating with Submarines', in *Jane's Defence Weekly*, 23 November 1985, p.1152.
23. Ibid., p.1153.
24. Beam. 'Resurrection of the ELF', in *US Naval Institute Proceedings*, April, 1983, p.117.
25. Swanborough and Bowers. *US Navy Aircraft*. Putnam, p.276.
26. Stefanick. *Strategic Anti-submarine Warfare and Naval Strategy*. Institute for Defense and Disarmament Studies, Lexington, 1987, p.147.
27. Spaven. op. cit., p.1154.
28. Beam. op. cit., p.117.
29. 'USN criticized for not using submarine laser communications', in *Jane's Defence Weekly*, 14 November 1987, p.1097.
30. Stefanick. op. cit., p.18.

CONVENTIONAL SUBMARINES

Within the élite club of nations possessing the capability to build and operate nuclear-propelled attack submarines (SSN) there is endless controversy regarding the continued construction of 'conventionals'. Where no such option exists the requirement for them is not questioned and numbers in operation worldwide are rising steadily. In 1954, outside the nuclear club, twenty fleets operated a total of 89 submarines. By 1984, twice as many fleets operated four times as many submarines.[1] Most, if they could afford it, would prefer SSNs. The 'club', on the other hand, has such a supremacy that it would be foolish to

make its technology generally available. Despite this, market forces show signs of being a more powerful factor. The unprecedented loan of an SSN by the Soviet Union to India has conferred prestige to the latter which it will not easily relinquish, while the United Kingdom and France are locked in commercial combat over a stated Canadian requirement for possibly a dozen SSNs. Should Saudi Arabia succeed in purchasing, or Brazil succeed in its stated aim of building, SSNs, the current power balance would be upset, with Argentina and Chile, for instance, willing to risk bankruptcy rather than see Brazilian supremacy. It is

The Italian *Salvatore Pelosi* (S 522) shows a clean pressure hull, but, perhaps surprisingly, an upper casing with sharp discontinuity at its junction with the hull, a feature that could reduce agility of manoeuvre. The three paired prominent sonar domes are probably associated with passive range finding (Italian Navy)

45

Repeated incursions by Soviet submarines into Swedish territorial waters have obliged the Swedish Navy to increase its ships' ASW potential, run down with the disposal of larger units. *Stockholm*-class corvettes not only have hull sonar and VDS, but have also trialled the Plessey COMTASS towed array. (AB Bofors)

only when compared with an SSN that a 'conventional' or SSK, looks deficient. In its own right it is a very effective platform and current technology is moving rapidly to improve it significantly, while maintaining the immense cost differential which separates it from the SSN.

The SSK's great advantage is silence, lacking, for instance, the gearing and circulating pumps that generate much of an SSN's noise. The latter, however, can produce oxygen, water and spare electrical power almost as a by-product, her endurance effectively being that of her crew. While inheriting her 'high-speed' hull, the SSK remains energy-limited, with high submerged speed being a luxury of short duration. One of the best of the current generation, the German-built TR-1700s constructed for Argentina, are reported to be capable of covering 460 sea miles at 6 knots submerged (i.e., about 76 hours' endurance) yet only 20 sea miles at 25 knots (48 minutes).[2] Such is the price of speed.

'Conventionals' should be regarded as complementary to SSNs and not an inferior replacement. From this standpoint, they offer advantages. Their superior stealth enables them to be particularly effec-

tive at waylaying nuclear boats obliged to transit shallow continental shelf waters or chokepoints. In essence, where the SSN has the speed and endurance to pursue a target and is, thus, best used in the open ocean, the SSK still needs to rely on its target coming to it, and needs to utilize geographical or contrived restraints (such as minefields) for the purpose.

Larger SSKs are roughly the same size as smaller SSNs, e.g., with a common hull diameter of 7.60 metres, the British *Upholder*s (at 70.26 metres) are little shorter than the 72.10-metre-long French *Rubis* SSN, while the Soviet export Kilo SSKs are an estimated 73 metres in length.[3] Conventionals of this size are for distant water use and contrast with 43–46-metre boats built by, for instance, Germany and Italy, for confined waters such as the Baltic and the Mediterranean.

Current SSK practice has adopted the hydrodynamics of the high-speed hull so that, on the surface, only a diesel exhaust really differentiates them to the casual observer. The more portly hull reduces surface area and, therefore, drag, while presenting a smaller cross-section to active sonars. It offers also the space for two decks over the battery stowage, an important habitability point when a 44-man crew carries out a 49-day patrol.

Weapons stowage is on an inferior scale to earlier days. The 35-year-old design of the British *Oberon*s, for instance, allowed for 28 torpedoes, four of them short AS weapons in stern tubes.[4] The *Upholder*s will need to manage on eighteen. Where it can be argued that the *Oberon*s needed more weapons for the purpose of salvo firing, it must be remembered that the new boats' 'one-shot, one-hit' armoury comprises two types of torpedo and, possibly, Sub-Harpoon or mines.[5] Prior to a patrol, therefore, due consideration must be given to tailoring load-out to mission, and to correct internal stowage so as to guarantee fastest response to situations as they develop.

For launching of weapons, the British prefer positive water discharge as being quieter than, for instance, the German 'swim-out' method. The latter demands also some of a torpedo's limited energy resources and is adopted, reportedly, because of tight power availability on German-designed boats.[6]

Australia has recently embarked on a six-boat *Oberon*-replacement programme. The Swedish *Kockums* Type 471, which defeated the *Upholder* in the design competition, is larger and comparatively more slender with a length/breadth (L/B) ratio near to 10:1, moving again farther from the 7:1 quoted by Friedman as ideal, and used in the pioneering Albacore high-speed experiments that began in 1953.[7]

The complexity of modern sonar suites is typified by that specified to be incorporated in the, Type 471s.[8] Complementing one another in the Thomson/Sintra 'Scylla' suite are a large, cylindrical (usually passive) array in the forward casing, an intercept array in a small dome above and an active array within the fin. For two-thirds of the length along each side are flank arrays while above these are three distributed passive ranging transducers. Completing the set is a mine-avoidance sonar and eight separate self-noise monitoring units.

Released drawings of both the *Upholder* class and the Type 471 show that conventional hull-piercing periscopes have been specified. The length of these, sufficient to give adequate submergence during observations, encourages mast vibration and influences the submarine's vertical dimensions.

Current state-of-the-art is typified by Kollmorgen's Model 76, a modular design with 'optional extras'.[9] The search periscope, first to be extended, can be topped

with a passive, radar-detecting ESM unit, which can incorporate a D/F (direction-finding) capability. Mast profiles minimize radar cross-section with reflection being reduced further by RAM (radar-absorbent material) coatings. To counteract submarine angular movement, the periscope head prism can be gyro-stabilized. An image intensifier can be built into the optical path for use in low ambient light conditions, or a Thermal Imaging Module, working in the IR bands, can be installed for use in total darkness. Inputs from these can be fed through split-field optics to a video rangefinder; if the target's overall height can be estimated correctly, its range is calculable. While an estimation is involved, the method is totally passive. Positive ranging is by an integral radar antenna or a less-detectable laser rangefinder. A built-in vertical reference unit permits the taking of starsights as an alternative to a satellite navigation (Satnav) antenna. For extended observation in low threat areas the periscope can be remotely controlled and its output viewed on a monitor. As improving autopilots better control a boat's periscope depth-keeping, shorter non hull-penetrating periscopes can be used. With modern proliferation of masts this also reduces congestion in the control room. Non-penetrating periscopes are housed entirely within the casing and fin, their sensor outputs electronically conditioned and passed into the hull by cable or optical fibre. These signals can be reconstituted on to monitors via the boat's video and data busses. Kollmorgen's Model 86 Optronic Mast is typical, utilizing a static lower mast optimized for low radar cross-section and minimum plume.[10] Only the sensor head needs to be rotated, greatly reducing power demand. To further reduce periscope indiscretion, Kollmorgen is developing offboard sensors and a periscope mounted on a towed buoy.

An 'indiscretion rate' (or ratio) is expressed as a percentage of a submarine's time spent necessarily in activities that may betray her presence. Typically, these include communication, observation, obtaining targeting data or weapon launch. Further, an SSK needs to recharge batteries by 'snorting' so that, despite her superior silencing, her indiscretion rate is far higher than that of an SSN.

Having cautiously come shallow, a submarine will typically first extend an ESM passive receiver antenna. This will be linked to a comprehensive ESM suite which may, as in the case of the Israeli-built Elbit TIMNEX-4CH, offer also a valuable ELINT (Electronic

Intelligence) capacity. A large number of individual emissions can be monitored over the full 360 degrees of azimuth, the Kollmorgen Sea Sentry III, for instance, processing up to 35 simultaneous inputs, analysing them and comparing them with a threat library to establish the fifteen highest-priority threats, whose data are displayed in real time with a bearing accuracy of better than ten degrees. The more specialized British Racal Porpoise 2 can reduce this to just three degrees.[11]

Submarine-launched anti-ship missiles have horizon-range potential (for instance the American UGM-84 Sub-Harpoon is reportedly effective out to sixty miles), but to realize this submarines must rely on passively acquired ranges and bearings (never very accurate), be indiscreet in order to gather positive targeting data, or risk communications with a third party.[12] Should the boat be unsupported and her target be observing electronic silence, she may be obliged briefly to 'go active', a risk second only to actual weapon launch in disclosing her position.

The conventional's greatest limitation remains its dependence upon atmospheric oxygen for battery-charging and the needs of the crew. Nuclear plant develops energy without the need of oxygen, with copious electrical power which can be used to generate both oxygen and water for the crew. With the 'conventional' market burgeoning, therefore, intense research is being directed to methods of air-independent propulsion (AIP). More than one viable principle may evolve.

Historical precedence is taken by the closed-cycle (or anaerobic) diesel and, considering their dependence on the satisfactory outcome of the U-Boat war, it is surprising that the Germans did not devote more effort into research in this direction prior to 1945. While schemes abounded for the addition of high-pressure oxygen to diesel exhausts in order to permit their re-ingestion, the culmination of extensive shore trials was the never-completed trio of Type XVII Ks designed for a submerged endurance of 120 nautical miles at 16 knots.[13] The development appeared to be rival to Walter's, in which the breakdown of hydrogen peroxide produced heat and oxygen, in which fuel was burned, the total heat being used to generate steam for the driving of a turbine. A single Walter unit could propel a Type XVII B 150 nautical miles at 20 knots submerged. As proper handling procedures had not been evolved, hydrogen peroxide proved dangerously unstable and, having side-tracked closed-cycle diesels,

was itself abandoned in favour of the long-lived high-speed 'electric boat'. The latter, still with us, is inherently safe, but, as yet, atmosphere-dependent.

Current contender to lift this dependency is the British Cosworth Argo unit. Claimed to be compatible with any turbocharged diesel, and being evaluated by both the Germans and the Dutch, the Argo continuously passes a diesel's exhaust through a seawater scrubber, removing impurities and replacing them with oxygen, stored under pressure, together with trace elements to guarantee full combustion. Cosworth claim that its system will already run continuously for three weeks submerged and will operate to a maximum depth of 500 metres.[14] The system's advantage is its compatability with existing diesel technology. Even if successful, however, a diesel running under water is still noisier than a conventional electric motor, a fact which has not deterred the Italian concern of Maritalia from pursuing a similar line of development.

German interest, notably that of IKL, is directed more toward fuel cells. Superficially explained, these work in a reverse manner to hydrolysis, i.e., hydrogen and oxygen are persuaded to react chemically to produce water and electricity. The former, a by-product, is pure enough to drink, while the latter is used to charge batteries. The process is noiseless and evolves little heat, important factors in signature reduction, while hydrogen hazards are reduced through storing it in the form of metal hydrides.[15] Following six years of testing, a full-size fuel cell module was inserted into the hull of the German submarine *U 1*. Trials commenced at the end of 1987 and are expected to have a profound effect on submarine design.

Yet another alternative is the closed-cycle Stirling engine, which operates without the need noisily to explode fuel injected into a cylinder. A double-acting device, it features a pair of mechanically coupled pistons, one operating in each of a hot and cold environment. Between the two pistons is a working gas, which is passed cyclically through a regenerator alternately to heat and cool it. Heat is derived from the chambered combustion of diesel fuel in pure oxygen. The oxygen is the limiting factor from the endurance point of view, but it is stored for greatest efficiency in the cryogenic liquid phase (LOX). Combustion products are water and simply dissolved carbon dioxide, cooled before discharge.[16] With standard combustion chamber pressures of 20–30 bar, operation without exhaust gas compression is possible down to 2–300m.

◄
Despite an early record of innovation in submarine development, the Spanish Navy now licence-builds French designs, such as the Agosta-class *Galerna*. Having Atlantic interests as well as playing a more significant role within NATO, Spain may well opt for larger boats of enhanced performance. (Empresa Nacional BACAN)

▶
Against the dramatic backdrop of the Hawaiian highlands, a Mk 48 heavyweight is eased into the torpedo hatch of a submarine. The ADCAP (Added Capability) programme will see these 55-knot weapons uprated to serve in the teeth of improved countermeasures until well into the next century. (Westinghouse Electric Corporation, Oceanic Division)

The TP 617 is the Swedish Navy's standard heavyweight torpedo, capable of being launched from surface ships as well as submarines. Unusually it derives energy from the combustion of alcohol in oxygen derived from the breakdown of hydrogen peroxide. This is cost-effective and allows for some 30 test launches, but makes for a longer-than-usual weapon. (FFV Ordnance)

Exercise head

Homing head
Tracking light
Balloon
Releasable ballast
Datarecorder

Warhead

Homing head
Charge
Safety device
Impact fuze

Electronics section

Computer unit
Control
Signal processor
Proximity fuze

Most of the world's submarines are still 'conventionals' and the most fundamental breakthrough for the near future would seem to be the development of a successful system for air-independent propulsion. The 10-year-old Swedish submarine *Nacken* is here being relaunched after the addition of a section containing two Stirling engines. (Kockums Marine AB)

▶▶

A Stirling engine on its test bed. Hydrocarbon fuel is burned under pressure in an atmosphere of pure oxygen in the domed vessel. The process is continuous, non-explosive and silent, and the products of combustion can be discharged directly down to operating depths corresponding to pressures of up to 30 bar. (Kockums Marine AB)

Currently marketed is the Swedish United Stirling's 4-cylinder V4-275R engine developing 100 kW (134hp) at a continuous 2,200rpm. Following three years of test, an additional section containing a Stirling module has been inserted into the Swedish Navy's submarine *Näcken* by Kockum Marine. This company was responsible also for the design of the new Australian Type 471s which could be retrofitted with Stirlings.[17]

In the *Näcken*, the Stirling supplements her conventional machinery. Starting with full oxygen tanks and fully charged batteries, she could be capable of running submerged for nine, snort-free days, typically cruising on the Stirling and conducting up to four engagements on higher-powered batteries. This sequence will exhaust the batteries to the 50 per cent capacity that demands a recharge, but represents a five-fold improvement in endurance between indiscreet snortings. Parallel with this development, the Soviets launched in 1987 the 'Beluga' conventional, a one-off, itself believed to be a test-bed for a new propulsion system, possibly based on Stirling-type machinery.

A further project is the imaginative French *SAGA I* submarine which, at 545 tons submerged displacement, is the largest commercial submarine yet built. Powered by two Stirlings, she can support 4–6 divers under saturation conditions and can work with mani-

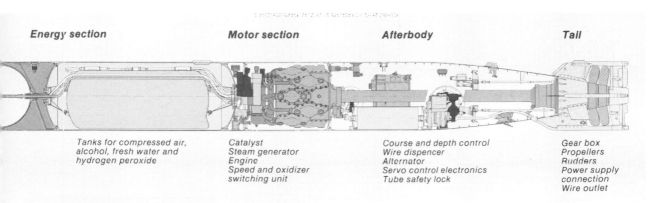

Energy section	Motor section	Afterbody	Tail
Tanks for compressed air, alcohol, fresh water and hydrogen peroxide	Catalyst Steam generator Engine Speed and oxidizer switching unit	Course and depth control Wire dispencer Alternator Servo control electronics Tube safety lock	Gear box Propellers Rudders Power supply connection Wire outlet

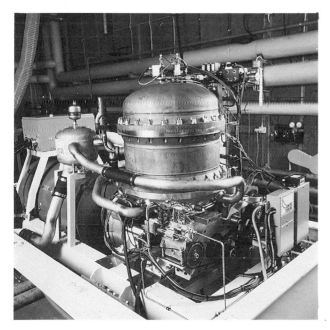

pulating tools down to 600 metres, for which further pressurization of the Stirlings' combustion chambers will be required.[18] Comex Industries, who run the project, are among the world's most experienced diving concerns and, though *SAGA I* is designed for commercial employment, her military uses are obvious. Her totally submerged operational profile allows for a double 150-mile passage, flanking a seven-day period of activities.

Kockums and United Stirling are researching beyond manned applications toward the Autonomous Remotely Operated Vehicle (AROV), combining the high energy density propulsion system with full auto-

mation to produce a compact military submersible with great potential. Working in the same direction, Comex Industries have teamed with the Canadians for the development of *SAGA II*. This, purely military, vehicle will incorporate a miniature nuclear power plant built by ECS (Energy Conversion Systems) which will run alongside conventional diesels. The Autonomous Marine Power Source (AMPS) works with low temperatures and pressures, so that a 100kW (134hp) unit, sufficient for a 200-ton coastal submarine, can be housed in a hull plug of 3.70 metres diameter and some 100 metres in length.[19] Heat derived from the reactor powers two Rankine-cycle engines and just 9 kilograms of fissile material is claimed to provide the energy necessary for 1,300 days of full-power submerged operation. AIP is obviously imminent. It will not improve speeds and it may increase a need for on-board oxygen without establishing a means of storing it, but it will reduce a major factor contributing to a conventional's indiscretion rate. Its introduction is well-timed to take advantage of the reduction and ultimate removal of the most inhibiting factor of all – the crew.

Unmanned submersible technology took off when offshore oil exploration moved from the benign waters of the Gulf of Mexico to the chill depths and harsh environment of northern Europe. Successive improvements in oil production methods led to work at depths where human divers can work only in expensive saturated conditions. Regular mandatory inspection and simple manipulative tasks are here best undertaken using remotely operated vehicles (ROV). This commercial requirement has resulted in considerable working experience being acquired in the essential areas of control, instrumentation, data handling/

transfer, and hull design, providing an invaluable technological base for military applications. Vivid recent proof was given by the exploring, and regrettable violation, of the *Titanic* wreck in 3,800 metres (12,500 feet) of water.

Any general war with the Warsaw Pact would involve the West's SSNs in the penetration of enemy 'bastions' and controlling access by his submarines to the North Atlantic through strategic 'chokepoints'. The West enjoys a slender numerical advantage in SSNs and, until recent years, these could individually rely on qualitative superiority, particularly in stealth. Soviet designs are fast catching up, however, and the advantage is eroded further when operations need to be conducted under ice. Simple accounting demands that Western boats ensure better than a 1:1 kill-to-loss ratio, but, for many scenarios, it is accepted that the loser in a duel would be he who first discloses his position, albeit by weapon launch. What is required is a force multiplier and that could well be the autonomous unmanned submersible. Its mode of use would relate to its capability, but its advantages are readily apparent. Cheap enough to be afforded in numbers it can, by being unmanned, be quite small, agile and, if required, able to work at considerable depths. Perhaps most importantly, it can be readily risked. A clue to possible size is offered by the Martin Marietta proposal for an Autonomous Underwater Vehicle (AUV), 9.14 metres in length and 1.37 metres in diameter, for use as SSBN decoys as well as unmanned functions in conjunction with SSNs and surface ships.[20] First-generation SSBNs, now decommissioning, could make carriers for, say, four AUV-sized vehicles, nested in the space vacated by missile tubes. These would be released and spaced along a barrier, each 'squadron' controlled by its parent, the line being backed by silent SSNs. Quiet enemy submarines need increasingly to be located by active sonars which, used by an SSN, betray its presence. Several active sonar-equipped AUVs would not only 'illuminate' an enemy but confuse it, concealing the presence of a torpedo-armed AUV or SSN. An AUV could easily imitate a high-value target to entice the enemy to reveal his position by attacking. Acoustically equipped AUVs could use noise as a weapon, saturating the area to screen a covert movement. Truly expendable, they can be used boldly, their applications at the moment limited only by real-time communication between parent and AUV.

A recent British study by SD Scicon suggests a similarly sized body of 10–11 metres by 1.80 metres which, it estimates, could be built at a current price of about £3 million.[21] Its primary role is seen as autonomous reconnaissance of up to two months' duration, using digital terrain-following navigational techniques. SPUR would cruise on a 9kW (12hp) fuel cell, switching to electric motor or closed-cycle internal combustion engine for attack or rapid evasion. Besides acting as an intelligence-gatherer, SPUR is seen as a weapons platform and, in the 'suicide' mode, as a weapon itself. Its current weakness, as with submarines themselves, is in communication, either to receive orders or to download data.

Limitations would appear to make it likely that direct submarine support will commence by one remote vehicle, tethered to its parent by an umbilical and used as a platform for countermeasures or an active sonar.[22] It could also be used to relay signals to further, free-ranging vehicles, thus avoiding the betrayal of the parent's position, and acting as a data relay if those vehicles are interrogated. An enemy would be unwilling to betray his whereabouts in order to attack a cheap, transmitting source knowing that it controlled other vehicles, yet undetected, some of which could 'illuminate' him for the benefit of attack by others. Even should such an engagement not account for the enemy, his position would be well-enough established for the ROV's parent to intervene.

Ranges offered by submarine-launched stand-off weapons are of little use without positive identification and targeting data. To remain discreet, a boat needs to rely on passive means, but, over this distance, range and bearing of a signal can be misjudged, while an acoustic signal can be degraded by sea clutter or noise of other ships, possibly neutral. Satellite observations may be of use, but these involve the submarine in communication, while the sensors aboard the satellite itself may not be able to penetrate poor weather conditions in the target's vicinity.

A possible answer is a remotely piloted vehicle (RPV). Those referred to elsewhere in this book would generally be too large, but not all RPVs need look and operate like aircraft.[23] For submarine use the rotary-wing type would appear promising, a good example being the Canadair CL-228, a VTOL device shaped rather like a peanut.[24 and 25] Its three-element shell accommodates power and propeller modules over a payload module. Currently the payload is 45kg and can equally well be used for target acquisition, jamming,

▶ At 500 tons displacement, the French *Saga I* is the world's largest commercial submarine. She can maintain 4–6 divers in saturation, allowing them to lock out for work down to 450 metres (later 600). With two Stirling engines she is capable of a 300-mile return trip and a week on station without surfacing. Her military potential is obvious. (Comex Industries)

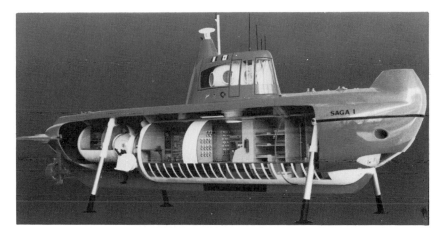

▶ Robotic submersibles, having no crew facilities, can be made small and used boldly. SD-Scicon's Patrolling Underwater Robot (SPUR) would be 10–11 metres in length and could be used as decoy, a sensor platform, surveillance vehicle or, in the attack mode, as a long-range torpedo/mobile mine in its own right. (SD – Scicon plc)

decoying, intelligence-collection or as a relay. As the vehicle can hover, a sonar element is a further possibility. With a take-off weight of 190kg the CL-227 has a 4-hour endurance and a 95nm (117km) radius of action. At recovery, the vehicle drops a fine Kevlar line, by which it is hauled down, its blades struck and the whole assembly stowed. As its body height is only 1.64 metres overall and its diameter 0.64 metres, handling from a modified submarine fin, with casing awash, is a real possibility, while the shape and signatures of the vehicle minimize the prospective target's chances of sighting it and being alerted. There is a long history of attempts to extend a submarine's limited horizons by aerial means; the requirement not only still exists but is also becoming more urgent.

Manned midget and miniature submarines continue to occupy much attention from designers. Despite the considerable allocation of resources to midgets during the Second World War their results, albeit occasionally dramatic, scarcely justified the effort. Of recent years, however, the increasing importance of élite special units in warfare has brought about a resurgence of interest. Soviet Spetsnaz forces are deployed with each fleet, with separate divisions tasked with reconnaissance, intelligence-gathering and covert operations, broadly paralleling the functions of others, such as the American SEAL and British SBS.[26] Small submersibles allow them, for instance, to lay, service and retrieve seabed sensors, tap communication lines, reconnoitre potential landing sites, deliver sabotage teams, lay mines or attack shipping. The Soviets have acknowledged[27] their regard for the unbalancing effect on the enemy of 'irregular' British operations in the Falklands during 1982 and, themselves, operate regularly and with a total lack of subtlety on the coasts of their neighbours, notably Sweden, where 'incidents' occur

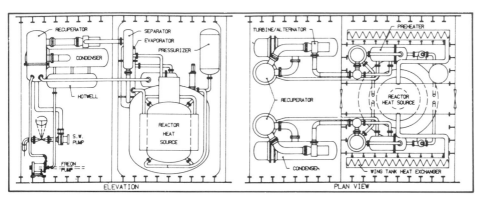

ELEVATION   PLAN VIEW

Should Canada's hopes for an SSN fleet founder finally on finance, the indigenous AMPS-powered SSN Nuclear Hybrid Submarine will look an attractive option for the mid-nineties. The addition of a 7.5-metre AMPS-N hull section to a 1,700-ton boat would add only 20 per cent to cost, but its 500 KW could provide a sustained 8-knot submerged speed. (ECS, Canada)

almost weekly.[28] They possess a wide range of vehicles from tiny submersibles to tracked seabed crawlers.

For operations farther afield, several miniature submarines are available, for the most part SSK dimunitives, such as Vickers' Piranha. The palm for originality, however, goes to the proposal by the Italian Maritalia firm. This is for a small submersible which is propelled by an anaerobic diesel, the problem of whose oxygen storage is met by constructing the hull from a large number of toroidal tubes, formed in a series of cross-sectional profiles and welded edge-to-edge to create a pressure hull.[29] Unlike the Swedish preference for LOX, the Italians store oxygen in these tubes in the gaseous phase at very high pressure. This type of construction has proved very robust, a trials vehicle collapsing at pressures equivalent to a depth of more than 1,100 metres. The proposed Maritalia 136-tonne (submerged) vehicle would have sufficient endurance

to cover the Mediterranean, and includes accommodation for four supernumeraries and a generous locking-out facility. It is stealthy and, as an alternative payload, it could carry four lightweight or two heavyweight torpedoes.

As a footnote, it may be mentioned that the Soviet Union still operates the majority of the world's conventionals and, of these, no less than 93 are listed as elderly Foxtrots and Whiskeys.[30] A recent publication remarks on their condition and block obsolescence.[31] It is unlikely that they could ever be replaced on a hull-for-hull basis and it is estimated that the Russian submarine fleet will be virtually halved, in terms of numbers, by the mid-nineties. There is a timely warning that the Soviets may make a virtue of a necessity and try to bargain away large numbers of 'rust buckets' in return for reductions in NATO strength, already inadequate.

References and Notes

1. Statistics from Submarine Supplement, *IDR*, May, 1986.
2. *Combat Fleets*, p.5.
3. *Combat Fleets*, pp. 134, 209 and 268.
4. *Jane's Fighting Ships*, 1981, p.560.
5. Vickers (VSEL) Publication, 'Type 2400 Class (*sic*) Submarine'.
6. Norman Friedman. *Submarine Design and Development*. Conway, 1984, p.138.
7. Ibid., p.139.
8. Pengelley. 'The Type 471SSK. Future cutting edge of the RAN', in *IDR*, May, 1988, p.527.
9. 'Model 76 Periscope Systems', Kollmorgen Publication ER.400 519/15. Rev.L.
10. 'Model 86 Optronic Mast', Kollmorgen Publication ER.400 649. Rev.S.
11. Sundaram. 'Surface and Survive. How EW assets help submarines', in *IDR*, July, 1988, p.822.
12. Norman Friedman. op cit., p.168.
13. Eberhard Rössler. *The U-Boat: Evolution and Technical History of German Submarines*. Arms & Armour Press, London, 1981, p.182.
14. Hewish. 'Air-Independent propulsion – trials get under way', in *IDR*, May, 1988, p.531.
15. 'Fuel Cells for Submarine Propulsion', in *Marine Propulsion*, May, 1987, p.25.
16. Nilsson and Gummesson 'Air-independent Stirling Engine – powered Energy Supply Systems for Underwater Applications', Published technical paper via Kockums AB.
17. Kinnunen. 'Kockums Marine AB', Press Release of 6 September 1988.
18. 'Presentation of the SAGA Project', Saga I/Comex paper AD.12.10.114 of April, 1988.
19. 'AMPS: a miniature nuclear power plant', in *IDR*, May, 1988, p.532.
20. *Combat Fleets*, p.721.
21. Barker and Tudor-Craig. 'SD-Scicon's Patrolling Underwater Robot (SPUR)', Concept Study, 1988.
22. e.g., *see*, Engelhardt. 'Soviet Sub Design Philosophy', in *US Naval Institute Proceedings*, October, 1987, p.199.
23. Stanley. 'RPVs on Submarines?' in *Jane's Defence Weekly*, 28 November 1987, p.1275.
24. Lowe. 'Advanced surveillance drones for now and the turn of the century', *World Aerospace Profile*, 1988.
25. CL-227 data publication SP 836 Rev. May, 1987 Canadair Inc.
26. Berkowitz. 'Soviet Naval Spetsnaz Forces', in *Naval War College Review*, 1988, p.9.
27. Ibid., p.13.
28. Leitenberg. 'Soviet Submarine Operations in Swedish Waters, 1980–6', in *The Washington Papers*, No.128, 1987.
29. Compton-Hall. 'Revolutionizing the Submarine' in *Jane's Defence Weekly*, 13 August 1988, p.266.
30. *Combat Fleets*, p.562.
31. Breemer. 'Soviet Submarines', Quoted in London *Daily Telegraph*, 27 February 1989.

Nearly three-quarters of the earth's surface is covered by water. Whether looked upon as a defensive moat, or a highway for trade or conquest, it forms a covered way for submarine operation. Where technologies change, the limitations imposed on them by the oceans do not, affecting both hunter and hunted alike.

Nuclear submarines are creatures of the deep ocean. The 'fleet' or 'attack' submarine (SSN) can here use its speed and manoeuvrability to the full; the strategic missile carrier (SSBN) can conceal itself. Both types, however, need to traverse various widths of shallow (up to, say, 200 metres) continental shelf waters while on transit. It is in these zones that the 'conventional' diesel-electric boats (SSK) can exploit their inherent advantages to meet the 'nuclears' on more like equal terms. Except for their Kamchatka-based Pacific Fleet boats, the Soviets face considerable stretches of these offshore shallows. The British and French are inconvenienced to a lesser degree, the Americans hardly at all.

Continental shelf waters would see much ASW activity in the event of war. Far from flat and featureless, their beds are moulded into topography reminiscent of that ashore, with valleys and ridges, plains, scarps and isolated hills. Many valley bottoms are cut by dense, cold water streams that yield features uncannily resembling those of river valleys ashore. At the edges of the shelves, where they plunge to the deep abyssal plains, steep canyons incise them. Submarines currently float over this dark territory like airships over an alien land, but, with improving sensors, a submarine will be able to 'see' around itself and use seabed topography to its advantage in concealment, stalking and ambush. Encounters may well come to resemble those between low-flying helicopters.

Surface winds and differential heating (by sun or through the earth's crust) provide energy to create ocean circulations on a titanic scale, particularly apparent in the upper levels where submarines operate. Ocean currents are less the mighty invisible rivers earlier imagined so much as a complex tapestry of whorls and eddies, meandering in a constantly varying pattern, visible only through the height advantage of a satellite. If able to conduct a dialogue with such a satellite, and knowing its own position exactly, a submarine can hitch a ride on a favourite drift, shut down to silent routine and ghost along unheard by passive sonars. The satellite's infra-red (IR) eye also detects eddies circulating about static cores of water at a different temperature.[1] A submarine lurking within such a system could be near undetectable.

Ocean circulation results in the formation of water layers of differing temperature or salinity, while temperature variation with respect to depth is dependent upon the unpredictable effects of the thermocline, which changes from place to place, from season to season. Both sides evaluate this three-dimensional battlefield with expendable sensors, but, in view of the expense of these and the finite number that can be

▶
The small, electrically-powered torpedo, configured for use with aircraft or standoff AS missile, is in wide use, but has to be of decreasing value when tube-launched from a surface ship, which is increasingly menaced from greater ranges by submerged submarines. A British Stingray is here seen being test-fired. (Marconi Underwater Systems)

◄
A British Hovercraft BH7 Mk 2 of the Royal Navy's Hovercraft Trials Unit fitted with a temporary trunk, housing a dipping sonar. This was used for trials in connection with mine counter-measures (MCM), but could easily be replaced by an inshore ASW sonar. The full flexible skirt has been demonstrated by the US Navy to be well-suited to over-ice roles. (British Hovercraft Corporation)

carried, fully recoverable systems will need to be evolved. An idea of the scale of this expenditure is given by a typical US Navy order, placed in April 1988, for 351,233 sonobuoys of three types, valued at 146 million dollars.[2] Submarines use a 'density layer' as of yore, something on which to ride silently, or to hide beneath when being hunted.

A new arena of immense strategic importance is the basin beneath the Arctic ice-cap. Much of it is 2,000 metres in depth with extensive tracts double this. Submarines 'going to ground' inside the ice edge are very difficult to find. The ice cap is neither continuous nor uniform in thickness. Ice-free areas, or 'polynyas', sometimes superficially covered in thin, 'one-year' ice, form up to 20 per cent of total area in summer, many persisting also through the winter.[3] In shallow water, ice may extend to the bottom, precluding all submarine navigation. In deeper water, hazards exist only immediately 'under the roof' where heavy weather may have shattered the ice, jumbled it and re-frozen it, so that it projects downward in vast rafts and keels.[4] To air-independent submarines, these features can be turned to advantage. Even in winter, polynyas large enough to permit surfacing for the purposes of communication or the launching of missiles are likely to be encountered at less than 25km intervals.[5] Like hunters expecting game at the waterhole, however, satellites can map the

day to day progress of such patches and direct hostile assets accordingly.

Anti-submarine warfare falls into the three phases of detection, classification and attack. Detection may be from aerial, surface or submarine platforms or from strategically deployed sensors. Maritime patrol aircraft (MPA) offer fast response and rapid area coverage, but can still detect deeply submerged submarines only by deploying and interrogating their limited number of sonobuoys, finally endeavouring to localize a contact through the use of their Magnetic Anomaly Detector (MAD). Even when built of standard high yield (rather than amagnetic) steel, however, a submarine's signature may be little greater than ambient terrestrial magnetism, particularly in strategically significant northern waters. The signal decreases as the cube of its distance from the detector,[6] which accounts for American MAD being reported as effective only to a 'few thousand feet'.[7] Improvements in signal processing will progressively extend this range.

An MPA benefits greatly from an input from a dipping sonar, which can be deployed as required, rather than positively committed, like a sonobuoy. Until recently only a hovering helicopter could deploy such a sensor, the helicopter having a performance in other respects greatly inferior to that of the aircraft. Bell-Boeing's V-22 (Osprey) tilt-rotor (see page 15) does, however, combine much of the flight envelopes of both helicopter and turbo-prop aircraft, being able rapidly to reach a point up to 500 miles distant from its flightpad, then hovering to deploy a sonar. Any hovering aircraft that is 'getting warm' is likely in the near future to be running the risk of being attacked by submarine-mounted point-defence missiles. At the moment, submarines, like tanks, are vulnerable to helicopter attack through their lack of a counter-weapon, but Stinger-type missiles in suitable fin-mounted containers must be a near development. Indeed, Soviet *Kilos* are already thought to have them.

Except through chance encounter or previous intelligence, an MPA is greatly dependent upon information from fixed ocean sensor chains to localize a target sufficiently to commence a search. Its task will benefit considerably through the development of satellite-borne non-acoustic sensors and data-processing gear.

A further alternative to both helicopter and tilt-rotor is the airship, used in ASW in both world wars. It can deploy dipping sonar and weapons, but where it lacks the aircraft's speed, it is vastly superior in endurance. If the airship proves to be successful in its proposed Airborne Early Warning (AEW) role, the infra-structure will be created which will then make it more attractive for use in ASW. It could be particularly valuable in the rapid establishment of a sensor barrier in a previously virgin area.

Helicopters are currently a frigate's major ASW system, and the enormous impact that they make on ship design is therefore justified. A possible cheaper alternative would be a frigate designed around a large, low-frequency sonar and an AS stand-off weapon. In the absence of helicopters from other vessels, a remotely piloted vehicle (RPV), demanding little space aboard, might be used to deliver a sonobuoy pattern out to the first convergence zone to gather data on a target detected initially by the ship's sonar.

As ASW platforms, surface ships are hostage to weather conditions. Hull-mounted sonars are subjected to noise from machinery, waterflow and wave impact. Reducing speed to a level that optimizes sonar performances renders a ship more vulnerable to attack and increases her response time except by helicopter or stand-off weapon. (SOW). Nevertheless, only a ship has the capacity to accommodate large, low-frequency sonars and their associated signal processing gear. Hull-mounted sonars suffer also from variations in water temperature, pressure and salinity, which affect speeds of propagation (and thus the calculation of range) and also distort energy paths. The variable depth sonar (VDS) was introduced as a means of deploying transducers at levels of more stable conditions beneath the thermocline or pronounced unstable ducts. In considerable depths of water, pressure creates an axis (the 'Deep Sound Channel') where propagational velocity is a minimum and about which energy from an active source is refracted in such a manner as to be reconcentrated at the surface at distances which can be calculated from ambient conditions. In these regions ('convergence zones') detection can be possible at considerable ranges. In continental

▶ The Italian carrier *Garibaldi* (C551) and cruiser *Veneto* (C550) at the centre of an ASW group escorted by *Maestrale* and *Lupo* class frigates. Before the completion of the carrier, with her Sea Kings, such a group would have fielded only AB-212s. The ships are particularly well equipped with AA and anti-surface ship missiles and should be well able to exercise submarine control in the Mediterranean Narrows, supported by shore-based Atlantic MPAs. (Italian Navy)

shelf soundings, deep refracted energy is intercepted and scattered by the seabed, causing spurious noise. By matching the wave-length of the transmitted energy to the roughness of the bottom, however, it is possible to use the latter as a reflector.[8] Such matching can never be exact, and the detector is unlikely to find itself in the convergence zone, so that means of improving these techniques might seem an attractive area of research in shallow-water ASW. This would complement the endless quest to extract minute useful signals from dominant background noise.

   Passive towed arrays eliminate most of a ship's self-generated noise and can be streamed at selected depths while being effective at higher speeds. They provide a long baseline from which the position of a noise source can be triangulated. Submarines, however, are getting quieter, making purely passive methods less effective. Active elements are therefore being introduced into

◄
Deployable from Sea King or EH101 (Merlin), the HELRAS (Helicopter Long Range Sonar) can be used in either active or passive mode. The large volumetric array retracts compactly into the central cylinder for stowage. HELRAS is a joint private venture between British Aerospace and Allied Bendix. (British Aerospace plc)

▲
With submarines becoming quieter and set to become indistinguishable from the ambient noise of the sea, it will be increasingly necessary to revert to active means of detection. British Aerospace's ATAS (Active Towed Array Sonar) can be deployed by ships as small as 250 tons. Some 900 metres of tow cable separates ship noise from the active element, and another 300 metres between this and the passive, inline array. (British Aerospace plc)

such arrays;[9] while their use will still alert a prospective target, they do not pinpoint the position of the transmitting ship, as they are remote from it. Even with the development of 'thin-line' arrays, their stowage and deployment gear is bulky, making a considerable impact on a frigate. Streamed, they inhibit her power of movement. For barrier purposes at least, it thus makes sense to remove the arrays from fighting ships and instal them aboard an auxiliary as the Americans have done with their T-AGOS ships. Given a secure and reliable data link, this releases warships for their primary missions. As warships rarely work in such ideal circumstances, however, they will tend to be encumbered with a full range of weapons and sensors.

Submarines, able to deploy active or passive sonar at a depth of their choosing and unaffected by weather, have emerged as the best ASW platforms. Until recently it was felt in the West that its quantitative inferiority in submarines with respect to the Soviets could be countered by qualitative superiority. A NATO boat is still capable of detecting its adversary first, but, with improved Soviet quieting techniques, this range is being reduced and will be still further reduced in shallow or ice-covered water.[10] A Western boat which has used its stealth to penetrate an enemy bastion is faced with a dilemma, being secure in the face of superior numbers only until she advertises her presence. If she launches a heavyweight torpedo at a target, her position is immediately compromised. The would-be target responds with spoofing, jamming, rapid manoeuvre – and a brace of torpedoes on a reciprocal bearing. Soviet submarines reportedly can go faster and deeper and, as the target is unlikely to be alone, the attacker becomes the attacked, and at a disadvantage. Stealth is, in itself, obviously not sufficient; in what would be attritional warfare, one-for-one kills would not be acceptable and a case can be made for greater numbers of less capable platforms to fit into a given budget, or the consideration of force multipliers.[11] A possible contender for the latter role would be unmanned submersibles (discussed above).

With hunters safe only if they withold their fire, alternatives such as the MPA with expendable sensors become more attractive, except that they cannot be employed in high-risk areas. For thirty years and more, lines of permanent sensors have been planted on the seabed, particularly at chokepoints, to monitor submarine movement. One line will yield a reasonable bearing on a noise source, a second will establish a 'fix'. Understandably, little is released regarding these installations, though the American SOSUS (Sound Ocean Surveillance System) has been mentioned.[12 and 13] It is likely that the oceans are well-populated with such systems, but, if they are to be

planted up forward where they can be of greatest use, it is likely that their positions are well known to a prospective adversary and that they will be destroyed during a build-up to full hostilities. Such semi-permanent assets thus need to be backed by means to establish an alternative barrier line, with mobile detection supported by attack platforms. Considerable American investment is, therefore, being made in SURTASS (Surface Towed Array Sensor) whose civilian-manned T-AGOS ships can deploy the 1,830-metre AN/UQQ2 arrays.[11] These can be used to establish a barrier at any chosen point, their acquired data being transmitted via satellite to a central point for analysis and resulting instructions to other assets, as required.

SURTASS ships operate for extended periods at low speed (typically three knots). Even when modelled on wide-beam supply craft, and equipped with flume-tank stabilization, they were hard on crews over a typical 98-day deployment. Later units are, therefore, constructed on the SWATH (Small Waterplane Area, Twin Hull) principle to impart steadier motion and the ability to operate in more extreme sea states. Without extensive cover, a SURTASS barrier remains highly vulnerable, while the data gathered is vital enough to consider more secure means of gathering. Again, the use of unmanned submersibles is a possibility. Slow and silent running, they could be placed by a mothership whose technology need be no more advanced than that of LASH, or commercial dock-ship designs. The submersibles would usually run shallow, continuously transmitting their data to the parent for onward transmission ashore.

Expensive new development can often be rendered unnecessary by the refinement of existing methods. An example of this is STRAP (Sono-buoy Thinned Random Array Project) whereby an MPA, in place of the limitations caused by the planting and interrogation of individual sonobuoys, processes their signal outputs in groups to permit 'beam-forming'.[15] By equipping one in five of the pattern with a low-power emitter, signals will be received and retransmitted by the remainder with time-lapses that will establish their exact spatial relationship. Interrogation of selected groups will then yield bearings of noise sources with reasonable accuracy, the use of two such groups producing a fix. Acoustic processors need the intelligence to reject system noise and spurious inputs such as from rain on the surface, fish, commercial shipping, drilling, etc.

Stealth techniques are continuously being refined to reduce submarine signatures further. Soviet boats have exaggerated curvature which will reflect a minimum amount of energy from an active sonar. They have special energy-absorbant covering to reduce the return even more, using a technique as old as the German 'Alberich' and 'Fafnir' which, as far back as the Second World War, was claimed to reduce reflected energy by up to 85 per cent.[16] Both the Royal Navy and the Soviets prefer shaped anechoic tiles, stuck to the hull. The latter experienced problems of adhesion, as evidenced by published photographs.[17] The US Navy stayed with applied coatings until recently, when it was announced that the new USS *San Juan* (SSN-751) would be the first American boat with appliqué material.[18]

Steady reduction in submarine noise has stimulated research into non-acoustic detection methods. Satellites, such as the US Navy's N-ROSS (Remote Ocean Sensing System) planned for 1991, will continuously update oceanic environmental data and, by highlighting areas most favourable at any time to submarine operations, indicate where concentration of ASW assets may be most beneficial.[19] As already noted, MAD gear is useful only at low altitudes, while a combination of new amagnetic submarine hulls and natural laws would seem to indicate little room for future improvement, except in data processing.

Because their hulls must displace water, submarines proceeding at shallow submergence produce a travelling 'hump' on the surface. Unless the boat is very shallow and moving at high speed, however, the hump

◄

A 150-ton, 10 × 15 metre array, consisting of 1440 Massa TR-IIC transducer elements. This could be lowered through the bottom of the *Mission Capistrano* for deep sound research at depths of about 1,500 feet. Known as Project Artemis, it proved during the 1960s that sound could be detected at ranges of hundreds of miles. Note crewmen at top. (Massa Products Corporation)

►

The active, transmitting element of ATAS is a vertical stave of lightweight flextensional transducers. Depending upon requirements these can be manufactured to emit acoustic energy at frequencies from 200Hz to 3kHz, the lowest frequencies demanding the largest assembly. The flextensional transducer was developed originally by the Ministry of Defence. (British Aerospace plc)

►

This unremarkable-looking device is the Massa TR-14IIA electro-magnetic transducer element which can be built into multi-component assemblies conformal with a hull, or cylindrical for 360-degree scanning. A stack of laminations is oscillated by the energization of magnets, vibrating the square diaphragm across a sealed airgap. Back radiation is low and the module is both rugged and shock resistant. (Massa Products Corporation)

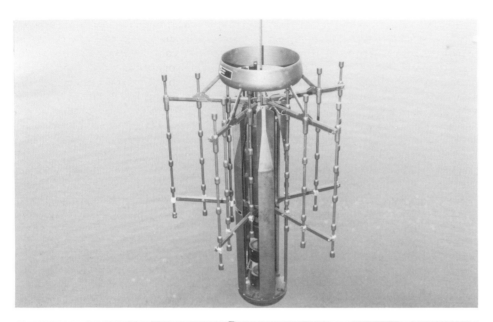

◀
Under evaluation for use by the American, British and Canadian navies is the Cormorant Advanced Lightweight Dipping Sonar, shown in the deployed configuration. It offers broad-band passive detection or a low-frequency active mode for long-range performance. All-up system weight is under 220kg. (Plessey Naval Systems Ltd)

◀
A towed array module in process of manufacture. A series of modules is connected in series to make up the full array, so that the elements next to the towing ship have to absorb all the drag as well as convey the large number of conductors for hydro-phone outputs, heading and depth sensors. All is contained in a neutrally buoyant, oil-filled hose. (Plessey Naval Systems Ltd)

is only a few centimetres in height. While invisible at surface level, it does have the effect of slightly modulating the overall surface wave pattern, and analysis of a satellite-based wide-aperture radar can reveal the distinctive Kelvin wave system of a ship's wake.[20] The provision of powerful on-board signal processors, necessary to detect this, will benefit greatly through new superconductive materials. Submarines tend to be warmer than the water through which they pass and, depending upon the characteristics of the thermocline, may produce a wake warmed sufficiently to reach the surface. Alternatively, it may displace water of a different temperature from that at the surface. Either effect could be observed by sensitive, satellite-based infra-red (IR) detectors.

Familiar to every sailor is the phenomenon of bioluminescence, the passage of his ship stimulating micro-organisms to emit a cold, blue-green glow, powerfully visible by night. Submerged submarines will promote a similar effect, although the resulting light is attenuated too rapidly to be visible from a satellite unless new types of detection can be developed. The blue-green band of the spectrum, though greatly affected by suspended particles, penetrates sea water best. Helicopter-borne blue-green lasers have been used successfully to detect the presence of mines down to 30 metres. If satellites can generate sufficient power for a submarine-detecting laser, this would need to be focused to a pencil beam, complicating scanning problems. Sufficient energy would need to be reflected by the target to reach the satellite's receiver sensor. One-way experiments must already have proved successful for, according to a recent report, Congress criticized the US Navy for not more quickly utilizing the Submarine Laser Communications Satellite System (SLCSAT).[21]

The second stage of ASW is Classification. Electronic intelligence (ELINT) is painstakingly garnered to provide a frigate with the characteristics of radar or any other radiating system being used injudiciously by a submarine which may be thus detected at greater than sonar range. For a submerged boat, however, acoustic means will still be the preferred method of indentification.

Machinery noise, distinctive enough to be narrowed to a particular boat, is much reduced through rafting and the use of flexible mountings to de-couple vibration from the hull. Propellers are easily detectable as single or twin. They rotate in a non-uniform wake field due to hull geometry, and consequently produce noise at blade-rate frequency. Propeller cavitation is noisy and unavoidable; careful design can move its onset to beyond normal operating parameters, but a better solution is the shrouded propulsor, usually known as a 'pump jet' and used also on torpedoes.[22 and 23] Best described as a single-stage, axial-flow compressor, its rotor blades work in a symmetrical flow, their noise being further screened, by the surrounding duct.

Cavitation can occur at any point where poor flow lines or excrescences can produce a local reduction in fluid pressure. Careful design and quality of manufacture can much reduce it, but, ironically, anechoic tiling, applied to reduce reflected sonic energy can, when individual tiles become displaced, offer such discontinuties. Average tiling is reported to be effective against active sonars working at frequencies above 10kHz.[24] At 1kHz, the frequency to which large frigate-mounted sonars are progressing, the tiling would need to be too thick to be practicable.

The final stage of ASW is the attack itself. Consideration here needs to take into account the possible use of tactical nuclear weapons. If the stakes are high enough, the uncertainties of targeting could well encourage their use, on the assumption that, as civil populations are not directly involved, low-yield warheads are unlikely to force an escalation to an all-out nuclear exchange. Suitable delivery would be by air-dropped depth-charge or by a submarine-launched vehicle such as the American Sea Lance, due to enter service in 1992 and effective out to the third convergence zone.[25] While the lethal radius of such warheads is subject to many variables, various sources quoted by Stefanick would indicate about one nautical mile for a ten-kiloton theatre weapon.[26] It should be emphasized, however, that with its inferior numbers of platforms, the West would be doing itself a grave disservice by initiating such an exchange.

Availability of Sea Lance would allow the final retirement of nuclear-tipped ASROC rounds and torpedoes (such as the US Navy's Mk 45), widely held to be as dangerous to the launcher as to the target. A further option is to fit the standard Mk 48 heavyweight torpedo with a so-called Sub-Kiloton Insertable Nuclear Component (SKINC) which can be engineered to give yields as low as 0.01 kiloton (equivalent to 10 tons of TNT).[27] Hot debate surrounds their mode of use, but they are held to be safe to use beyond 1,500

▶

FFV's TP43XO electric torpedo is primarily for use against silent submarines in shallow water, but, being less than half the length of a heavyweight, can also be stowed in tandem in a standard submarine tube for use against smaller surface targets. Being wire guided, it can even be launched in emergency by simple slide from a fishing vessel. FFV is developing an anti-torpedo torpedo. (FFV Ordnance)

◀

The air-dropped depth-charge is, and is likely to remain, a highly effective AS weapon, particularly in shallow water. It can also be used against surface ships. Shown is the Mk II Mod. 3, which can be carried by helicopters as small as the now phased-out Wasp. Its weight, including 80kg of explosives, is 145kg. (British Aerospace plc)

metres, lethal to a submerged target at 150 metres, and capable, through shock, of disabling its vital equipment at 300 metres. A drawback is a 'blue-out', or temporary degradation of own sonar following such a burst. Such weapons can only encourage designers to follow the Soviet regression to double-hulled boats. A water-filled cavity theoretically offers little protection from shock, but it allows the working-in of deeper frames, separates the immediate explosion of a conventional warhead from the pressure hull, and gives scope for the location of anti-surface ship missiles in pressure-tight silos between the hulls. No double hull, however, could withstand the 300kg warhead of a Mk 48 torpedo launched by another submarine. Released from a comparable depth, it is unlikely to be either out-run or out-manoeuvred. Currently undergoing an added capability (ADCAP) upgrade to take it through to the next century, the Mk 48 weighs in at 1,633kg, is capable of

a maximum speed of 55 knots and has a range of 50,000 metres.[28] The same source credits the new British Spearfish, planned to enter service in 1990, with a weight of nearer 2,000kg, and a maximum speed of about 70 knots.[29] Range estimates vary from about 65,000 metres to only 40,000 metres.[30 and 31] Currently, submarines can counter such monsters only with 'soft-kill' techniques, a situation analogous to a frigate lacking point-defence or CIWS in the face of missile attack. It is reported, however, that the Anglo-American Surface Ship Torpedo Defence System (SSTDS), still under development, will eventually be adapted for submarine use.[32]

Unlike Soviet practice, the West limits many of its surface ships to deploying the same ASW torpedoes as its aircraft. With tight size and weight constraints, airborne torpedoes need to accept limitations in specification, but it seems unnecessary to confine a ship to

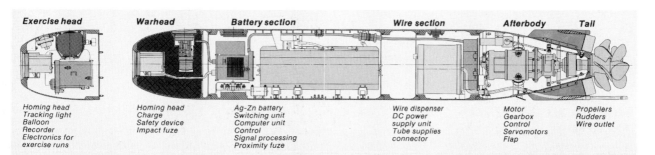

Exercise head	Warhead	Battery section	Wire section	Afterbody	Tail
Homing head Tracking light Balloon Recorder Electronics for exercise runs	Homing head Charge Safety device Impact fuze	Ag-Zn battery Switching unit Computer unit Control Signal processing Proximity fuze	Wire dispenser DC power supply unit Tube supplies connector	Motor Gearbox Control Servomotors Flap	Propellers Rudders Wire outlet

similar limitations. Indeed if an ASW vessel is close enough to a submarine to launch a lightweight torpedo it could be argued that she will already have been destroyed by a submarine-launched heavyweight. Capability is largely a function of weapon volume and that of the British Stingray ASW torpedo has barely a quarter that of the Spearfish.[33] Various sources allude to the Stingray's difficulties when, newly-operational, it was obliged to 'go active' when searching for quiet targets in shallow water around the Falklands in 1982.[34] Building on this experience, the French Murene is reported to be effective in water only forty metres in depth, which is probably more important than its ability to operate 'below 1,000 metres'.[35] Besides intelligence and warhead size, the major parameter to suffer from small size is endurance. Murene's speed is quoted as 38 knots during its search phase and 53 knots for attack; it can run for six minutes at top speed. Pitted against a Soviet Alfa submarine (up to 45 knots at 'over 700 metres' depth) its margin is too slender to hope for an interception in a tail chase. It does, however, possess a combination of ahead-looking and flank array sonars which, feeding data into the weapon's intelligence, allow it to assess the target's course and speed; it can then assume a constantly updated intercept course rather than indulge in a wasteful tail chase.

A long-established alternative is to locate the much larger target offered by wake turbulence, a technique known to be used by the Soviets, and by the Americans in the old Westinghouse Mk 37 ('Freedom') torpedo.[36] Having detected a submarine's wake, the weapon turns in the direction of greatest effect and, while noisy itself, is likely to go undetected as it approaches in the target's blind sector, where turbulence blinds his sensors.

While improvements to discriminate decoy from target, to increase battery power densities, and to

design warheads to defeat widely separated double-hulled submarines, are refining the torpedo – they *are* only refinements and a radical re-think will soon be necessary. For a given volume it is unlikely that torpedo prime-movers can be designed to develop significantly more power than at present. Heavyweights use thermal engines whose noise is of little consequence as long as they can outrun the target and still have sensors capable of effective active or semi-active homing. Small ASW torpedoes are electrically powered, much quieter and prefer passive sensors.

Half a century ago it was still necessary to aim the submarine like a gun, whose barrel was the torpedo tube. Long, cylindrical weapons were thus required, their shape owing little to hydrodynamic laws. This tyranny of shape is no longer relevant and, as long as sonars can be made conformal, there seems little reason why torpedoes should not be profiled to minimize drag and use either discardable 'sabots' to discharge them from larger-calibre tubes, or swim them out from external, pressure-tight containments (although the latter option may be noisier and use some of the weapon's stored energy). Improved hydrodynamics would see the torpedo go farther and/or faster on the same energy, but one could also question whether the rotating propulsor itself could be replaced or complemented. Its great advantage is a relative lack of noise, enabling on-board acoustic sensors to function. Rocket propulsion, though degraded by increasing depth, would impart far higher speeds for a limited period, but at the cost of a high noise level.

One could, therefore, visualise a hydrodynamically optimized vehicle capable, even now, of being driven at 90 knots by a rotating propulsor and using passive sensors to overtake its target and take up a designated firing position relative to it. At this point it would discharge a group of rocket-propelled unguided submunitions before, possibly, completing the attack by hitting the target itself. Conceivably, the vehicle itself could be viewed as recoverable once it had carried out its attack and if operational circumstances permitted.

To become operational in 1992, as a SUBROC replacement, is Sea Lance. Capable of being launched from '80 per cent of an SSN 688's test depth' in an encapsulation, the two-stage, inertially guided rocket vehicle fires on approaching the surface, thence flying 'better than 100 miles' before releasing its payload. [37] This will usually be the new Mk 50 Advanced Light-Weight Torpedo (ALWT) which itself may have difficulty in overhauling a deep-running target bent on escape. Sea Lance, being manoeuvrable in flight, should be a major advance over the long-serving ASROC which followed a ballistic trajectory, whose 9,000-metre maximum range was regulated only by rocket burn time, preset from sonar data.[38] This weapon thus suffered from 'dead-time' as well as the performance of the dated Mk 46 torpedo that it carried.

By the early 1990s a vertical-launch (VL) compatible ASROC round will be available but, beyond a hint that guidance will be provided during the initial, or boost, phase, further improvements are not known.[39] While its relative cheapness permits the advantage of salvo firing, its range would now be a major limitation in a confrontation with, say, a Soviet Charlie I submarine, whose eight SS-N-7s can be submerge-launched against surface targets out to 50,000 metres.[40]

With respect to surface-launched stand-off AS weaponry, the Soviet fleet is better equipped than those of the West. The early Anglo-Australian Ikara was bulky and also delivered a Mk 46 (reportedly to 18,000 metres) but is now all but extinct.[41] As helicopters are already over-tasked and, indeed, many ships do not have them, the need for a replacement SOW is evident. The private-venture Super Ikara is being flight-tested. Capable of a simple canister-launch, it can reportedly carry the much-improved Stingray torpedo out to 90–100,000 metres. Matra/OTO Melara are using the Mk II Otomat to deliver a Murene to 40,000 metres. None of these weapons is better than the torpedo carried, but will be effective until submarines acquire a 'hard-kill' torpedo defence (a sort of anti-torpedo torpedo analagous to a surface ship's point-defence missile system).

Still common aboard most ships that need to conduct ASW in shallow water are mortars, although the Royal Navy's Limbo has virtually disappeared. Sophisticated homing torpedoes still do not work well against silent targets, bottomed in shallow water, where the small ship with a classification sonar and a mortar may have a distinct edge. The most common weapon in the West is the 375mm Bofors launcher which, even in the twin-barrelled version, can get off six rounds within 60 seconds against targets out to 3,600 metres. Its rocket-propelled bombs cannot be decoyed or jammed, and give the target virtually no warning.

Either side is likely to be deploying towed torpedo decoys. Current Western technology is typified by the Graseby software-controlled vehicle that interfaces directly with the host vessel's sonar, so that it can be near-instantaneously tuned to counter any incoming seeker.[42]

Mines, in deep-laid barriers athwart routes that submarines are obliged to use to and from their bases, will continue to pose hazards significant enough to encourage the means of their sweeping, e.g., the Royal Navy's EDATS (Extra Deep Armed Team Sweep) sweepers of the 'River' class.

Mobility will increasingly blur the distinction between mine and torpedo. A nice terminological point is that moored mines were, earlier, termed 'torpedoes', which accounts for Farragut's immortalized order at the Battle of Mobile Bay in 1864 – 'Damn the torpedoes! Full speed ahead!'[43]

Best known is the venerable Captor (Captive Torpedo), now thirty years old and comprising a Mk 46 in a buoyant encapsulation which can be moored in up to 300 metres.[44] A barrier weapon, it lies dormant in a group or 'stand-alone' mode until triggered by an incoming acoustic signal whose harmonic content matches that preset into its threat library. While Captor itself is now dated, its concept is not and its current updating will see it valid until the entry into service of the Advanced Sea Mine (ASM), now out to tender to Anglo-American consortia.[45] It is reported to be deployable down to 600 metres, with a similar slant range.

A further development is the American Submarine-Launched Mobile Mine (SLMM) which utilizes Mk 37 torpedoes as vehicles for the planting of ground mines (which could be the torpedoes themselves) in positions inaccessible to a submarine. Presumably the torpedo's speed is greatly reduced to increase its range, improve control and to decrease noise.

Depth-charges, the classic ASW weapon, are nowadays associated mainly with aircraft, but are still valid and effective when deployed by minor combatants (of which the Soviets have many) in shallow water. Recent

▶
Anti-submarine rocket projectiles are designed for use in restricted and shallow waters which limit sonar range and generate false echoes. In this environment AS missiles and torpedoes are unsuitable. The Bofors 375mm projectile can range to 3,600 metres and be used in an auxiliary howitzer role. It is being developed as an anti-torpedo weapon. (AB Bofors)

▼
Many future frigates, to be affordable, may have to forego the full facilities for the large helicopter necessary to prosecute submarine contacts to the limits of detection. One partial solution would be to utilize fully the spacious facilities aboard the replenishment ship. The Dutch *Poolster* pioneered this departure with three Lynx ASW helicopters. (Netherlands Navy)

◄ From ahead, there is little to be seen aboard the Type 22 *Brave* that connects her with her ASW speciality. She differs from the remainder of an already diverse group of ships in being trials ship for the Rolls-Royce Spey SMIC engines. Her machinery is COGOG connected, so that the power of the cruise Tynes cannot be added to that of the Speys. (Rolls-Royce plc)

transfer of elderly Golf II SSBs to the Baltic, from where even their old SS-N-5s could reach much of mainland NATO with little warning, is a reminder that the latter could well find shallow-water ASW a pressing necessity.

With the reduction of long-standing tensions between East and West comes the likelihood that the fleets of either will most likely become involved with those of lesser powers. As these can also purchase the latest arms and control technology, they can pose major problems, as evidenced by the British inability to account for German-built Argentinian submarines during 1982. It is a valid point that groups of high-value surface ships, be they combat or mercantile, offer attack submarines their most attractive targets. The corollary of this is that in their vicinity is the best place to concentrate mobile ASW assets, which should be equipped with this in view.

References and Notes
1. Stefanick. *Strategic Anti-Submarine Warfare and Naval Strategy*. Institute for Defense and Disarmament Studies, Lexington, 1987, p.224.
2. 'Recent Government Contracts', in *Jane's Defence Weekly*, July, 1988.
3. Stefanick. op. cit., p.315.
4. Le Schack. 'Understanding Sea Ice', in *US Naval Institute Proceedings*, October, 1987.
5. Stefanick. op. cit., p.318.
6. Stefanick. op. cit., p.17.
7. Tierney. 'The Invisible Force', in *Science '83*, November, 1983.
8. Stefanick. op. cit., pp.238–40.
9. British Aerospace Systems and Equipment (BASE) Active Towed Array Sonar (ATAS) News Release B Ae 171/88.
10. Stefanick. op. cit., p.50.
11. Nylen. 'Mêlée Warfare', in *US Naval Institute Proceedings*, October, 1987, p.57.
12. Norman Friedman. op. cit., pp.171–3.
13. Stefanick. op. cit., pp.38–41.
14. *Combat Fleets*, p.795.
15. 'Sub location by STRAP', in *IDR*, January, 1986.
16. Hackman. *Seek and Strike*. HMSO, 1984, p.321.
17. e.g., *Jane's Defence Weekly*, 21 November 1987.
18. *Jane's Defence Weekly*, 20 February 1988, p.287.
19. 'N-ROSS: a new ASW dimension', in *US Naval Institute Proceedings*, September 1987.
20. 'The Non-acoustic Detection of Submarines', in *Scientific American*, March, 1988, p.25.
21. *Jane's Defence Weekly*, 14 November 1987, p.1097.
22. Norman Friedman. op. cit., p.137.
23. Wettern. *Warship World*, Autumn, 1988, p.6.
24. *Maritime Defence*, October, 1988, p.378.
25. *Combat Fleets*, p.692.
26. Stefanick. op. cit., p.28.
27. 'The Implications of Sub-kiloton Nuclear Torpedoes', in *US Naval Institute Proceedings*, August, 1987, p.102.
28. *Combat·Fleets*, p.694.
29. Ibid., p.203.
30. Ibid., p.203.
31. 'Anti-submarine Weapons', in *IDR*, March, 1987, p.308.
32. *Jane's Defence Weekly*, 4 June 1988, p.1087.
33. *Combat Fleets*, p.203.
34. e.g., 'Lessons of the Falklands', in (US) *Naval Engineers' Journal*, July 1983, p.131.
35. 'ASW Weapons', in *IDR*, March, 1987, p.308.
36. e.g., *see* Corlett. 'Nuclear Submarine Warfare in the 21st Century', in *Maritime Defence*, November, 1980, p.408.
37. *Combat Fleets*, p.692.
38. Ibid., p.692.
39. *IDR*, March, 1987, p.314.
40. *Combat Fleets*, p.563.
41. Ibid., p.202.
42. Royal Navy Equipment Exhibition report, in *IDR*, November, 1987, p.1543.
43. e.g., *see* Potter. *Illustrated History of the US Navy*, 1971, p.107.
44. *Combat Fleets*, p.694.
45. *IDR*, March, 1987, p.315.

THE FRIGATE

Warships are notoriously difficult to categorize and the term 'frigate' had a more precise meaning in Nelson's fleet than it has today. In general, it denotes a ship whose primary function is anti-submarine (ASW) capability depending on size or how much she will be expected to operate autonomously. Applied to Soviet ships, the term is misleading in that northern conditions dictate that ASW be undertaken by much larger units. For instance, 32 of the 36 listed Krivak 'frigates' are termed by the Russians simply 'patrol ships'.[1] Only the four final Type III variants combine a helicopter platform with a VDS to make a

capable ASW frigate, yet these serve the KGB's 'Maritime Border Guard'. The smallest ships carrying Soviet ASW categorization tend to be called 'destroyers' in the West due to their size, speed and multi-function weapon fits.

The most prolific category of surface combatant in the majority of fleets, the frigate is in a state of continuous evolution. It is required effectively to counter submarines that enjoy varying degrees of attack superiority and to defend itself against increasingly sophisticated means of attack, while being sufficiently inexpensive to allow significant numbers to

► Lead ship of a class of 51 frigates, the *Oliver Hazard Perry* (FFG-7) shows the 'boxy' layout typical of the current generation. With the after end devoted to hangar and flight pad, electronics had to be crowded on to masts bunched well forward. A squat, large-diameter funnel casing lowers the IR signature of the two LM2500 gas turbines, whose uptakes protrude from the top. (General Electric Marine and Industrial Engines)

be built. The inevitable compromise will always exhibit shortcomings. Quality conflicts with quantity. The best of frigates cannot be in more than one place at a time, yet it is worse than useless to commit a ship poorly equipped for the task in hand.

Size will tend to increase. Hull steelwork is cheap compared with its contents, particularly when expressed as a proportion of through-life cost. Longer hulls are more easily driven and are better seakeepers. If ships remain efficient in severe sea states, they effectively increase platform availability without increasing numbers. Longer ships have kinder motion, extending the envelope of helicopter operability. Longer ships allow armament and sensors to be sited with minimum mutual interference. Larger ships have greater endurance, potentially superior 'stand alone' capacity and a better ability to absorb and survive battle damage. Larger ships have the capacity for later modernization, particularly as data-handling tends to be demanding of volume. It is unlikely that frigates displacing less than 3,000 tons (standard) could be sufficiently versatile to meet the requirements of a modern, front-line fleet.

It is noteworthy that world-wide frigate development has produced a genre of remarkably consistent specification. For armament, a single medium-calibre gun is complemented with light automatic weapons and/or, increasingly, by a close-in weapons system (CIWS). Larger examples are also acquiring point-defence missile systems (PDMS). Space permits only one major missile system, the choice of which reflects operational constraints – western European ASW helicopter-equipped units favour four/eight anti-ship SSMs;

American frigates tend to an area-defence SAM; while Soviet frigate-sized ASW ships, having no helicopter, take bulky stand-off ASW weapons. Such commitment of a ship to a major role will be relaxed with the increasing use of vertical-launch systems (VLS) where the type of missile loadout will be related to mission. Further stimulation to size increase is the growing tendency to ship two helicopters. These are used not only for ASW but also for over-the-horizon (OTH) targeting and weapon guidance, for deploying electronic support measures and for deploying anti-ship missiles (ASM). So essential are they to a frigate's potential, that the availability of at least one is vital.

Hull-mounted sonars are still specified, increasingly matched with towed arrays. Variable-depth sonar (VDS) is common in Soviet ships, but, in the West, is more usually confined to a helicopter's dipping ('dunking') sonar. Speed is necessary for tactical reasons yet is detrimental to sonar operation. Towed arrays allow sonars to be distanced from ship noise, while the latter can itself be reduced by careful design.

High speeds are, currently, almost invariably derived by gas turbine propulsion, but tactical manoeuvring is undertaken with gas turbine or diesel. Neither of these is as quiet as might be desirable, and the British Type 23 will break new ground with diesel-electric secondary machinery, the prime-movers raft-mounted above the waterline and the propulsion motors running silently under accurate speed control without need of gearing.

For an allied group of fleets, such as those of NATO, a standard frigate is the ideal. Commonality of design and specification would allow for keen competition,

A *Kortenaer*-class frigate of the Netherlands Navy fitting out afloat in the covered facility at de Schelde, Vlissingen. One of NATO's difficult problems is that each member has yards capable of constructing first grade ships; in short, peacetime overcapacity and more expensive ships. Note the rounded sheer strake and avoidance of vertical planes. (Netherlands Navy)

The Greek frigate *Limnos* was the second of two taken from the Netherlands Navy's production series of *Kortenaers*. While the large force of Greek Second World War-vintage destroyers is totally obsolete, their replacement by such ships as *Kortenaers*, tailored for Atlantic operations, would seem questionable, the *Doorman* (M-class) looking more suitable. (Royal Schelde)

Intended as replacements for the *Leander* and *Rootfiler* classes, the Dutch *Doorman* or M-class frigate has emerged considerably larger than the ships that it replaces, a not uncommon failing. (Royal Schelde)

with builders and equipment suppliers benefiting in turn from a coherent construction policy and economic production runs. Mixed-flag NATO groups would also work together more simply. With this ideal in mind, a NATO Project Group has formulated a specification, agreed by Canada, France, West Germany, Italy, the Netherlands, Spain, the UK and the USA, for a common frigate replacement for the 1990s.[2] Its target standard displacement of 3,500 metric tons is a reasonable mean of those operating currently

under those flags. The project will not be easy because, although the ASW element introduces a strong common link, the environment in which they will operate varies considerably. Facing an Eastern Bloc enemy, for instance, AS ships working the western Atlantic would face a markedly lower level of air threat than those controlling the GIUK gap. Ships operating in the Mediterranean require speed rather than the endurance necessary for those operating in the ocean. Full advantage should be taken of vertical launch

systems (VLS), whereby the missile loadout can be varied as required between SSMs, SAMs and the vertical-launch version of the ASROC, when it becomes available in the early nineties.

Comprehensive levels of interchangeability, and the natural desire of each nation to retain its design-and-build capabilities, will cause the NATO frigate to be long in gestation, despite its optimistic label of 'NFR 90'. Indeed a recent report stated that 'an as yet unfinished study on threats and budgets has indicated alternative hull designs to best meet different missions'.[3] That delay to the NFR 90 is accepted within NATO is demonstrated by the recently announced German intention to acquire a new class of frigate, the Type F123, four of which are planned to supplement the F122 (*Bremen*) class by 1994–5.[4] They are 'advanced Bremens' differing primarily in the adoption of a VLS and, in view of the target displacement for the NFR 90, their 4,100 tonnes is significant, not least for being not far short of the later British Type 22s which have the dubious distinction of being the world's largest frigates. It is, however, probably a realistic assessment of the likely size of a future 'survivable' escort, while the same report speaks of a likely requirement for 58 'NATO frigates' of an 'envisaged 5,000-tonne design starting at the turn of the century. Fully committed to the project, the Germans refer to the ship as their 'Type F124', which will certainly incorporate a measure of the modular fitting-out concepts pioneered by Blohm & Voss for their MEKO

frigate range and believed to be incorporated in the projected F 123s. It is understood, however, that while the NFR 90 design group, ISSC, is Hamburg-based and stresses the requirement for a standard platform with interchangeable modular combat suites and equipment, it has not (at the time of writing) selected the MEKO philosophy outright.[5]

While the Americans and British have been leisurely examining the possible advantages of modularization, the German firm developed the concept whole-heartedly and, following a slow acceptance period, is deservedly enjoying in export sales the fruits of its enterprise. MEKO is an acronym for Mehrzwecks Kombination (multi-function) and comprises a standard hull whose fitting-out accepts a variety of modular 'functional units' which slot into standard apertures, built into the structure. These functional units (FU) already include a range of medium-calibre guns, from the American FMC 155mm vertical-load weapon to the Bofors 57mm. They embrace a variety of Close-in-Weapon Systems (CIWS), including the three most popular – Goalkeeper, Phalanx and Sea Zenith. There is a choice of 40, 35 or 30mm automatic weapons or of seven modularized point-defence missile-launchers, including Lightweight Seawolf and the still-under-development Rolling Airframe Missile (RAM). Vertical-launch Seawolf and Seasparrow are offered as well as 8-, 16-, 32- or 64 -cell VLS assemblies. Fourteen search/surveillance radars, ten fire control systems, ESM, sonar, communication and navigation

◄
A Rotating Airframe Missile (RAM) streaks from a prototype launcher on the starboard quarter of the US destroyer *David R. Ray* (DD-971). The General Dynamics RAM is an international collaborative venture, for a point-defence missile to replace, from 1992, the venerable Sea Sparrow, whose 8-cell launcher can be seen in the foreground. The 21-cell launcher will permit inexpensive salvo fire, but could be superseded by guns firing course-corrected ammunition. (German Navy)

One impression, based on the MEKO 360, of how the NATO frigate for the 'nineties may look. While the all-diesel propulsion permits a funnelless layout, the resultant 27-knot maximum speed would be insufficient for some fleets. Phased-array radar and, 'four-corner' CIWS armament are also noteworthy. (Blohm & Voss)

Technology transfer. Lead ship of a class of six, all of which will be built in Argentina, the *Espora* is an example of the MEKO 140, a small versatile frigate of 1,560 tons. She is fitted for, but not with, a telescopic hangar, and the four planned MM40 Exocet SSMs are missing from the after deck. All six ships are reported to be for sale. (Blohm & Voss)

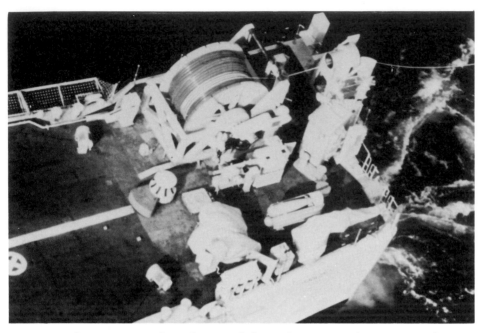

◄

Towed arrays are effective against surface or sub-surface targets, but may produce data that requires skilled interpretation. Quieter sources are demanding that an active element be also incorporated. The after end of the British frigate *Sirius* shows the impact on the ship's layout. (Plessey Naval Systems Ltd)

►

The complexities of modern electronic warfare is well illustrated by the foremast of a frigate completed recently in France for Saudi-Arabian account. ECM and ESM antennae have a wide frequency coverage for threat detection, surveillance, electronic intelligence (ELINT) and self-protection, such as by the round, flat JANET jammer. (Thomson – CSF)

units are also represented. Only area-defence SAM systems are currently too large to be suitable candidates for the MEKO.

Advantages stressed by Blohn & Voss include hull erection being a purely shipyard activity, separate from weapon or sensor manufacture.[6] Items in the latter categories can thus be assembled, set to work and stored under ideal conditions, being transferred to the shipyard only when required, there to be slotted into the hull with no duplication of effort. Repair is possible by replacement, in much the same way that a gas turbine exchange has taken the place of weeks alongside a dockyard wall, cleaning and re-tubing boilers *in situ*. With the unit cost of warships spiralling, life expectancies of 30 years and more are not unreasonable. Technological advances are continuous and the prospect of 'rolling modernization' by replacement, rather than major mid-life rebuilding, must be attractive. MEKO critics speak vaguely of weight and volume penalties, but Blohn & Voss equate each to just 2 per cent. It is a fact that all the nations participating in NFR 90 can build a first-class frigate; it is equally a fact that the great majority of these are too expensive to attract an export order or to be acquired in adequate numbers. Shortcomings or not, MEKO comes currently in three basic hull sizes – 3,600, 2,000 and 1,400 tonnes displacement – which

can be contracted comparatively inexpensively, the outfit (the expensive part) following later to spread the budget if necessary.

Besides the German F123 programme, the Canadians have needed to order a second batch of *Halifax*-class frigates and, if their ambitious schemes for an SSN fleet also go ahead, the chances of their acquiring NFR 90 in addition look bleak. France continues to build indigenous frigates and is linked with the NFR 90 project primarily because of the market that it will afford the proposed FAMS weapon system (in which Italy, Spain and the UK participate). The United Kingdom, meanwhile, will soon need a replacement programme for the Sea-Dart armed Type 42s, while the US Navy, having just completed a long series of FFG-7 *Perry*-class frigates, has more of the type than it requires. With so disparate a range of participants, the road to NFR 90 realization looks stony.

A frigate is of little use if, though an excellent ASW platform, she cannot defend herself. The Falklands War came as a shocking reminder that today's opponent, even if lacking a technological base, can purchase the latest weaponry and sensors in a readily accessible market. Many of today's submarines can not only outrun a frigate, but, through the use of stand-off weapons, can also out-range her. Included in a minimum outfit, a frigate needs ESM which reliably locates

and classifies incoming threats, 24 hours a day. This must be linked to both decoy ('soft kill') and weapon ('hard kill') systems. The electronics need to be able to grade incoming threats in order of urgency, allocating the correct countermeasure to each. Seconds count, so systems should operate automatically and manoeuvre the ship appropriately. Earlier defensive systems were limited by radars and directors to addressing perhaps only one or two targets simultaneously. Tomorrow's war will feature saturation attack through multiple threats, so a multi-function radar will be essential to provide sufficient track and guidance channels. For 360-degree protection, four decoy launchers should be provided, with automatic, rather than manual, loading and the ability to adjust chaff size to match the wavelength of the radar illuminating the ship at any time.

She requires a medium-calibre, rapid-firing gun, to engage at least one threat at maximum range, and with correct ammunition. The choice is not easy. While the American and British prefer 5-inch and 4.5-inch guns for their value in shore gunfire support, the characteristics of these weapons are not ideal for engaging, say, an SSM. In this role, a 76mm OTO-Melara Super Rapid gun fires to 8,000 metres at 120 rounds per minute, while the British 114mm (4.5-inch) fires to 23,000 metres at 25 rounds per minute.[7] A wave-hugging SSM is unlikely to be detected at better than 8,000 metres, a distance which, at only trans-sonic speeds, it will cover in about 30 seconds. For safety, the

▶
Only the indigenous Meroka CIWS on the hangar roof really distinguishes the Spanish-built *Santa Maria* from American FFG-7s. Full-scale warship design capability is extremely expensive, but Spain's mature shipbuilding industry has allowed for successful adaptation of American, French and German designs. (Empresa Nacional BACAN)

SSM needs to be destroyed at least 1,000 metres from the ship, leaving about 26 seconds' firing time. During this period the 76mm will loose more than 50 rounds to the 114mm's eleven. OTO-Melara and British Aerospace are further developing ammunition capable of being slewed through about ten degrees for course correction in flight.[8] While effective against missiles, however, the Italian's 6kg projectile weight cannot compete with the 21kg of the larger gun for use against surface or shore targets. Even the smallest of the 'medium calibre' guns, the Bofors 57mm, is a very effective weapon with high reaction rates, throwing at a rate of 220 rounds per minute out to about 6,000 metres.[9] With a claimed system precision of two milliradians and proximity-fuzed projectiles sensitive to seven metres, every round should hit or damage its target at 3,500 metres. Optional extended-range ammunition allows for engagement of thin-skinned surface targets out to 17,000 metres. Bofors state that, in the vital first 30 seconds of an engagement, the 57mm will put more explosive on target than a 100mm gun of orthodox configuration.

Roughly similar in range are Point Defence Missile Systems (PDMS), where excellence is very much a function of size and cost, and beyond the scope of many austere frigate designs. The British Seawolf here remains in a class of its own, but, though combat-proven, it has not sold for export despite VLS and lightweight launcher versions having been developed. It is not clear whether this is due to cost or security restrictions. Bidding as rival is the MATRA-built SADRAL from France. Its rounds are only a quarter of the weight of a Sea Wolf's, but, with a Mach 2.5 speed and range from 5,300 down to 500 metres, it is very effective against aerial targets with low crossing rates.[10]

Other French giants, Aérospatiale and Thomson-CSF, are developing a co-ordinated family of SAMs ('Aster') and control systems, the latter based on the new Arabel multi-function radar.[11] Arabel's phased-array antenna is not static, like the four-quadrant American Aegis, but rotates to give a 360-degree coverage with an elevation up to 70 degrees. Beam aperture precision enables up to fifty threats to be tracked and 'at least' ten engagements to be controlled simultaneously, to defeat saturation attack. The Aster 15, known as SAAM (Surface to Air Anti-Missile), will cope with Mach 2.5 seaskimmers manoeuvring at up to 15g and missiles diving at up to Mach 3.5. Supersonic targets will be intercepted at between eight and ten thousand metres, subsonic at 15–17,000 metres. Aster's agility in the terminal stage results from lateral, as well as axial, thrust. Under the umbrella title of Syrinx, the overall package may provide the basis for FAMS (Family of Anti-Air Missile Systems) in which Italy, Spain and the UK also participate. This is seen

◀ Here seen aboard a Swedish corvette, the Bofors 57mm Mk 2 mounting has such versatility as to be chosen for the medium-calibre gun for the current building programme of Canadian patrol frigates. With a rate of fire of 220rpm and proximity fuzing it can engage aircraft or sea-skimmer. Extended-range ammunition carry to 17,000 metres for surface warfare. (AB Bofors)

▲
Shown aboard the French AA frigate *Cassard* is the sextuple stabilized launcher of the Sadral point-defence system. A single operator can utilize radar, a fire control unit, IR or optical means to control his Mistral missiles. (MATRA)

▶
Marconi's 1802 CW tracker radar is associated with the Royal Navy's Seawolf missile, for which it offers full blind fire control. Both missile and target are tracked, their relative positions computed and the missile given continuous guidance commands over a fully redundant link. Thermal imaging or TV is supplied for passive surveillance or tracking. (Marconi Radar Systems)

as an alternative to NAAWS (NATO Anti-Air Warfare System), also multinational in origin but with the powerful American representation of Westinghouse and General Electric/RCA.[12] Both are likely contenders to arm the NFR 90.

Even the best missile defence will be 'leaked' by the odd SSM, against which the Close-in Weapons System (CIWS) is the accepted defence. Autonomous gun/radar assemblies, they have the advantage of having no minimum range of engagement. The original example of the West, the American Vulcan/Phalanx, though technically effective, fired 20mm projectiles against which SSMs could be hardened. Versions now available include 4-barrelled 30mm and a 5–7 barrelled 25mm Gatling-type guns. If the mounting weight can be tolerated, the 30mm is the better choice, with high-inertia projectiles or proximity fuzing. Indeed, the British are turning over from the earlier Vulcan/Phalanx to the 30mm Goalkeeper, whose General Electric cannon is controlled by a Dutch Signaal radar. Such weapons, to be effective, need to be mounted high up to command wide arcs, so the six tons per mounting could be inhibiting for smaller frigates.

On balance, the versatility and relative cheapness and simplicity of guns suggest that they might be preferable to PDMS, with one or two 57mm being a satisfactory combination with a CIWS. Threats are changing, however, and, on the design horizon, looms

A trials shot of the Turkish frigate *Yavuz*, lead ship of a quartette of MEKO 360s. Both the 5-inch/127mm gun and the superimposed quadruple 25mm Sea Zenith CIWS, mounted on their modules, can be clearly seen. Nets are rigged around the larger weapon to catch the shell cases of a pending firing trial. (Blohm & Voss)

the hypersonic anti-ship weapon. While official test programmes have been cancelled, both LTV and General Dynamics (Convair Division) are reported to be still researching into composite-bodied vehicles capable of withstanding local temperatures of 3,500 degrees F in Mach 17+ flight at high altitude.[13] Such vehicles would be targeted at 'high-value, time-urgent targets' which, of course, could be just about anything posing a threat at a specific time. While guidance methods remain unclear, such weapons would be virtually undetectable on approach, and possess a momentum unstoppable by any gun or point-defence system fast enough to react. Fortunately, hypersonic weapons appear to be about as far from reality as the directed energy weapons that would be their probable counters.

Suitable equipment to distract and divert the current generation of SSMs ('soft-kill') is inexpensive in through-life terms by virtue of being reusable, but can equally well be complemented by careful design. The unusual television homer can (once identified as such) be defeated by a simple smoke-screen. Those that home on signal emissions can be thwarted by frequency shifting or, albeit inconveniently, by electronic silence. The commonest varieties, the infra-red (IR) and semi-active radar homers, still pose problems. Hot spots around machinery and uptakes are being designed-out, but, in suitable conditions, the exhaust plume can be detected from over the horizon.[14] Currently exhaust gases are elaborately cooled before discharge, but, with ever more sensitive IR detectors, they will need eventually to be vented below the waterline, making a funnel-less frigate a probability. This will be simpler on diesel-driven ships than on those with gas turbines, which exhaust vast quantities of hot gas. It is possible that a necessity may be transmuted into a virtue by discharging the exhaust in the form of the bubble curtain now reportedly being fitted to surface ships to absorb hull-generated noise.[15]

Even as acoustic sensors are now fitted to monitor self-noise, so are fibre-optic loops being evaluated in continuous check of the ship's surface temperatures.[16] Some of the light directed along such cables is reflected back to source, the amount being temperature-related. With the aid of a dedicated micro-processor, such variables can be analysed, updated and displayed up to five times per minute. In difficult areas, water sprays or curtains may be specified for cooling.

Though inevitably becoming big and 'boxy', a frigate can have her radar cross-section significantly reduced by design detail. Sharp edges are rounded, gun mountings multi-faceted, 'vertical' surfaces are given varying degrees of tumblehome or flare. Such measures serve to scatter radar energy rather than reflect it back towards its source. Progression may well be to higher-freeboard, well-rounded hulls with super-structure suppressed in favour of greater underdeck capacity. The form of future frigates remains uncertain. The US Navy, never an innovator in frigate development, sees itself as being well-provided with what it views as a 'defensive' class of ship. Following the débâcle of the *Stark* incident in the Persian Gulf in May 1987, Congress apparently favours the conversion of this numerous (FFG-7) class from primarily ASW to AAW.[17] This policy would seem mis-directed, as the *Stark* was not a victim of poor equipment so much as a refusal to believe she was being attacked.

To keep ASW numbers to strength, the US Navy will need to consider the form of life-extension programme involving the 46-ship FF-1052 (*Knox*) class. These austere, single-screw ships have their share of critics,

and their steam propulsion demands 285 crew compared with the 225 aboard a gas-turbine driven FFG-7. Re-engining is advocated as an obvious means of taking the ships economically to the year 2015 but this, together with updating, is thought not to be cost effective.[18] One definite improvement will be the upgrading of their SH-2F Kaman LAMPS I helicopters to an effective 'G' variant, which aircraft looks set to populate other LAMPS I-equipped ships.

NATO fleets will require to develop smaller and cheaper frigates if they are to field anything like the number required. If such as helicopters, towed arrays and data processing serve to increase unit size and cost, it makes sense to examine means of removing such items to complementary platforms. When the British Type 23 was first conceived, it boasted only flight pad and basic helicopter facilities, the aircraft itself being garaged and maintained aboard the new-style, one-stop AOR (supply ship) that would accompany her group. It would seem that it was then realized that frigates do not fight wars while organized in tidy, conformal groups, but need instead to be able to deploy their full ASW potential while defending themselves with, if possible, the margin to assist further in group defence. The 23s, therefore, acquired a large helicopter and full facilities, taking them beyond the cheap, export-attractive design they were first intended to be.

To break this mould, a recoverable, remotely piloted vehicle (RPV) could be considered. It would need to lay sonobuoy patterns, deploy a dipping sonar, relay data, and deliver weapons besides deploying an ECM/ESM package when required – in fact it needs to be an unmanned helicopter. The Americans tried this years ago with DASH, which was a failure only because it was a bold concept ahead of the technology of the time. Technology has advanced and the idea needs re-examining, possibly as an enlarged version of the Dornier, or Canadair double-rotor vehicles now available, the advantage of which are their VTOL characteristics.

With new, thin-line versions becoming available, towed arrays are less bulky but, even so, there are too few frigates to devote their time to trolling back and forth on barrier duty. It is not beyond possibility, if T-AGOS-type ships are too vulnerable or too expensive, to build unsophisticated manned submersibles for the purpose of deploying barrier arrays, their data being transmitted over a secure link for action to be taken by appropriate platforms. Should technology allow them

Immediately identifiable by virtue of the black protuberances ahead of the engine intakes, a Kaman YSH-2G Super Seasprite pre-production unit is seen undergoing sea trials on an FFG-7 flightpad. The forward fixture is a temporary instrumentation boom. No RAST system or fantail extension is necessary for an FFG-7 to embark on '2G'. (Kaman Aerospace)

This impression of a US Navy SWATH of the T-AGOS 19 series shows clearly the type's characteristic features – deeply submerged twin hulls supporting a spacious rectangular deck through slim, surface-piercing pylons. Visible are the after stabilizer fins which, being set at an angle, act also as rudders. (US Navy)

An Australian S-70 B2, an 'export' version of the Sikorsky SH-60B LAMPS III. Despite the vast area of ocean for which the RAN is responsible, only six FFG-7s are able to carry helicopters on a permanent basis, and the new *Anzac* frigates are required urgently. The chin fairing houses an MEL 'Super Searcher' radar in place of the LAMPS III's LN-66. (MEL Avionics System)

Component parts of the MEL Super Searcher, here with a planar antenna. The operator can use it in the 'stand-alone' surveillance mode, or integrate it with other sensors to coordinate ASW, vector fighters, provide OTH guidance or guide air-to-surface missiles such as Penguin or Sea Skua. The radar is frequency-agile for difficult environments and incorporates customized software. (MEL Avionics System)

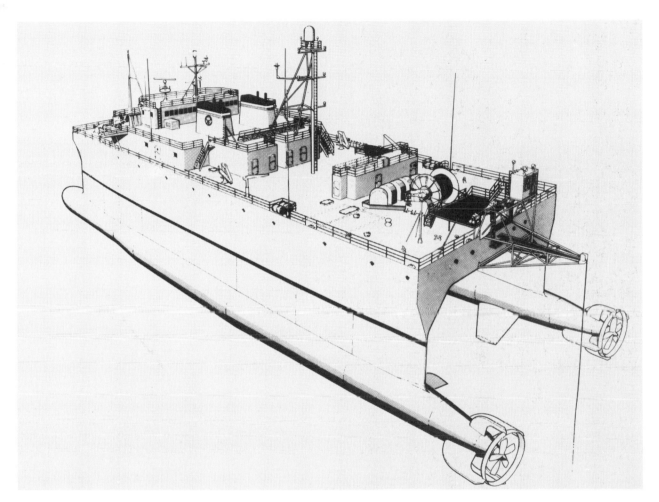

to be unmanned, the submersible could be risked through the incorporation of an active element in the array, for the purpose of final target localization immediately prior to attack.

The Type 23s are reported to be the first Royal Navy frigates with a bow sonar, the all-round 2050.[19] It is larger, because it operates at lower frequencies, which would not only give it longer range but also devalue the effectiveness of the acoustic tiling used on Soviet submarines.

The reverse to removing helicopters from frigates is to acknowlege their primary role and re-design the ship around them. This makes the Surface Effect Ship (SES) attractive. Following experience with two 100-ton prototypes, the Americans have already built the SES-200, whose 160 × 39-foot (48.75 × 11.9 metre)

overall dimensions gave an unencumbered rectangular flightdeck, and a steady and fast ride in sea states that would have obliged a monohull to slow to avoid slamming. It is forecast that the next step should be to a 1,500–2,000-tonner which, while smaller than the 3,500-ton monohulls considered minimum-sized for American service, would enjoy a comparable performance envelope.[20] Such a ship could deploy the V-22 Osprey Tiltrotor aircraft, would be virtually immune to submarine torpedoes and be able to pace the submarine itself in poor conditions. Extrapolations from SES-200 performance figures suggest the 2,000-tonner's maximum calm weather speed to be of the order of 41 knots; that of a 4,000-tonner would be 46 knots.[21] Progress on the SES has, no doubt, suffered from the failure of the MSH coastal minesweeper

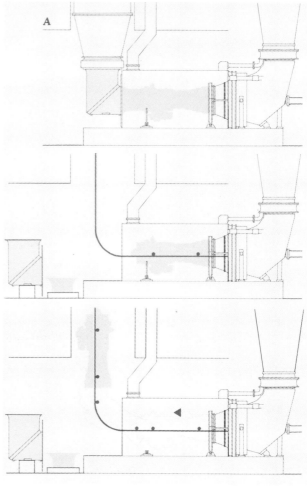

which attempted to incorporate too many untried technologies in a single design; this example, however, should not militate against the SES concept.

The French, meanwhile, are constructing the 250-ton (full load) *Agnes 200*, planned to start a year's development trials in the spring of 1990 and leading to the production of a 1,400-ton prototype ASW SES by the year 2000.[22] Designated the *Eoles 1200*, this 89 × 21-metre craft is, perhaps optimistically, projected to be capable of 52 knots over calm water and maintain 35-40 knots in sea state 5–6. Well-suited to sprint-and-loiter patterns, she will be evaluated as a possible replacement for French ASW frigates then nearing the end of their useful life. The *Eoles 1200* will be propelled by twin waterjets, whose diesel drive is configured to

provide power for the low-speed 'boating' mode or the high-speed hover mode, where power is also diverted to the lift fans.

As mentioned earlier, the British Type 23 also features innovatory propulsion. On passage, each of the ship's twin shafts is powered by a Spey gas turbine which, unaided, can propel her at 28 knots. For silent ASW operations the shafts can, alternatively, be powered by DC motors, deriving current via thyristor convertors from the ship's four multi-purpose AC diesel-generator sets, which are mounted high in the ship to reduce noise transmitted to the submerged hull. For full speed, the gas turbine and motors can be combined in a unique CODLAG (Combined Diesel-Electric and Gas Turbine) arrangement. Such a

◄◄
The quiet revolution. Two Spey SM1C modules installed in the forward machinery space of the British frigate *Brave*. The contrast between this and the labour intensive steam plant of earlier generations of ships is dramatic. Each SM1C is rated at 18 MW continuous. (Rolls-Royce plc)

◄
Repair by replacement. Earlier ships requiring machinery repair needed to lay alongside for the duration. Today, two men can remove and replace an SM1C'S gas generator or power turbine rotor in the simple stages shown, getting the ship back into service with minimum delay. This policy will become standard for all systems. (Rolls-Royce plc)

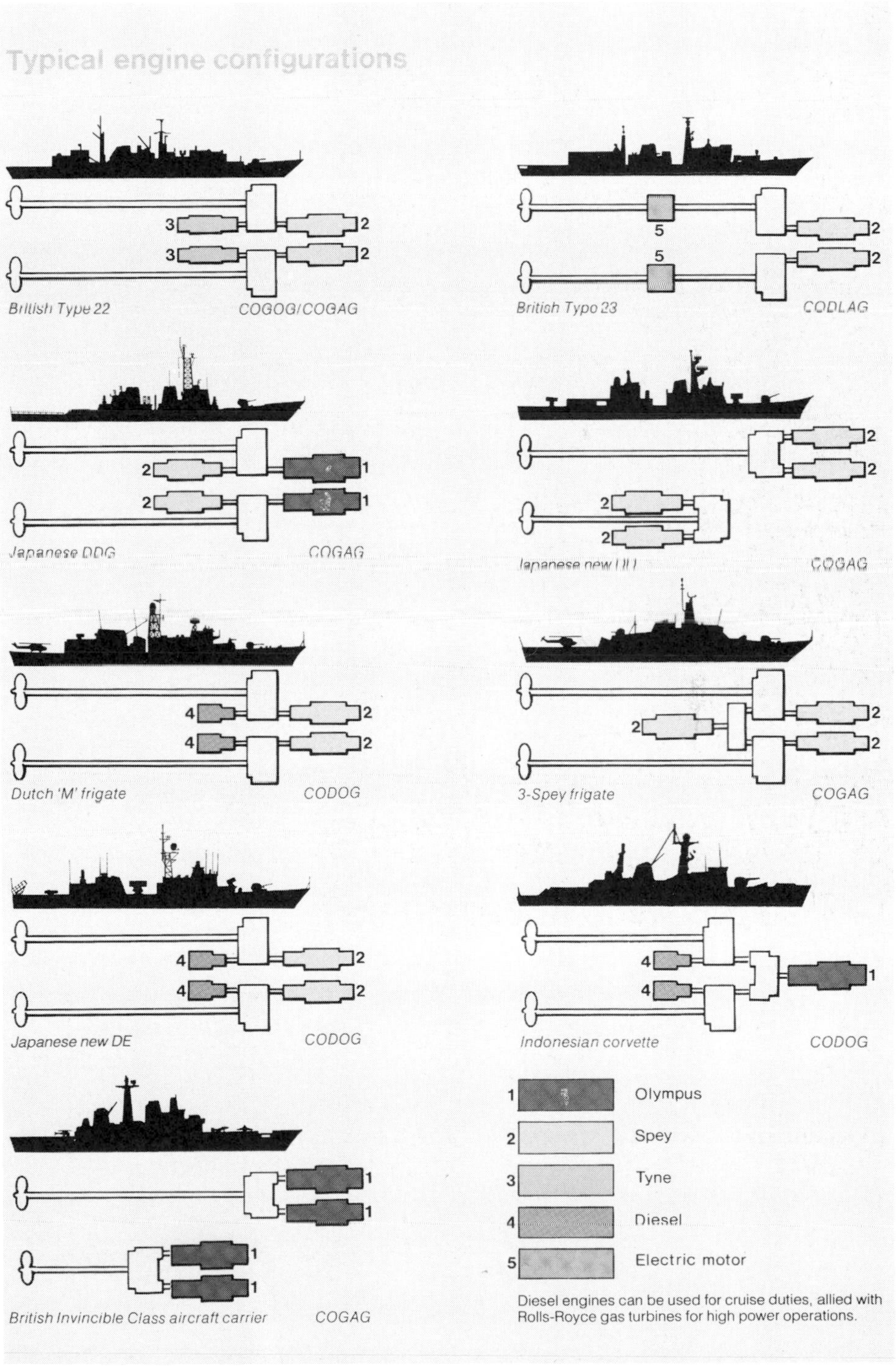

Typical engine configurations

British Type 22 — COGOG/COGAG

British Type 23 — CODLAG

Japanese DDG — COGAG

Japanese new DD — COGAG

Dutch 'M' frigate — CODOG

3-Spey frigate — COGAG

Japanese new DE — CODOG

Indonesian corvette — CODOG

British Invincible Class aircraft carrier — COGAG

1	Olympus
2	Spey
3	Tyne
4	Diesel
5	Electric motor

Diesel engines can be used for cruise duties, allied with Rolls-Royce gas turbines for high power operations.

►
Where steam plant was once tailored to a specific hull, the choice of Olympus (21MW), Spey (19,5MW), or Tyne (4MW), in combination with diesels or electric motors, gives a designer the necessary power and arrangement to satisfy any operational envelope. All units are repaired by replacement. (Rolls-Royce plc)

Conceived as a small, no-frills, inexpensive, export-orientated frigate, the Type 23 (*Norfolk*) has grown by stages to become a viable *Leander*- replacement for the Royal Navy. Even so, it is reported that the third batch to be ordered will be about seven metres longer. Note the VL Seawolf and eight conventional Harpoon launchers, rather exposed forward. (Yarrow Shipbuilders Ltd)

machinery package is heavy, complex and expensive, justifiable only because of the overriding requirement for silent running. It is remarkable how, in a design which has grown from a cheap exportable craft to one costing £150 million – some three-quarters that of the cost-criticized Type 22 – not even a single CIWS is shown on official impressions.[23] Indeed only recently have these shown a second radar-tracker for her vertical-launch Sea-Wolf defence.

Silent electric propulsion may well be realized with the promised breakthrough in super-conductivity, if this can reduce the present 10–15 per cent losses to the order of the 2 per cent typical of a gearbox.[24] The world's first superconductive-powered demonstrator is due to go operational in 1990.[25] This, the 150-tonne Japanese Yamato I, is only 22 metres in length, with machinery designed to develop a propulsive thrust of 8,000 Newtons (about 800kg force) for a modest eight knots. Even this limited venture entailed investment of five billion yen, but represents a sum which should yield substantial return.

References and Notes

1. *Combat Fleets*, pp.617–20.
2. Wright. 'The NATO Frigate Project', in *Naval Forces*, vol.5, No.2, 1984, p.36.
3. (American) *Naval Engineers' Journal*, September, 1988, p.19.
4. 'West Germany sets up frigate project', in *Jane's Defence Weekly*, 1 October 1988, p.795.
5. Letter to Author from Blohm & Voss dated 9 November 1988.
6. 'FES – Functional Unit System', Blohm & Voss publication, WS-001-0388-02.
7. *Combat Fleets*, pp.201 and 299.
8. Hewish and Turbe. 'Anti-ship Missile Defence', in *IDR*, October, 1988, p.1307.
9. 'Bofors Naval Weapons. The 57mm Mk 2 all-purpose gun', Bofors publication, PB-06-P284E.
10. 'Mistral for Naval Use', MATRA publication, 1988.
11. 'Aster and SAMP/SAAM', in *Maritime Defence*, October, 1988, p.380.
12. Hewish and Turbe. op. cit., p.1301.
13. Reported in *Jane's Defence Weekly*, 22 October 1988, p.1023.
14. 'Reduction of IR signature' *Naval Forces*. Special supplement on the Blohm & Voss MEKO 200, p.51.
15. 'Five areas of stealth for RN Type 23s', in *Jane's Defence Weekly*, 22 October 1988, p.998.
16. 'USN trials for temperature sensor', in *Jane's Defence Weekly*, 5 November 1988.
17. Metcalf. 'Frigates: Quo Vadis?' in *US Naval Institute Proceedings*, May, 1988.
18. Metcalf. ibid., p.71.
19. *Combat Fleets*, pp.202 and 213.
20. Butler. 'The Surface Effect Ship', in (US) *Naval Engineers' Journal*, Supplement, February, 1985, p.209.
21. Butler. ibid., p.216.
22. 'The next generation of ASW escorts?', in *IDR*, October, 1988, p.1240.
23. Hewish. 'New Frigate Designs for NATO Navies', in *IDR*, April, 1988, p.416.
24. Gates. *Surface Warships*. Brassey, London, 1987, p.75.
25. 'Japanese Shipbuilding – Sunrise or Sunset?', in *The Naval Architect*, October, 1988, p.E307.

MAJOR ESCORTS

Since the Second World War, the term 'destroyer' has changed its meaning entirely. From a fast ship, built around a torpedo armament and designed to operate (at least ideally) in independent flotillas, the destroyer has become associated with anti-air warfare (AAW). As capability and firepower increased, the category of 'cruiser' was re-introduced. Both terms thus now apply to predominantly AAW ships, the choice of term referring to individual potential. It is futile to criticize such regrading of terminology, which has been normal throughout the evolution of the warship itself. (For instance, the cruiser of the Second World War did much the same job as one of Nelson's frigates, while the *Warrior* of 1864, the most effective battleship in the Royal Navy, was, technically, also a frigate.)

Destroyers in their later, AAW, guise have always tended to be larger than ASW-orientated frigates, due to their bulkier missiles, magazines, handling and launching gear, and directors. Surface to air systems have the built-in disadvantage of having to control their missiles until they are close enough to their target to acquire it for themselves in the terminal phase. Even with semi-active homing, the ship could engage no more targets than she could illuminate, and each illuminator needed to be dedicated for a period long in comparison with the potential firing rate of the launching system. With only one or two illumination radars per ship, defence saturation was a real danger.

As far back as 1958, therefore, the Americans, who led the field in this type of technology, began the development of a 'super' version of the Tartar missile, then entering service.[1] Together with an up-rated Talos, this weapon would have constituted the medium/long-range Typhon system. This would have featured a new-style control radar with, in place of rotating antennae, fixed arrays composed of a large number of phase-shifting elements, switched electronically at very high speed to permit multi-target tracking with very fine beams. Although it went to sea for trials in 1964, the Typhon radar was shortly afterwards abandoned on grounds of cost and size.

The work was not wasted, being ploughed into a new Advanced Surface Missile System (ASMS), also aimed at defeating saturation attack and, following the Eilat incident of October 1967, meeting the additional threat posed by the SSM. ASMS became Aegis and, because of the new guidance methods employed, a new complementary missile was also developed in the Standard SM-2. Aegis searches and tracks simultaneously with hundreds of pencil beams, but, instead of requiring several 'paints' by a rotating scanner to establish targets' position, course and speed, any contact on Aegis will attract multiple 'dwells' in quick succession from beams so fine that they provide data 'of fire control quality'.[2] Thus, in place of a dedicated illuminator providing reflected energy pulses continuously to guide a missile to target, Aegis employs command guidance, sending flight corrections directly to the missile.

A further advantage is in Aegis' ability to compute a continuously updated intercept course, flying the missile by the most economical route rather than, as with semi-active homing, obliging the missile always to point at its target. Firing similar missiles, an Aegis ship (currently the CG-47, *Ticonderoga* class) can out-range another by as much as 55 per cent.[3] Precision illumination is required only in the terminal phase, when one of the CG-47's four directors is slaved for a few seconds on to coordinates supplied by the SPY-1A radar, which is the heart of the Aegis system. Many more missiles can, therefore, be simultaneously controlled than there are illuminators, making saturation attack difficult.

Aegis has set a standard which others must follow. It remains, however, a large system with a great impact on superstructure layout, its fixed, multi-element arrays needing to be set at an angle to the vertical in each of the four quadrants, and with clear arcs in each. Initial attempts to design it into a nuclear escort resulted in the half-billion-dollar CGN-42 Strike Cruiser which, like Typhon before, fell to an economy axe. It was, therefore, decanted into a DD-963 (*Spruance*) hull, which had to absorb an extra 1,100 tons on full load displacement, with an attendant increase in draught of nearly half a metre. A major sacrifice was more than 2½ knots in speed, inhibiting its flexibility as an escort. Extra capability saw the destroyer categorization elevated to 'cruiser', without any increase in physical size. The CG-47's four arrays are arranged axially and abeam, an arrangement that gives all-round coverage, but dictates two superstructure blocks. More austere, the currently constructing DDG-51 (*Burke*) class of 'destroyer of the nineties' has adopted the four panel, 45-degree layout first proposed for the aborted Strike Cruiser. While these can all be accommodated in the bridge block, there would appear to be a blind sector dead astern, caused by the two substantial funnel casings. Though

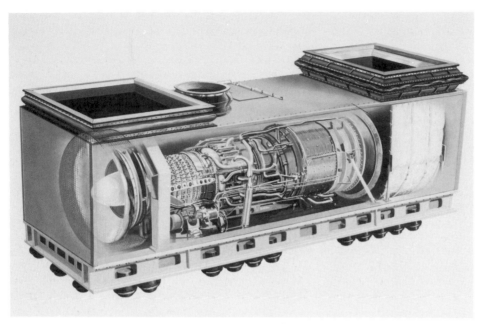

An LM-2500 gas turbine assembly, looking from the inlet pump end. The shock and acoustic decoupling mounts can be seen protruding from the base. Self-contained at about 22 tonnes weight, the LM-2500 can be rated to produce up to 26,600hp (c.20,000 kW). While interchangeable the record for an installed unit is 15,500 hours running – and still running. (General Electric Marine and Industrial Engines)

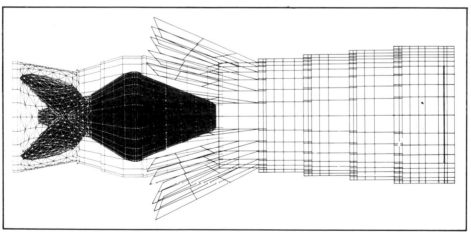

Infra-red (IR) signature reduction. The DRES Ball features film-cooled outer duct and centre body followed by a multi-ring entraining diffuser. The device dilutes exhaust gases with cool air and ensures that all visible metal surfaces are cooled. This finite-element analysis diagram assists in vibration and shock design. (W.R. Davis Eng. Ltd, via General Electric Cincinnati)

little smaller in displacement than the CG-47s, the *Burke*s will have very different proportions, the former's more traditional waterline length/ beam (L/B) ratio of 9.7:1 being reduced to only 7.9:1, with a move towards hulls of larger waterplane areas.[4] The superior stability range that results has been bought at the expense of some speed, although the extra beam also improves resistance to missile strike. In this context it is interesting to note a margin of 'over 130 tons' for armour protection.[5] Splinter protection is being increasingly worked-in in way of vital spaces and equipment and, with the current rapid developments in light composite materials, this trend will accelerate.

Composites commonly comprise fibre laid in an epoxy or metal matrix. While the current front runner is Kevlar, a para-aramid, the new Dynemma SK60 already exhibits a specific strength some 40 per cent greater on a density more than one-third less.[6] If quantity production can force down costs, a likely development would be composite internal ship structural panelling taking the place of protective additions in sensitive areas.

A striking feature of the DDG-51's appearance is the lack of vertical surfaces, with even the mast becoming a heavily-raked tripod to minimize radar signature. While a modified Aegis system has been accommodated, it has been at some cost. Legend endurance has been criticized as inadequate and only three SPG-62 illuminators are provided for the ship's primary AAW role. As there is no point-defence missile system, incoming SSMs have to be dealt with by only a pair of 20mm Vulcan-Phalanx CIWS. More seriously, no ASW helicopter is embarked (though there is a flight pad aft) so that, until the introduction of an ASROC round compatible with the ship's Mk 41 VLS, she has little AS potential. Although the VLS ASROC will allow for any mix of weapons 'on the rail', submarines can now mount OTH missile attacks against surface ships, and the stand-off qualities of a LAMPS III are essential rather than merely desirable.

An interesting comparison, on virtually the same length and displacement, is afforded by the Soviet *Sovremennyy*. Double-ended, her paired SA-N-7 (Gadfly) systems have an estimated forty missiles, capable to a range of 28km (17.5 miles), some 70 per cent of the Standard SM-2's advertised range. She has a 3-D phased array radar, not in the massive Aegis arrangement but in the form of a pair of back-to-back rotating antennae (known as 'Top Plate'). Not as capable as Aegis, it does not, nevertheless, require the ship to be designed around it. No less than six of the compact Front Dome tracker-illuminators ensure all-round coverage for an adequate number of SA-N-7s simultaneously. In place of the DDG-51's single 5-inch gun, the *Sovremennyy* has four slightly larger 130mm weapons. She, too, carries no point-defence missile system where an SA-N-9 could be expected. Her four 30mm CIWS are, however, far superior to the Americans' two 20mm mountings. The DDG-51's superiority lies in her ability to salvo-fire Harpoon SSMs if the VLS is so loaded, enabling her to out-shoot the Soviets' eight SS-N-22s. Both weapons are sea-skimmers, using active radar terminal homing because of the difficulty of illumination in close proximity to

▶

Hard and low. The aircraft-launched anti-ship missile is not as immediately destructive as a torpedo, but disables a large target by destroying much of the upper structure in the area of the hit. If the target is not sunk by fire or structural failure she would probably need to be scuttled as irrecoverable in an operational situation. Here a West German Kormoran is about to strike a *Fletcher* destroyer target. (German Navy)

A Seawolf point-defence missile streaks from its launcher aboard the British Type 22 frigate *Brave*. This class is the last to be fitted with the sextuple mounting which, loaded, weighs a reported 3.5 tonnes. At the masthead is the back-to-back antenna of the Type 967/968 target designation radar and, partly visible over the bridge, the Marconi Type 911 search and track radar. (British Aerospace (Dynamics Division))

The Goalkeeper CIWS, fitted to both Dutch and British escorts, links a 7-barrel 30mm GAU-8/A Gatling gun with a surveillance radar, a dual-frequency tracking radar, a fire control unit and 1,190 rounds of ammunition on an all-up weight of about 6,100kg. Tungsten alloy penetrators ensure a kill of even hardened missiles. Incoming SSMs seek to be inconspicuous in a sea clutter and through the increasing use of stealth techniques, particularly in radar absorbent materials (RAM). Goalkeeper uses dual frequency detection, the broader I-Band for tracking and continuous-wave illumination, and the concentric pencil beam K-Band to pinpoint the target without multi-path effects. (HSA)

Test-firing a vertical-launch (VL) Seawolf from the trials vessel *Longbow*. Comparison with the picture of the *Brave* launching shows the extra boost motor which lifts the missile prior to capture and toppling. Vertical-launch will be fitted to British Type 23 (*Norfolk*) frigates and AORs, going far toward the defeat of saturation attack. (British Aerospace (Dynamics Division))

the surface. Each, therefore, is vulnerable to ECM, where the Americans should enjoy the edge.

Building in parallel with the *Sovremennyy* class, in a programme likely also to extend well into the nineties, are the *Udaloy* AS destroyers. With signs of a cutback in Soviet naval expansion, emphasis on a more 'defensive' posture and priorities given to the operation and countering of submarines, it may well be that the *Udaloy*s flourish in numbers at the expense of the *Sovremennyy*s. In other fleets, ships given primarily to ASW would likely be termed 'frigates', but there is nothing frigate-like about an *Udaloy*. As with a *Sovremennyy*, she is a slender, high freeboard ship, credited with 35 knots. The first of her type with two AS helicopters, she also ships two quadruple SS-N-14 ('Silex') ASW missiles of 30-mile range, together with eight large torpedo tubes. Defensively, the *Udaloy* has no less than eight, 8-cell SA-N-9 point-defence missile systems. Capable of a 15km (c. 9-mile) range, these missiles are associated with only two tracker/illuminators, the Top Plate, whose antennae are mounted high on the mainmast, being able to keep several missiles in the air at once, while detecting any further threats as they materialize. Any missiles 'leaking' past

the SA-N-9 barrier will be engaged by one of four 30mm CIWS. *Udaloy* is a formidable ASW ship, that should prove difficult to sink, even by all-out missile attack.

Destroyer-type fleet escorts are, of course, built elsewhere than the USA and the Soviet Union. From the mid-nineties, Japan should start to commission a quartet of Aegis ships. Still resisting the formation of a large armaments industry, the Japanese buy most of their technology (not always the latest) from the Americans. Italy, on the other hand, has developed a thriving technological base, actively seeking foreign partners in more expensive collaborative projects. Except, therefore, for common Standard SM-1 systems, their ships have a largely home-produced sensor and armament fit. The two Italian *Animoso*s, due for completion in the early nineties, have adopted CODOG propulsion, based on two licence-built General Electric LM2500 gas turbines. Where earlier steam plant was tailored to a specific hull, aircraft-derived GTs are of fixed maximum rating so that these ships, shorter and beamier due to the accommodation of a pair of EH101 helicopters, will necessarily be slower than older destroyers.

British escorts have a history of being designed down to an artificially low size and cost, requiring later stretching to improve their capacity. Yarrow, with long experience in destroyers, built all four of the Batch 1 Type 22s of which the first, *Broadsword*, is shown on full power builders' trials in the Clyde estuary. (Yarrow Shipbuilders Ltd)

First of the 'Batch 3' Type 22s, HMS *Cornwall* has gained a 114mm DP gun, the four MM38 Exocets being replaced by twice that number of longer-ranged Harpoons, resited in a more sheltered position abaft the bridge. Light automatic weapons,

which earlier flanked the bridge, have been replaced by the infinitely more effective centreline Goalkeeper CIWS. A second Goalkeeper to give all-round coverage, was cut for economy. (Yarrow Shipbuilders Ltd)

▶
'Batch 2' Type 22s were lengthened by more than 14 metres, not in order to increase armament directly, but to enable them to accommodate the EH101 helicopter and a large towed array. HMS *London*, last of the four Yarrow-built Batch 2s, shows a fine 'rooster tail' and her double-ended Seawolf armament to advantage. Lack of offensive armament is very evident. (Yarrow Shipbuilders Ltd)

Still adhering firmly to the concept of the slender-proportioned destroyer are the French, whose C70 AA (*Cassard*) type has a length/beam ratio of 10:1. Although fiercely nationalistic in equipment procurement, the French have also remained with the Standard missile, actually building new ships around systems removed from discarded units. As with the Italians, and the continuing lack of a British Sea Dart replacement, it points up the enormous cost of new SAM systems and the urgent requirement for the new so-called Family of Anti-Air Missile Systems (FAMS) currently under development. Escorts of the calibre of the *Cassard* are required to offer not only area defence, but also close-in defence, sufficient to protect the ship and to contribute to the integrated coverage of a group. Through digital data links, French SENIT combat information systems interface with those of other platforms, but the *Cassard* is pioneering a new passive detection and tracking system based on infra-red (IR) emissions.[7] Its Vampir panoramic search unit is sited on a stabilized platform high on the lofty mast favoured by French designers, where its elevation and reduced sensitivity to sea clutter give it a claimed 10km detection range against aircraft or wave-hugging missiles. It works simultaneously on two discrete wavelengths and its one-milliradian accuracy in azimuth allows the associated Pirana IR tracker to be laid on to an emitting source with great precision. Once locked, the tracker slaves the gun or Sadral point-defence system, but, as usual, the limitation of the system would appear to be its ability to cope with multiple targets.

Not the least interesting feature of the *Cassard*s is in their being the largest all-diesel (CODAD) warships of modern times.[8] While having no native gas turbines of any size, the French have amassed considerable medium-speed diesel experience through their SEMT-Pielstick concern, a controlling interest in which has now been acquired by the German MTU agglomerate. Unlike gas turbines, diesels can be run economically over a wide band of power, but have not been popular in larger installations, mainly because of their inherent noise. This limitation would seem to have been reduced, or accepted as being less important to an AAW ship than to one engaged in ASW; the *Cassard*s employ a total of 64 cylinders to develop 30,000 kW (*c.* 40,000shp) for a surprisingly low legend speed of 29.5 knots. Resiliently mounted machinery rafts and flexible

An artist's impression of the ASW version of the Osprey tiltrotor, the SV-22, staging from a DD963 destroyer. For stowage, the wing is rotated in line with the fuselage and the rotor blades folded. With a 300-knot maximum speed, the aircraft combines rapid reaction to distant contacts with a sizeable payload. (Bell Helicopter Textron)

▶
Lead ship of a class of eight, the Japanese *Asagiri* has recently joined a fleet expanding rapidly to take a greater share of national defence. While weapon systems still show dependence on foreign supply (the eight Harpoon SSMs are missing), electronics and sensors are increasingly of home supply. Rolls-Royce Spey gas turbines are licence-built by Kawasaki. (Rolls-Royce plc)

transmissions are commonly used to de-couple most noise and vibration from the hull. While fitted initially with a DRBV 15 search and low-altitude air search radar, the *Cassard* is due to exchange this with the new DRBJ 11B, which enters service in 1989. This is a Thomson/CSF multi-function radar (MFR) of the new generation, capable of undertaking long-range and horizon searches, together with surveillance, detection and tracking of multiple targets. It can further support the area-defence SAM system by transmitting guidance corrections to missiles in flight while providing target illumination as required.[9]

In a manner similar to that of the original Aegis SPY-1A, an MFR uses a large number of electronically switched phase-shifters, but may be fixed or rotating. Fixed Aegis arrays are each 12.5 feet (3.8 metres) across and comprise 4,480 elements. By comparison, an MFR, will employ between 1,000 and 1,500 elements in total. Though more compact, therefore, it cannot have the comprehensive coverage offered by Aegis and benefits from integration with other ship-borne sets. Whether MFR arrays should be fixed or rotating depends on application. Fixed arrays are larger, more versatile and mounted lower in the ship,

a feature critical to some vessels. Rotating arrays are cheaper and have little impact on ship layout, so can be retro-fitted. Being lighter, they can be sited higher, improving their chances of detecting the sea-skimmer.

Ultimately, there remains the choice between a highly capable shipborne radar coupled with relatively simple missiles, or a basic outfit aboard a ship whose lack of sophistication is offset by more intelligent weapons. As SAMs need to remain as small and as agile as possible, the trend (despite micro-electronics) will usually be towards the refined shipboard end, able to guide pairs of missiles in a number of simultaneous engagements while tracking and assessing the largest possible number of other threats. Varying market demands will see a range of product options being offered; for instance, the back-to-back rotating antenna of Selenia/Marconi's EMPAR or the four (or even five, with the fifth covering the zenith against terminal divers) fixed arrays of the ARE/Plessey MESAR.

Other than in exceptional climatic conditions, radars are horizon-limited, but, at very low frequencies, different factors become more significant. At 200 MHz for instance, a 1.5-metre target approximates to one wavelength, causing a resonance which can be detected beyond the horizon, though not yet with an accuracy sufficient for targeting. Physical size limited early experiments to land-based equipment, but progress is set fair to produce a shipborne radar with a range of 100km (c.63 miles). [10]

Use of radar renders the user liable to detection by the would-be target's ESM, followed by possible countermeasures such as jamming or attack by an anti-radiation missile. A promising advance, therefore, is a new Phillips radar, which relies on a frequency modulated continuous wave rather than the usual pulsed transmissions. [11] Above 2,500 metres, ESM equipment, though aware of the radar, cannot derive sufficient data to initiate contermeasures. Known as Pilot, the radar is effectively covert until the inevitable antidote is developed, and it is suggested that it be mounted on a common back-to-back rotating pedestal with a conventional radar to allow the operator to select that which best suits the situation. Such a dual antenna would put an extra 90kg at masthead height.

As the oceans remain an effective hiding-place, even for the largest group, it must be assumed that much research is being invested in satellite search and surveillance. Operational or pending, for instance, are the American N-ROSS and the Soviet RORSAT (Radar Ocean Reconnaissance Satellite). By the turn of the century, such vehicles will be used more actively in targeting or, possibly, as weapon platforms in their own right. It is not surprising, therefore, to see the American request for substantial budgeting to develop a shipborne anti-satellite (ASAT) weapon system incorporating both kinetic (KE) and directed energy (DE) principles. [12] They are certainly not alone. Superficially, the production of such a weapon sounds common sense, but it will promote massive controversy. Military satellites allow superpowers to monitor effectively such matters as major disarmament agreements. As about 70 per cent of American overseas military communication is routed via satellites, disruption would degrade their ability to control a crisis. [13] Satellites are an integral part of deterrence, and deterrence prevents war. Proven ability by either superpower to destroy satellites would prove desta-

bilizing in peacetime. Nevertheless, in the absence of a formal treaty banning it, research continues in both camps. As military satellites need to orbit as low as 150km (about 94 miles)[14] to acquire useful data, they become vulnerable to attack from an air-launched weapon such as the American Miniature Homing Vehicle (MHV) which, launched from a high-flying F-15 in a 1985 demonstration, destroyed a satellite target at a height of 345 miles (approx 550km). Such prodigious quantities of power are required to destroy a satellite from a ground station that it is difficult to see a DE/ASAT system at sea in the near future.

Soviet *Sovremennyy*-class destroyers have what appears to be a laser device atop their bridge structure; this has been claimed to have been used to irradiate (*sic*) a Western patrol aircraft.[15] Another source mentions 'anomalies', attributed to laser illumination, experienced by both American and British satellites overflying the Soviet Union.[16] While the American Mid Infra-Red Advanced Chemical Laser (MIRACL) successfully destroyed a drone target in 1987, it was stated that the use of lasers at sea, in place of even conven-

tional CIWS, was 'years away'.[17] As MIRACL is only one of several avenues of laser research associated with the SDI programme, it is the future of this that may dictate the timing of the laser as a weapon rather than as a range-finding device. Stabilizing it accurately and for sufficient duration to enable it to damage a satellite's optical sensors from a moving ship would prove a difficult task in itself, but it would take a bold prophet to say that it could not be done.

Within the timespan under consideration, other novel types of weapon may appear on escorts, at least in prototype form. Advances in higher-temperature super-conductivity have improved the potential of smaller hulls to generate the immense, short-term energy levels necessary to power pulsed electro-magnetic weapons such as the rail gun, which would destroy with the kinetic energy of its super high-velocity projectiles, or a directed energy weapon whose destructive power is vested in an aimed pulse of energy, the effect of which would be much the same as that of the Electro-Magnetic Pulse (EMP) associated with a nuclear burst

◄
The Netherlands *Jacob van Heemskerck* is one of two *Kortenaer*s to sacrifice helicopter facilities for a Standard MR area defence SAM system. In conjunction with the space devoted forward to the Sea Sparrow and its reload facility, it is evident that space could be saved by a vertical launch system (VLS). Missing are the eight Harpoon SSMs amidships and the Goal-keeper CIWS from its deckhouse right aft. (Netherlands Navy)

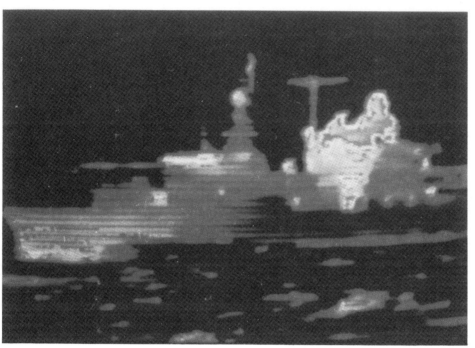

This IR photograph, taken during the initial trials of a MEKO 360 H2, shows warmer spots around the forward accommodation, wheelhouse, uptakes and exhaust plume. Further cooling of the latter may be effected before discharge, existing surfaces water-cooled or re-sited to avoid heating. The image perceived by an IR seeker is less precise. (Blohm & Voss)

▶

The Argentinian MEKO 360 *Almirante Brown* has an all-Italian armament, the AAW component of which is the Aspide version of Sea Sparrow, with two twin 40mm Breda mountings at each end, each pair controlled by a LIROD radar/optronic director. The 40mm calibre makes available a wide range of ammunition. (Blohm & Voss)

◀

A small radar cross-section reduces the ship's chances of being detected or successfully targeted by an active missile seeker. Note how a 'conventional' profile gives powerful returns on either beam and from astern and, how, through careful alignment of planes and avoidance of 'corner reflectors', the radar signature can be dramatically reduced. (Blohm & Voss)

▶

Blohm & Voss' MEKO concept embraces a range of hulls, each fitted with standard apertures and access paths for the fitting of Functional Units – gun, missile, fire control, etc. Any FU can be quickly removed for repair or exchange for another FU of the same class. Function chains, e.g., search radar, fire control and gun, are selected to be compatible. (Blohm & Voss)

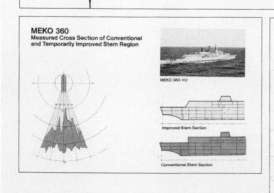

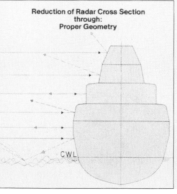

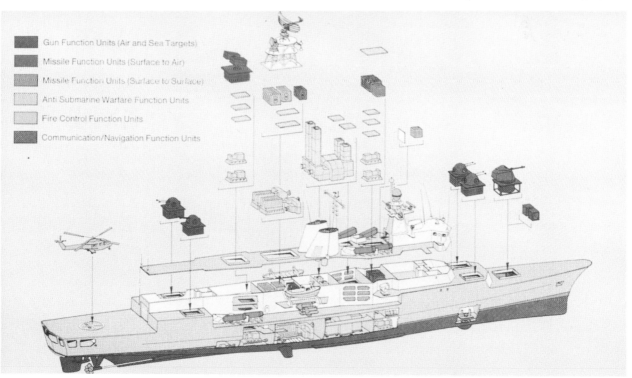

Gun Function Units (Air and Sea Targets)

Missile Function Units (Surface to Air)

Missile Function Units (Surface to Surface)

Anti Submarine Warfare Function Units

Fire Control Function Units

Communication/Navigation Function Units

▲
Long-range anti-ship missiles, such as this quadruple Harpoon mounting on the Turkish *Yavuz* will continue as a major escort's primary surface weapon. (Blohm & Voss)

▶▲
A complete quadruple 25mm Sea Zenith CIWS constructed as an inter-changeable MEKO module, which permits rapid replacement. (Blohm & Voss)

▶
Layered response to the threat of aerial attack will be ever more essential to a ship's survival. Visible here are the threat warning ECM atop the foremast, DA-08 airsearch radar with IFF, an 8-cell Mk 29 launcher for Sea Sparrow point-defence missiles and two Sea Zenith CIWS flanking their dedicated Siemens Albis optronic director. (Blohm & Voss)

References and Notes
1. Norman Friedman. *US Destroyers*. Arms & Armour Press, London, 1982, pp.222–3.
2. Meyer and Mura, 'Aegis', in *US Naval Institute Proceedings*, February, 1977, p.93.
3. Norman Friedman. op. cit., p.225.
4. *Combat Fleets*, pp.727–33.
5. Ibid., p.733.
6. Data from Dyneema Vof (Nederland) publication, TEN Int., 1987.
7. 'French Naval Applications of IR Detection and Tracking', in *Armada International*, May, 1988, p.85.
8. 'The French naval defence industry', in *Maritime Defence*, October, 1988, p.375.
9. Hewish. 'Trends in Shipborne Radar', in *IDR*, June, 1988, p.667.
10. Ibid., p.671.
11. Pengelley. 'Philips Pilot covert naval radar', in *IDR*, September, 1988, p.1177.
12. '(Funding sought) for ASAT research', in *Jane's Defence Weekly*, January, 1989.
13. Quoted by Stein, 'Satellites, Anti-Satellite Weapons and Security', in *RUSI Journal*, Winter, 1988, p.48.
14. Ibid., p.50.
15. Liebig. 'Radio-Frequency Weapons: Strategic Context and Implications', EIR Special Report, February, 1988, p.47.
16. Stein. op. cit., Quoting Aviation Week & Space Technology.
17. Norman Friedman. 'World Naval Developments/US NAVY DEVELOPS MIRACL Laser', in *US Naval Institute Proceedings*, March, 1988, p.178.

AMPHIBIOUS WARFARE AND THE SURFACE ACTION GROUP

'US naval forces have largely exceeded the limits needed for defence . . . There is practically no other country in the world where the navy and air force are numerically stronger than the land forces . . . US naval forces are meant mostly not for defence but for conducting active operations in the oceans, in regions unrestricted by any boundaries. The large primary role in their structure belongs to attack forces . . . battleships (all of which carry long-range cruise missiles) . . . and powerful amphibious forces capable of simultaneously moving task forces across great distances'. Thus Marshal of the Soviet Union Akhromeev, writing recently in *Pravda* and underscoring the continued Russian concern for American potential for 'power projection', a concern that has existed since 1945.[1]

At this date amphibious forces, with overwhelming seapower in support, had just decided the outcome of the Pacific War, and the Cold War had begun. The Soviet Union could be defeated only by land, but its leaders, who understood little about seapower, were deeply worried that a foreign power could turn Russian coastal waters from a defensive moat into a highway for landing a hostile army and for outflanking defences. This threat was both the impetus for Soviet fleet expansion and the factor that decided the form of that expansion.

A table accompanying the report showed that 65 per cent of American naval forces are considered 'ocean capable' as opposed to only 12 per cent Soviet, while no less than 52 per cent of Soviet strength was directed to 'coastal defence' to only 6 per cent American.[2] It is not clear on what the Marshal based his definitions or whether he referred to tonnage or numbers of ships. Even if he has presented biased figures to support his argument, however, it is still obvious that the fleets have differing roles.

The standing American amphibious squadrons are vehicles for the US Marine Corps which, with an authorized strength of 199,600, number three times the manpower of the British Royal Navy and the Royal Marines combined.[3] Though now faced with a possible 10 per cent cut following the well-funded Reagan years, the Corps is a powerful spearhead force with dedicated hardware ranging from F/A-18s to a new generation of amphibious warfare ships. Also in the pipeline are tilt-rotor aircraft and heavier armour, though critics of the latter argue that it makes no more sense for the Marines to assume the Army's armoured role than it does for the Army to form its new proposed 'light divisions'. Marines operate 'in support of land campaigns associated with naval operations . . . [and] as an expeditionary force in readiness, prepared to engage in low-intensity conflict'. While these terms of reference are broadly true for Marine-type forces world-wide, governing their equipment and means of deployment, only the USMC is large enough to initiate a landing and, in terms of limited warfare, follow through to a military conclusion unassisted by the Army. The USMC has long voiced misgivings regarding seaborne fire support. The disappearance of gun-armed combatants, and the abandoning of the projected lightweight 8-inch (203mm) gun, left the 5-inch (127mm) as the only suitable weapon, at the rate of no more than one or two per ship. Prepared shore defences are little affected by 5-inch rounds, however, while air support is no substitute, being less accurate, and wasteful of highly expensive assets in the shape of both aircraft and crews. Primarily for this reason, and as a means of boosting progress towards the now-abandoned goal of a 600-ship navy, the four *Iowa*-class battleships, with their 16-inch main batteries, underwent their controversial rehabilitation. It is because of this close relationship that amphibious warfare and surface action groups are here being considered together. It should be appreciated that, in peacetime, 'amphibious warfare' is not synonymous with another Okinawa-style operation, as lifting capacity for only a spearhead force is maintained. Follow-up capacity would need to be improvised.

It is worth looking briefly at the evolutionary forces that have brought about current developments. The Pacific War was brought to its triumphant conclusion in 1945 due largely to amphibious warfare. This required vast assemblages of shipping to lie offshore for extended periods, a situation previously acceptable with superiority in both air and seapower, but obviously not possible with the arrival of nuclear weapons, the delivery of just one of which could destroy an armada. What was required was a means of rapid shuttle movement from a safe range, preferably from over the horizon (OTH).

The helicopter, still a newcomer in 1945, was seen as this means and developed steadily until it was common practice to transfer two-thirds of the assault force by air and only one-third by surface craft.[4] Once landed, of course, such units were light infantry, their armour, artillery and transport being scaled to be air-portable, while larger helicopters were developed to carry them.

◄

Whether a 45-year-old battleship would be viable in a full-scale modern shooting war, only a shooting war is likely to prove. As a peacetime symbol of seapower, however, *Missouri* (BB-63) has considerable 'presence'. The Vulcan Phalanx CIWS and the armoured box launcher (one elevated) for Tomahawks are evident, high on the superstructure. (US Navy)

◄

A Tomahawk cruise missile blasts off from an armoured box launcher aboard the reactivated battleship *New Jersey* (BB62). The weapon would normally be the BGM-109B anti-ship version. While this is effective to 250 miles, the ship carries no dedicated means for precise targeting at this distance. (General Dynamics Corporation)

There seems to have been something of a design conflict between the CH-46 Sea Knight, which can lift 18 combat-ready troops, and the twice-as-heavy CH-53 Sea Stallion, with its capacity of 38 troops or four tons of internal freight. The early-sixties design of the 8,300-ton *Raleigh*-class LPDs could spot up to six CH-46s at a time, while the 11,850-ton *Whidbey Island* LSDs of two decades later can handle simultaneously only two CH-53s.[5] The weakness of this style of assault is its vulnerability to ground fire, and the introduction of reliable shoulder-launched, ground-to-air missiles in recent years has made it necessary to mount simultaneous defence-suppression flights, necessarily from other decks.

An unfortunate side-effect of the OTH heliborne assault concept was to see it achieving its aim through total surprise; gunfire support would be unnecessary, indeed, counter-productive in giving prior warning to the defenders. This, however, was to ignore the fact that defences had to be subdued before landing craft could follow up with the main body and their armour. During the period of build-up it is also necessary, for instance, to break up enemy armour concentrations at a considerable distance inland, at least seventeen miles being desirable.[6] Even with extended-range (ER) ammunition, the 5-inch 54 cannot reach this. The abandoned lightweight 8-inch 55 is quoted as having had twice the range of the 5-inch, four times the penetrating power, six times the fragmentation power and a laser-guidance capability.[7] With ER rounds it could range 30–40 miles with the capacity to launch sub-munition rounds for area denial.

While helicopters retain their major assault role, therefore, both Americans and Soviets have looked for a complementary means of mounting an assault from a maximum range, with gunfire support as required. For this the Russians have retained solidly built (by modern standards) *Sverdlov*-class cruisers, each carrying a dozen 155mm (6-inch) guns. The US Navy still had its four 16-inch *Iowa* battleships and three large 8-inch *Des Moines* cruisers (as yet un-rehabilitated).

The gun, it must be stressed, is not an out-moded weapon. Both it and the missile have their virtues, their weaknesses – and their place. Advantages for the gun are the relative cheapness of its ammunition, its resistance to counter-measures (at least with conventional rounds), its ability to fire at targets with no signatures and its capacity for indirect fire. Only in recent years have terrain-following techniques conferred the ability for cruise missiles to strike at a set of anonymous coordinates well inland, but its 450-odd kilograms of high explosive is less than the content of a single 16-inch shell. (Even the proposed modification of the cruise missile to a propfan drive will not change the equation significantly).[8] An *Iowa* can deliver 18 conventional rounds per minute to more than 40,000 yards (*c.* 36,500m) and the same number of laser-guided 'specials' to a reported 88,000 yards (80,500m).[9] Even more potent from the gun-support standpoint, is the amount of explosive delivered on target per hour. As quoted, a *Nimitz*-class supercarrier, crewed by 6,600 men, uses and risks expensive aircraft and aircrew to place less than 27 tons of explosive.[10] An *Iowa*, with a quarter of the crew strength, can off-load no less than 1,458 tons, with minimal risk to equipment or personnel. Only when the battle has penetrated more than 50 miles inland does the carrier come into its own (although longer over-flying further increases risk) but, by this stage, the amphibious force has long broken out from its beachhead. The adoption of ER ammunition will necessitate the upgrading of the *Iowa*'s fire control from the present 40-year-old electro-mechanical technology to a version of the Mk 160 digital system fitted to CGs and DDGs.[11] Extra range is gained through the use of saboted, sub-calibre projectiles, propelled by an unchanged weight of charge. The projectile carcasses are packed with sub-munitions in support of the attack scenario.

This sees a surprise OTH-mounted landing quickly securing an initial perimeter defence line, sufficiently far inland to enable the main surface-borne force to be put ashore unopposed, except by defenders already threatened from their rear. A containing counter-attack is then seen as likely to develop within six hours. As all likely operations are against forces of, or modelled on, the Eastern Bloc, this response is anticipated to be by one or more motorized rifle divisions. At normal strength these each comprise 13,000 personnel, 270 tanks and a large number of 'soft' vehicles and artillery pieces. In deploying prior to engagement, this force occupies a front estimated at 2,000 yards (*c.*1,830m) by six miles (*c.*10km) deep. Even in such a densely populated zone, a conventional 16-inch round would cause only local damage, but the ER round can be an airburst weapon, detonated after a predicted flight time and scattering its sub-munitions over a wide area.

For the purposes of surface warfare at sea, the *Iowa*s retain the traditional 2,700-pound (1,227kg) armour-piercing (AP) and 1,900-pound (864kg) high-capacity (HC) projectiles, though these now represent only the innermost of three bands of engagement.[12] Of these, the outermost is the perlieu of the 250-mile Tomahawk cruise missiles, 32 of which are carried in eight, four-cell armoured box launchers. While these are non-reloadable at sea, ships of this size and stability range could easily ship more. The tactical naval version (BGM-109B) relies on inertial guidance over the featureless sea, but can be interchanged with the 'C' or 'D' versions carrying a blast warhead or sub-munitions respectively. These, using terrain-comparison guidance, can accurately find a target designated at up to 1,400 miles (2,240km) distance. Mid-band engagement is with the RGM-84 A/D Harpoon, which version is credited with 'over 60 miles' range.[13] It will be apparent that either of the SSMs will require targeting and identification assistance from a third party if their full ranges are to be utilized. Current satellite coverage (as discussed elsewhere) is unlikely to be able either to positively identify or to target with sufficient accuracy. An SAG, unsupported by a carrier or MPA, would therefore be obliged to use helicopters for the purpose.

While the battleships can carry up to four helicopters apiece there are no hangar facilities, and presumably all would need to be flown off or jettisoned before the after turret could fire. In practice, the problem may well not arise. Major justifications for the rehabilitation of the *Iowa*s were, officially:

(a) To reinforce carrier battle groups operating offensively in high-threat environments.
(b) To operate as the centre of a group without carriers in lower-threat areas.
(c) To support amphibious groups.
(d) To undertake offensive operations against surface and shore targets.
(e) To establish a 'presence'.

With respect to (a), the battleship will gain both air cover and targeting information from the carrier. In return, it offers long- and medium-range enhancement of the group by a total of 32 Tomahawks and 16 Harpoons, little enough in comparison with the strike power of the carrier itself, and hardly half the capacity of a single VLS-fitted *Ticonderoga* (CG-47) or *Spruance* (DD-963).

If (a) appears an expensive luxury, more serious misgivings arise at (b) and (c). During the Second

◄
Filling Drydock One at Long Beach Naval Shipyard, the bulk of the battleship *New Jersey* (BB-62) undergoes modernization. The quest for speed is evident in her hull – elongated bows and forward entry, bulbous forefoot and all vertical armour flush with the shell plating rather than added externally. (US Navy)

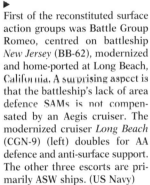

►
First of the reconstituted surface action groups was Battle Group Romeo, centred on battleship *New Jersey* (BB-62), modernized and home-ported at Long Beach, California. A surprising aspect is that the battleship's lack of area defence SAMs is not compensated by an Aegis cruiser. The modernized cruiser *Long Beach* (CGN-9) (left) doubles for AA defence and anti-surface support. The other three escorts are primarily ASW ships. (US Navy)

World War – now nearly a half-century ago – 32 gun-armed capital ships were lost. Of these, only seven were sunk in surface combat, three by submarine, but no less than fourteen by direct air attack.[14] Since then, aircraft have advanced immeasurably in potential and have been joined by the SSM. Despite this, the battleships have been updated only with 'bolt-on' weaponry, which cannot include area defence SAMs. An abandoned Phase II conversion included a VLS along with a raised flight deck aft. Point-defence Sea Sparrow was also abandoned (at a reported saving of 68 million dollars) as being too fragile to withstand the shock and blast from the main battery. Four 20mm Vulcan Phalanx CIWS are useful only for 'last-ditch' defence and modern hardened SSMs could well defeat even these. As the twelve original 5-inch 38s can be discounted in an AAW role, the battleships depend entirely upon their accompanying ships for AA protection. This is an interesting reversal of the Pacific War days, when battleships stayed close aboard the carriers to give them close-in AA coverage.

In contrast, the Soviet *Kirov*-class large cruisers, of about half the *Iowa*'s tonnage, can offer their SAGs twenty SS-N-19 SSMs (four more than the *Iowas*' Tomahawks, with about 300 nautical mile range (*c*.550km) compared with 250 nautical miles (*c*.460km) in the anti-surface version). No medium-ranged SSMs are carried, the ship carrying SS-N-14 anti-submarine stand-off weapons to emphasize her different role. Where, however, the *Iowas* have effectively no AA defence, the *Kirovs* carry 96 area-defence SA-N-6s with a 45 nautical-mile (*c*.83km) range together with 40 point-defence SA-N-4s.[15] There are also eight 30mm CIWS, with a hitting power sufficient to disable any SSM. When considered in a general SAG role, the *Kirovs*' lack of major gunpower is an irrelevance, since gunnery duels are unlikely to be fought. A *Kirov* can, therefore, not only hit harder than an *Iowa* at long range but is able to defend herself and her group from air attack.

The direct aerial threat to an *Iowa* is not easily quantified. Most Second World War sinkings were by air-dropped torpedoes or armour-piercing glide bombs, neither of which appears in today's inventories. While SSMs have the momentum of a large projectile, they would probably break up against the armour while, of course, doing no damage below the waterline.

A fair assessment, then, is that, operating as the centrepiece of an SAG, an *Iowa* could be damaged by aircraft but destroyed only if their missiles were nuclear-tipped. She would be vulnerable therefore to a range of Soviet ASMs carried in several varieties of strike aircraft. For long-range surface action she can offer less than a CG-47; against air assault she can offer nothing. As the torpedo, by striking below the water-line, totally by-passes the battleship's protection, the primary danger would appear now to be from the nuclear attack submarine. Half a century ago, the battleship depended upon her screen for AS protection. She still does. Unfortunately, she was designed at a time when radiated noise was of little consequence, which increases the chance of her being detected while degrading the sensors of her own escort. On balance, a battleship SAG is not really secure unless accompanying a carrier battle group (CVBG), while increasing the latter's potential by only a limited amount.

A lesser, peacetime, priority for the *Iowa*s is 'establishing a naval presence' and for this they are better than any submarine, or even carrier. The Soviets have discovered the benefits of port visits by such impressive units as the *Kirov*s and high-profile calls by the *Iowa*s can do much to offset these. Statistically, warships occupy most of their lives in peacetime activities and, failing general hostilities before the end of the century, the world's last battleships should see out their final years in much the same role as well-considered but venerable statesmen. In a time of increasing financial strictures, however, it will not go unnoticed that the 1,500-plus crew of a single *Iowa* could man four highly capable CG-47 cruisers or seven FFG-7 frigates.

If the cost of operating gun support ships were to prove prohibitive, a possibly useful weapon, though by no means a substitute for the gun, is the Assault Ballistic Rocket System (ABRS). This is configured around a 12-round launcher which can be fitted simply to the assault ships themselves. The system is credited with an effective range of more than 36km (40,000 yards) and being capable of saturating an area with sub-munitions.[16] If major assault ships are expected to remain over the horizon, the vehicle for ABRS would

probably be the LSTs that actually need to 'take the beach'.

At the time of writing, the American amphibious potential is being rapidly increased. Although this is due much to the requirement for recognized Third World involvements, the expansion is obviously causing disquiet to the Soviet Union, against which it could similarly be directed. In service, building, or 'in the pipeline' are four classes of major amphibious warfare ship, the 'Marinized' MV-22 Osprey Tiltrotor aircraft, the surface-effect LCAC landing craft, the Advanced Assault Amphibious Vehicle (AAAV)[17] and the comprehensively equipped forces of Maritime Prepositioning Ships. The influence that is shaping such assets is the requirement for over-the-horizon (OTH) assault. Central to this aim is that most successful application of the hovercraft principle to date, the LCAC (Landing Craft, Air Cushion). This 150-tonner can carry a 60-ton payload (75 tons at overload), equivalent to a single main battle tank, or four light armoured vehicles and 24 combat-ready troops.[18] Unloaded, the LCAC can better 50 knots; loaded, depending on conditions, between 30 and 40 knots. Truly amphibious, it can cope with heavy surf, submerged obstacles, marsh or saltings. Almost impervious to mines, it can deposit its cargo well inland of the shoreline if required. Because of the LCAC's wide tolerance of conditions, it is claimed that it can work over about 80 per cent of the world's beaches – or four times those accessible to conventional craft.[19] This factor alone causes an opponent to dilute his defensive strength further in order to cover a threat.

First assault is undertaken from about twenty nautical miles (37km) out, beyond the range of most mobile artillery, but, in the follow-up, the LCAC scores over both the standard LCU or LCM-8. Comparison can be made between a two-unit LCAC working from five nautical miles (more than 9km) off the beach, a two-unit LCM-8 'nest', and a single LCU, each of the latter working from a more vulnerable distance of 5,000 yards (*c*.4,500m).[20] Cargo capacities are, respectively, 120, 130 and 150 tons, but, due to varying speeds and turn-round times, the cargo delivered and offloaded on the beach in a 120-minute period is 360, 130 and 150 tons respectively. In fairness, this schedule, extrapolated to 144 minutes, yields 360, 260 and 300 respectively though, at this point, the LCACs will have commenced their fourth run to the beach, their turnrounds speeded by their double-ended

▶
Lead ship of a planned 90 units, LCAC-1 demonstrates why the Marine Corps is so keen on air cushion landing craft. With four armoured personnel carriers as cargo, the craft effortlessly crosses the boundary between land and water. Such truly amphibious craft considerably extend assault options. (Textron Marine Systems)

▶
An ALQ-66 mine counter-measures sled cuts a broad swathe while under tow of an MH-53E Sea Dragon. Normally based ashore at Norfolk, Va. and Alameda, Calif, the US Navy's MCM squadrons are deployable worldwide in ships of the amphibious force. Visible are the aircraft's side sponsons/floats, each containing 1600 US gallons of fuel, and the refuelling probes. (United Technologies Sikorsky Aircraft)

◄
Half helicopter, half aeroplane, the MV-22 Osprey would allow the Marine Corps to deploy 24 fully-armed troops (or 6,000 pounds/2,700kg of cargo) to 430nm (790km) combat range, even with VTOL. Its cruise speed of 275 knots is almost twice that of the heavy helicopters which an economy-minded Congress is suggesting as a substitute. (Bell Helicopter Textron)

access. Of the 90 LCACs funded, fifteen had been delivered by the end of 1988, with nine more programmed per year until 1994. At the time of writing, LCACs were making only their fourth fleet deployment and operating doctrines were still being evolved.[21]

The second pillar of the new-look assault is the Bell-Boeing MV-22 Osprey Tiltrotor aircraft, which will share with helicopters the task of inserting spearhead personnel to secure key points prior to the main landing. This operation would normally be covered by the Marines' own AH-1Ws and AV-8Bs, but, if cover were dispensed with, the MV-22 could work from 400 miles (more than 640km) out.[22] The aircraft's ability either to hover or to cruise in level flight at about 320mph (c.150kph) is as applicable to Marine requirements as to ASW. Production should commence in 1991 with an operational target of 1994. Incorporation of much composite material has resulted in a 25 per cent reduction in the MV-22's weight, as compared with an all-metal structure, but, at its maximum take-off weight of 55,000 pounds (25,000kg), it requires a short take-off, limiting its use to larger decks. Only at

a reduced weight of 45,000 pounds (c.20,500kg) could it work in a vertical take-off mode from the smaller facilities of battleships, destroyers or AORs.[23] At this weight there is sufficient margin to transport 24 combat-ready troops or 6,000 pounds (c.2,700kg) of cargo over 500 miles.

The current American amphibious fleet of about 65 ships was built over a short space of time and faces block obsolescence at the turn of the century. In response to this threat, four classes of ship are under construction or planned. Most ambitious of these are the five Wasp-class LHDs (Helicopter/Dock Landing Ship), essentially up-rated Tarawa LHAs, which themselves date from only 1976–80. The programme for the latter was drastically cut due to financial pressures, and the Wasps mark a reinstatement. Their dimensions are much the same, due to the eternal limitations of the Panama Canal locks, but they are far more capable. Experience with the Tarawas has shown a need to increase aircraft spots, so the LHDs have adopted carrier-style deck-edge elevators and have sacrificed two forward-mounted 5-inch 54s in order to square-off

▶
Despite her size, the Italian *San Giorgio* (L9892) is designed to take the beach to offload vehicular cargo over a bow ramp. The 'ducktail' aft serves as a base for the stern gate and a suppressor of the stern plume, increasing efficiency. Five helicopters can be carried but not struck below. *Impavido*, *Maestrale* and *Alpino* class ships in background. (Italian Navy)

the flightdeck. On paper, some shore gunfire support capacity has been lost, but, in practice, it would seem to have been inadvisable to bring so valuable a unit to within 5-inch range of the shore.

The docking well of the LHAs was configured around four LCU 1610s in a two-by-two arrangement, but that of the LHDs is narrower to accommodate three LCACs in line ahead. These operate 'dry', obviating the requirement to flood down, a procedure for which the LHAs took on 15,000 tons of water.[24] Where the LHAs have an all-helicopter aviation complement, the LHDs fill six slots with AV-8Bs to assist in their assault role. A secondary role for the ship, however, is in ASW, or with a twenty V/STOL/ASW helicopter mix. Flightdeck layout to maximize deck spots has not allowed space for a 'ski-jump' so operations will need to be reconfigured around rolling take-offs for the AV-8Bs.

One reason for the funding of the LHDs was the prospect of the seven-ship class of *Iwo Jima* LPH (Amphibious Assault Helicopter Carrier) attaining the end of its useful life during the 1990s.[25] While these ships will then be in their third or even fourth decade,

this is not old by American standards. It would seem to be logical to demote them to the less-demanding ASW role, with a helicopter minesweeping capacity, sparing the billion-dollar-plus LHDs from a secondary role in which they are really too valuable to be risked. Where all-purpose LHDs occupy the glamorous end of the amphibious spectrum, even acting as command ships when required, the workhorses remain the Dock Landing Ships (LSD). Again, the most recent of these (*Anchorage*, LSD-36, class) had a well docking configured to minor landing craft, but the currently building octet of *Whidbey Island*s (LSD-41) can accommodate four LCACs. On completion in 1990, the class is scheduled to be followed immediately by six 'cargo variants' (the *Harper's Ferry*, or LSD-41CV type), with only two LCACs but greatly enhanced cargo and vehicle stowage. Beyond these is the LX, still in the definitive stage. Like the LSDs, it carries helicopters and troops and, with a 'dry well', LCACs only.[26] Smallest of the new-look fleet, is the Advanced Amphibious Assault Vehicle (AAAV). Again not fully defined, it will take part in an OTH assault, ideally carrying a squad or more of infantry, a 25mm cannon and protection against the 30mm fire expected from Warsaw Pact LFVs.[27]

Of recent years, the Soviet Fleet has, in contrast, slowed its rate of expansion. Unlike the Americans, the Russians place little public emphasis on 'force projection', and do not possess high-profile amphibious groups. Nevertheless, they have the capacity to mount a sizeable operation, spearheaded by their 15,000-strong Naval Infantry. The fleet still enjoys a junior place in the Soviet military heirarchy and amphibious operations are viewed primarily as means of securing the army's flanks or, more ambitiously, the seizure of strategically critical ground. In the latter categories one could instance the Black Sea or Baltic Sea exits, or even Iceland if a protracted Atlantic war looked likely. Air cushion assault was adopted by the Soviets from the early seventies and they are now credited with nearly eighty assorted hover vehicles. Of these, the Lebed can accommodate two light tanks, and fit three at a time in the well of an *Ivan Rogov* assault ship. The 360-ton *Pomornik* is credited with being the world's largest SES warship.[28] Too large to be deployed by an assault ship, it is intended probably for short-range thrusts, as would be required in the Baltic.

By far the most advanced concept, however, is the long-heralded Wing-in-Ground (WIG) vehicle. In appearance resembling a stubby-winged flying-boat, the WIG takes ground-effect to the limit by ducting its forward-mounted engines downward to produce the rolling air bubble on which it rides at an altitude of, perhaps, twenty metres, below most radar cover. Hard data remains sparse, varying from the reported 60-metre long Orlan type,[29] configured to amphibious assault, to the generally similar Ukta, armed with anti-ship missiles.[30] While WIG principles are well understood in the West, the concept has, so far, attracted little interest. The Russians are great innovators, but the chances of combat survival of a craft the size of a 747, flying at treetop height at the speed of a DC-3, must be debatable. Its dependency on calm water or flat ground must also be inhibiting. In war, however, it is the bold and unexpected that carries the day, and no developments should be under-estimated.

During a period of heightening tension, a self-sufficient amphibious force can, by its positioning, send a clear political signal without the involvement of a third party.[31] Its presence keeps the defence spread thinly to cover any eventuality and, should diplomacy

triumph, it can withdraw as unobtrusively as it arrived. Many states maintain token amphibious forces; most lack a clearly defined role and exist mainly for prestige. Within NATO, however, individual fleets have fully designated responsibilities for specific tasks. It is surprising, therefore, to see the United Kingdom, charged with the deployment and support of the Anglo–Netherlands Amphibious Force on the Northern Flank of the NATO area, so tardy and apparently unwilling to provide the means. Not until four years after they had proved their continuing worth in the South Atlantic in 1982 were the Royal Navy's two elderly LPDs finally freed from the earlier imposed threat of scrapping. This preceded a series of ambiguously worded official statements of intent which culminated in the soliciting of proposals from several yards with respect to the various merits of modernization of the existing ships, building replacements, or conversion of selected mercantile hulls. The process continues.

Exercises have shown that mere appropriation of passenger/vehicle ferries is not enough; in the weather-blighted NATO North they are too dependent on port facilities. Without substantial modification, such RoRo ships have shown themselves to be dangerously unpredictable with even small amounts of water on the open freeboard deck. Time, money and imaginative re-design can transform merchantmen into efficient auxiliary warships, as evidenced by the recent conversion of the *Contender Bezant* container ship into the 'Aviation Training Ship' *Argus*. Her usual peacetime complement of 6–12 helicopters can be exchanged in a crisis for a dozen V/STOL fighters, though her tight layout precludes the benefit of a 'ski-jump'. Late in 1988 the British Government issued invitations to tender for an Aviation Support Ship (ASS), yet undefined but apparently in place of a mooted conversion of the *Bezant*'s sister-ship.[32] Unlikely to be a reality much before the end of the nineties, the ASS will accommodate a Royal Marine Commando Group, with its own helicopters, vehicles and equipment.

The South Atlantic campaign of 1982 underlined again the requirement for enormous quantities of mercantile support tonnage, which total depends as much on the distance at which the operation is mounted as on the scope of the operation itself. As has happened in the past, the Americans have acted on British experience more positively than the British themselves. Colonial bases are getting ever fewer, while

▶ As an autonomous CIWS system, weighing under five tonnes, the Spanish Meroka can be easily fitted to high-value mercantile units or auxiliaries. Unusually, it works not on the Gatling principal, but consists of twelve separate 20mm barrels, giving an exceptionally high rate of fire of 9,000 rounds/minute. Note radar and optronic directors. (Empresa Nacional BAZAN)

▶ The concept of 'one-ship' replenishment, with one ship sustaining an entire task group for a specified period, is producing very large and valuable vessels, such as the new 31,600-ton *Fort Victoria* for the Royal Navy. Though she is equipped with 32 vertical launch Seawolf and three large helicopters, her defence would be a matter of concern. (Harland & Wolff plc)

friendly governments may decline assistance on political grounds, so that the provision of suitable tonnage, its concentration, loading and safe passage over considerable distances is both a task of magnitude and a means of giving a prospective adversary generous advance warning and the chance to attack. To speed the process, the US Army evolved the 'light division', felt by the Marine Corps unnecessarily to

duplicate its own functions. In parallel came the concept of 'prepositioning'. The prevailing trade recession made technologically advanced ships, with rapid transfer facilities cheaply available. These were taken on 25-year charters and modified to store between 20 and 25 per cent of the across-the-board requirements of a Marine Expeditionary Brigade (MEB). Thirteen such ships have been organized into three Maritime

Prepositioning Squadrons, based on the US Atlantic coast, at Diego Garcia in the Indian Ocean, and at Guam/Tinian in the Western Pacific.[33] This choice of basing allows any crisis point to be reached in 7–14 days, though the crews maintain what must be a debilitating waiting brief of four-months-on, two-months-off. Only every two to four years are the ships unloaded in entirety for full maintenance. Forward deployment of such valuable units as these and the 21 Afloat Force Prepositioning Ships would be hazardous in anything but peacetime police-keeping, and full hostilities would probably see them pulled back to areas where they could be more readily protected. Nevertheless, these two groups of ships, together with ten specialized Auxiliary Crane Ships, constitute the first element of the strategic sealift force.

The second element, of 'surge shipping', would be available within three weeks of mobilization and drawn from the Ready Reserve Force (RRF).[34] At the end of 1988 the RRF comprised 106 ships, acquired and brought up to specification prior to lay-up. By 1992, the planned strength of the RRF is 120 hulls, much of the highest class RoRo and high-speed ex-container tonnage, LASH carriers and modern tankers, purchased for the most part at rock-bottom prices.

The final element in freight movement is re-supply shipping, and it is here that doubts exist.[35] As with most traditional maritime nations, the USA has seen its fleet virtually priced out of a cut-throat and shrinking market. To survive, owners have 'flagged-out' vast tonnages to 'convenience' registers, where they can benefit from tax concessions and the employment of low-paid Third World crews. In 1987, however, it was demonstrated that owners do not necessarily have a legal right to recall their ships to the colours in times of crisis. Thus both the United States and European NATO could face a shortfall in tonnage, a shortfall that will increase with every month of government indifference to ship owners' problems. To its credit, the US Commission on the Merchant Marine and Defense (CMMD) has both recognized and defined the problem, recommending a programme to expand the fleet to 650 suitable vessels by the year 2000. Such an expansion would, however, be entirely artificial, bucking market trends and, in view of the decline in defence dollars that will characterize the Bush administration, the proposal will remain unrealized. The long-term effects run deeper. With general employment of Third World crews, the ready pool of trained, home-flag seamen

Opposite page, top: The light-weight Barricade decoy system can be installed rapidly on any auxiliary going 'in harm's way'. (Wallop Industries)

Opposite page, bottom:Expendable jamming devices, such as that shown, can be rapidly tuned and fired, degrading the anti-ship missile's seeker capacity while chaff/IR provide a more attractive target elsewhere. (Thomson – CSF)

▶
The surreal pattern caused by the burst of a GEMINI chaff and infra-red (IR) round. (Loral Hycor Inc)

diminishes, training facilities run down through lack of demand and the 'tradition' of seagoing is slowly eroded. This is not vain sentiment, for NATO depends today as much on shipping and free-trade as it ever did.

Not governed by market forces, the Soviet merchant fleet expands. In 1986, at a time when the British-flagged fleet had slumped to 2,256 ships of 11,567,117 gross registered tons, and was still declining rapidly, that of Russia was 6,726 ships of 24,560,888 grt.[36] Near self-sufficient, Soviet Russia has a merchant fleet far and away in excess of its needs. In peacetime it acts as a general gatherer of intelligence and a valuable earner of foreign exchange. As much of the latter is gained by undercutting established conference agreements, the process is doubly valuable in forcing the opposition out of business. In time of war the fleet, which is technically advanced and of recent vintage, acts as an auxiliary to the regular fleet, with such as RoRos, docklifters, barge carriers and sea/river traders (with low air and water draught) well adapted to an amphibious warfare role. No arms limitation agreements are likely to affect so valuable a force and the Soviet mercantile ensign can be expected to become ever more familiar. It is likely still to share ports and sea lanes with well-found shipping of the traditional maritime powers, though this will be increasingly graced with the colours of Cyprus and Malta, the Somali Republic and Singapore.

References and Notes

1. 'Alarm at arms race in the seas', as reported in Jane's Defence Weekly, 26 November 1988, p.1360.
2. Ibid., p.1360.
3. Scharfen. 'The Marine Corps in 1987', in US Naval Institute Proceedings, Naval Review, 1988, p.163.
4. Alexander. 'Amphibious Warfare. What sort of future?' Assault from the Sea (ed. Bartlett) US Naval Institute Press, 1983, p.419.
5. Combat Fleets, pp.712, 756 and 757.
6. Weller. Naval Gunfire Support of Amphibious Operations, Dahlgren, 1977; quoted by Herrmann. 'Closing the Gun Gap' in US Naval Institute Proceedings, November, 1988, p.105.
7. Weller. ibid., p.105.
8. 'Propfans for cruise missiles studied', in Jane's Defence Weekly, 23 April 1988, p.784.
9. Bailey. 'The 16-incher: Big, big gun', in US Naval Institute Proceedings, January, 1983, p.106.
10. Muir. The Iowa-class Battleships. Blandford, 1987. (Typical bombardment rates), p.151.
11. White and Antoniuk. 'The improved 16-inch Gun Weapon System', in (US) Naval Engineers' Journal, May, 1988, p.194.
12. Figures from Muir. op. cit., p.142.
13. Missile ranges taken from Combat Fleets, pp.690–1.
14. Statistics from Hough, Dreadnought. Patrick Stephen, Cambridge, 1975, p.234.
15. Wetterhahn. 'Frunze – a Kirov with a difference', in IDR, December, 1984, p.1798.
16. Herrmann. 'Closing the Gun Gap', in US Naval Institute Proceedings, November, 1988, p.106.
17. Karch. 'The Corps in 2001', in US Naval Institute Proceedings, November, 1988, p.44.
18. Poyer. 'LCAC. Amphibious Breakthrough', Textron Marine Systems Publication, p.70.
19. McKearny. 'Launching the New Assault Wave', in US Naval Institute Proceedings, November, 1987, p.43.
20. Ibid., p.46.
21. Howe. 'Tomorrow's Gator Navy', in US Naval Institute Proceedings, December, 1988, p.66.
22. Pitman. Interview in US Naval Institute Proceedings, August, 1988, p.40.
23. Data from 'The V-22 Osprey', Bell-Boeing Publication, 4-87/20M/HER.
24. Terzibaschitsch. 'US Navy's LDH', in IDR, April, 1988, p.427.
25. Ibid., p.425.
26. Howe. op. cit., p.65.
27. Karch. op. cit., p.44.
28. Combat Fleets, p.640.
29. Ibid., p.640.
30. USDOD/USIS artist's impression, featured in RAF recruiting advertisement in the UK national press, October, 1988.
31. e.g., see, Garrod. 'Amphibious Warfare: Why?', in RUSI Journal, Winter, 1988, p.25.
32. Ibid., p.30.
33. Wells. 'Maritime Pre-positioning – a new dimension for rapid deployment', in Armed Forces, March, 1988, p.125.
34. Combat Fleets, p.807.
35. Truver. 'Crisis in US Strategic Sealift capability', in Jane's Defence Weekly, December, 1988.
36. Combat Fleets, pp.119 and 562.

'Dusk off the Foreland – the last light going
And the traffic crowding through,
And five damned trawlers with their sy-reens blowing
Heading the whole review! . . . '

Thus Kipling's slightly romanticized minesweepers of seventy and more years ago. While technologies have changed, and are changing, however, the order has not, and the traffic must still follow the 'sweepers.

Ultimately, in order to sink a ship, she must first be flooded, and the mine and torpedo, assaulting from below the waterline, remain the best weapons for the job. Mines are relatively cheap, stockpile easily and can be periodically updated. Mines are highly cost-effective; an 'incident' (or even the threat of one) causes expensive traffic delays and even more expensive countermeasures to declare an area safe. Mines are simply laid, but swept only with difficulty. During the Second World War a ship was lost for every 29 to 32 mines laid. Mines are now even more effective and the Soviet Union alone is reported to have stockpiled between 300,000 and 400,000.[1] The traditional image of the mine, horned and sinister, riding silently to its cable, is not totally outdated. Indeed, weapons of this type embarrassed even the might of the US Navy during its rather heavy-handed convoy operations in the Persian Gulf during 1987–8. The Americans turned to their European allies for assistance and found these, in turn, to be so ill-equipped that ships of the quality of the British *Hunt* class (replacement cost £35-40M) needed to be deployed to tackle antiques that would have been disposed of equally simply by a brace of Kipling's trawlers.

Controlled minefields will have continued validity in appropriate geographical situations. To Sweden they may become increasingly important, as the approaches to her sensitive naval bases are subjected to seemingly endless incursions by Soviet 'midget' submarines. Going largely unreported due to Swedish sensitivities on neutrality, these incidents were running at 40–60 annually during 1982–4.[2] Offshore skerries create a multiplicity of miniature, shallow chokepoints where bottom-laid 'magnetic loops' will indicate the passage of an intruder. Swedish patience could be tried to the point where these indications could be used to detonate reduced warning charges or, ultimately, full-charge ground mines. For the greater part, mines remain autonomous, ground-laid in shallow water, riding buoyantly to cables in deeper area. They are still triggered by one, or a combination, of the signatures used for the last half-century – magnetic, acoustic or pressure. These signatures remain so much more dominant than others that they are unlikely to be superseded in the near future.

Current technology is typified by the SM G2 ground mine developed by Dornier for the West German and Danish Navies, which share the responsibilities for controlling the shallow Baltic exits. The section con-

◄
The re-constituted image of a Second World War-vintage submarine as 'seen' by a side-scan sonar in a Tow Fish. She is seen sitting on a hard, level bottom with negligible scour, and from an elevation of about 30 degrees. Before a 'picture' can be made from the sonar data, corrections must be made for depth/speed variation, bottom texture, etc. (EG & G)

MINE WARFARE

▶
Things to come. The West German drone-minesweeper control ship *Wolfsburg* (M-1082) with two of her three F-1 Troika MCM craft. Mine counter-measures is a dangerous but ordered occupation, well suited to remote-control methods which reduce the risk to both personnel and equipment. Other areas of naval warfarc will follow suit. (Gcrman Navy)

taining the charge can be configured to individual targets and launching platforms, but the instrumentation section remains the same, adapted as required through modifications to its software.[3] It maximum effective depth is 70 metres. On-board digital processing allows the weapon to 'acclimatize' itself by measuring ambient sea noise. This enables it to recognize a target the more easily, when compared against a pre-programmed profile. Continuous sampling establishes target speed, course and (with knowledge also of depth) its closest point of approach. Only if optimal requirements are satisfied will the mine be detonated and then at the moment calculated for greatest effect. Target data is filed in the mine's computer through a simple coupler, which renders it easy to programme the mine virtually up to the moment of laying. Elaborate mathematical modelling techniques are used to establish the correct number and disposition necessary to achieve an ideal field (though actually laying this

may well prove more difficult!). Buoyant, tethered influence-type mines laid in deep water can be tackled by mechanical sweeping. Ground-laid in shallow water, they may or may not respond to sweeping, in which case they must be cleared individually by a minehunter. Ground-laid, pressure-actuated mines remain virtually unsweepable.

Developed for deep water barrier use, but likely to be modified increasingly for shallow water, is the mobile mine. Targeted primarily at submarines, and already operational over two decades, is the American Captor. This is, essentially, a torpedo moored in a buoyant capsule and launched at a target located autonomously or through the sensor chain associated with thc barrier. Whereas Captor is based on the small Mk 46 ASW torpedo, the new Anglo-American Hammerhead is built around a full-sized 21-inch weapon.[4] This, while considerably extending lethal range, will, due to its size, reduce the choice of delivery platform.

◄ All naval first-of-class units are subjected to a range of realistic shock testing, this being the only manner in which a true evaluation of a ship's resistance can be made. In this case a British Hovercraft SRN3, involved in mine countermeasures (MCM) trials, demonstrates the immunity conferred by an air cushion to a mine-sized explosion. (British Hovercraft Corporation)

◄ Still unique in the West is the US Navy's helicopter minesweeping force. Shown is the foil-born sled of the EDO Mk 105 and ALQ-166 countermeasures outfit for sweeping both magnetic and acoustic influence mines. The device on top is a radar reflector to permit the sled's track accurately to be monitored. (EDO Corporation)

Hammerhead goes operational in the mid-nineties, demonstrating that the original Captor concept was sound and will be improved primarily through successive changes in components and intelligence.

The effectiveness of a mine's explosion degrades rapidly with range, giving rise to the concept of the rising mine. Typical of these is another Anglo-American project, the Crusader.[5] This orientates itself vertically on the seabed, classifies and identifies a target autonomously and releases a rocket-propelled sub-munition. The latter is aligned toward the target by thrust-vectored control, using similar techniques to those in vertically launched SAMs.

Perhaps the most menacing aspect of the mine is its rapidly improving intelligence. Even the simplest can be set to a sequence of active and inert phases or, by a 'ship counter', to ignore a given number of stimuli before going active. Either of these measures renders even several passes with sweeps an unreliable guarantee of safe water. Much data has been accumulated about the magnetic and acoustic signatures of a wide variety of warships. Such 'footprints' can be analyzed and stored in a mine's memory for the purposes of specific targeting. On-board sensors can then define such a signature, the signal's energy spectrum then being extracted by Fast Fourier Transform techniques. If it agrees with that in the memory bank, detonation is initiated. It will be obvious that

sweeps will require to generate a convincing signature to hope to persuade such a mine to explode to order. A mine can use several signatures in the course of actuations.[6] Reasonably, it should expect first to hear a target. This stimulus can be used to initiate a timing sequence. Proceeding at average speed, a true target could be expected to offer additional magnetic and pressure signatures within a reasonable time span, causing detonations. A minehunter, however, creeps at low speed and on unpredictable courses. As her pattern does not follow that of a defined target, the mine can recognize her and 'shut down' for a predetermined period, ignoring even the most sophisticated influence sweeps. Alternatively, the MCMV herself is such a scarce and expensive asset that it would be worth 'guarding' a minefield with mobile mines that recognize her irregular behaviour and low signature specifically to target her. An ideal weapon for the purpose would resemble the Bofors 'Rockan', a device of irregular shape and low metallic content which, partially silted, might well go unnoticed by an MCMV presented with more obvious targets. Responding only to the irregular and cautious progress of the MCMV, the weapon would be analogous to anti-personnel mines scattered to deter the clearance of buried minefields ashore. Anti-sweep devices to protect moored mines typically target the sweep. For instance, the Americans list the Mk 53, a 225kg 'mine sweep rig

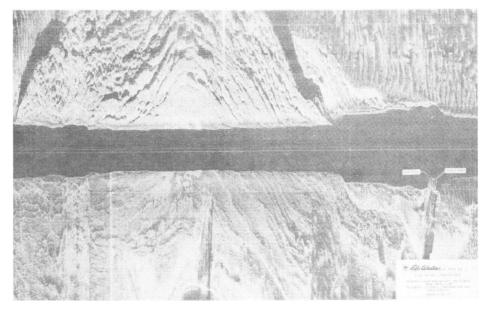

▶ An excellent example of bottom detail reconstituted from a side-scan sonar pass. The subject is slumped sediment in the lower Mississippi and the Edo Western Model 602 tow vehicle was operating ten metres above the bottom in thirty metres of water. As the area immediately beneath the vehicle cannot be 'seen', it shows as a black band. (EDO Corporation)

obstruction weapon'.[7] Future efforts to sweep a field of deep-laid mobile mines could, however, find the swept weapon actually re-selecting its target on being thus disturbed, and attacking its would-be sweeper.

Mines may be laid by surface, submarine or aerial platforms. Surface layers have the greatest capacity and, potentially, work with greatest precision. On any scale, however, they are now limited to defensive lays. Gone are the days when a destroyer flotilla could penetrate enemy waters, lay a field and be clear by daybreak. With modern surveillance there is no cover in darkness. Historically, disguised merchantmen have enjoyed a limited minelaying success, particularly in a war's opening phase, and would probably do so again. Recent experience of the nuisance caused in the Gulf of Suez by a Libyan RoRo simply rolling mines over her stern ramp constitute a sharp reminder, but such operations do not amount to an offensive. Dedicated surface layers for defensive work have all but disappeared as many types of mercantile craft can be fitted with stockpiled gear for the purpose. An example is the

Babcock High Volume Minelaying System, which utilizes standard pallets containing mines pre-stowed in expendable pallets. Air-or ship-compatible, the system allows the mines to be simply gravity-laid.

Certain shallow-water fleets, particularly the Swedish, rely heavily on mine warfare. Most of their warships are fitted for, or with, minelaying rails, while simple systems have been developed to allow even a fishing lugger to lay when required. The aforementioned 'Rockan', for use down to 100 metres, is designed to be laid simply by releasing it down a tracked slide. It is shaped ingeniously to glide from the point of release and alight on the seabed at a position distant by twice the water depth. Simply by aligning the mines in sequence, a craft of opportunity can, by following a single track, lay three parallel lines of mines simultaneously.

As offensive minelayers, submarines are both covert and precise, but limited in shallow water by the minimum depth in which they can safely manoeuvre. Except in specialized boats, however, mines have

◄
The stylish Italian Lerici mine countermeasures vessels (*Milazzo* in illustration) proved an instant export success, an advantage in greatly offsetting design and development costs. Although two remotely operated vehicles are carried for the location and disposal of mines, neither is visible in this view. (Italian Navy)

▶
A Belgian *Aster*-class MCMV prior to launching by shiplift. The so-called 'Tripartite' design of composite construction is common also to ships built in France and the Netherlands, and stands as an excellent example of the benefits to be gained by standardization. The centreline diesel-drive propeller and two electrically driven 'active rudders' are evident. (ACEC (Division Défense))

▶
A close-up of the portside 'active rudder' on a Belgian MCMV. The ducted propeller is driven directly by an 88 kW motor, giving silent and responsive thrust directly in line with the rudder. They are used in conjunction with a pair of bow thrusters for accurate manoeuvring during mine-hunting operations, but can also drive the ship unaided at 7 knots in emergency. (ACEC (Division Défense))

Mines are not only comparatively inexpensive and tolerant to long term stockpiling, but lend themselves to straightforward and regular updating to keep them abreast of mine countermeasures technology. As part of a programme to install new Sensing and Processing Units to Mk 12 ground mines, a modified battery chassis is here seen being fitted. (British Aerospace plc)

Minehunting is a complex and patient undertaking that requires a high level of realism in training. The Versatile Exercise Mine (VEM), shown here being assembled, simulates a mine not only in physical size and shape but has an algorithm that enables it to be programmed accurately to portray any combination of influence mine. It monitors the minehunters' efforts to sweep it as well as its and its sweep's signatures. (British Aerospace plc)

always needed to be shipped at the expense of torpedoes. Indeed, submarine-launched mines are of the same order of length as a torpedo (e.g., the American Mk 65 Quickstrike is quoted at 3,250mm compared with the 3,467mm of a Mk 37 torpedo.[8] The mine, however, contains a probable 950kg charge compared with the torpedo's 148kg). Both the Germans and the Swedes (in their 'Bunny' system) adopt the solution of fitting the submarine with a temporary girdle, a veritable 'bandolier' of mines that can be ejected on demand. Following this, the girdle is jettisoned and the submarine, her conventional weapon stowage unaffected, can proceed to a useful offensive patrol instead of returning 'in ballast'. There are drawbacks to the system in that the mine cargoes are vulnerable to external over-pressures from depth or explosion, while the mines themselves cannot, at present, be re-programmed once stowed.

A neat reversal of the mine-delivered torpedo is the torpedo-delivered mine. The American Mk 67 SLMM, or Submarine-launched Mobile Mine, is based on a converted Mk 37 torpedo, whose 483mm (19-inch) calibre presumably requires sleeved tubes. Designed to be launched at sites that are inaccessible to the submarine, its exact mode of operation is not yet clear. It probably runs at low speed to conserve power and to minimize noise and, if wireguided, be both tracked

and controlled to plant it at or near a desired point. A better means of mining such important but inaccessible spots is afforded by Soviet activities in Swedish waters. Specially adapted 'seagoing' submarines lay at the outer edge of the archipelago, transfer crew to a miniature submarine or tracked seabed vehicle carried as cargo on their casings, and loiter to await its return. Such craft can plant and service minefields with great precision, and show an interesting historical continuity with submarines of the Second World War, which towed or launched canoes, 'Chariots' or X-Craft for use against clearly defined targets.

Air-laid mining is less accurate, rapid but less unobtrusive than formerly, again through improved surveillance. During the Second World War, related aircraft losses were on a light scale in comparison with results achieved, but aircraft best-suited to the task can now operate only at great risk and with a high probability that the exact coordinates of their lays would be logged with precision by coastal defence radars. Nevertheless, the C130 (Hercules) capacity of eighteen 2,000-pound (c.900kg) or thirty 1,000-pound (c.450kg) mines is not inconsiderable.

As types of mine and the means of delivering them continue to proliferate so too do types of counter-measures vessels (MCMV) and methods for clearance. The minehunter emerged in the mid-sixties as a

► Though considerably smaller than the Royal Navy's 'Hunts', the Dutch Tripartites were equally able to operate in the Persian Gulf, during the recent war. Shown is *Maassluis* which, with *Hellevoetsluis*, formed the Netherlands contingent. The Dutch Government has enjoyed export success by being ready to sell units from home production runs. (Netherlands Navy)

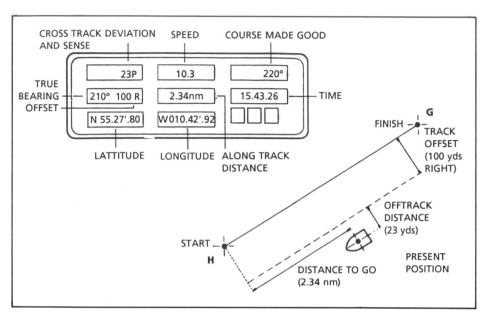

CROSS TRACK DEVIATION AND SENSE
SPEED
COURSE MADE GOOD

23P	10.3	220°
210° 100 R	2.34nm	15.43.26
N 55.27'.80	W010.42'.92	

TRUE BEARING OFFSET

TIME

LATTITUDE LONGITUDE ALONG TRACK DISTANCE

FINISH — G
TRACK OFFSET (100 yds RIGHT)

OFFTRACK DISTANCE (23 yds)

START — H
PRESENT POSITION

DISTANCE TO GO (2.34 nm)

◄ Various displays are available to the Mine Hunt Director (MHD). The track to be followed by the MCMV is defined before the operation and identified by lettered waypoints. In the Track Guidance Mode, the display is here showing the craft proceeding from point H to point G. She is 23 yards to port of a desired 100-yard offset track. (Racal Marine Systems Ltd)

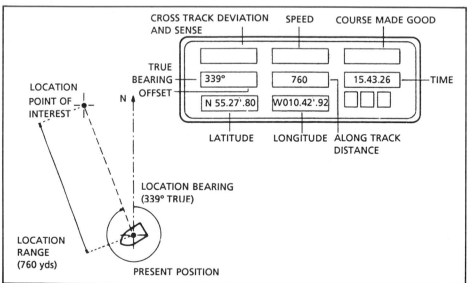

CROSS TRACK DEVIATION AND SENSE
SPEED
COURSE MADE GOOD

339°	760	15.43.26
N 55.27'.80	W010.42'.92	

TRUE BEARING OFFSET

TIME

LATITUDE LONGITUDE ALONG TRACK DISTANCE

LOCATION POINT OF INTEREST

N

LOCATION BEARING (339° TRUE)

LOCATION RANGE (760 yds)

PRESENT POSITION

◄ During the investigation of a particular contact, the MCMV will shift from propulsion to hover mode, maintaining her relative position in wind and tide. The display here shows the vessel at a point 760 yards from the point of interest, which bears 339 degrees true. Data is continuously updated and superimposed. (Racal Marine Systems Ltd)

platform for the painstaking clearance of mines that could no longer be guaranteed neutralized by standard sweep techniques, but this is not to say that the minesweeper is obsolete. Moored mines used in shallow water are now unusual; they are, however, cheap and of considerable nuisance value, as events in the Persian Gulf in 1987–8 illustrated. They will never entirely disappear, though they are comparatively easily swept, can break adrift or drag in heavy water, and are unable to maintain desired depth in tidal waters or in pronounced currents. In 'deep water' however, out to the 200-metre limits of the continental shelf, deep-laid moored mines are a menace to submarines (as they were in the Dover Strait or Northern Barrage as far back as the First World War). They are tethered on short scopes, close to the seabed, and can

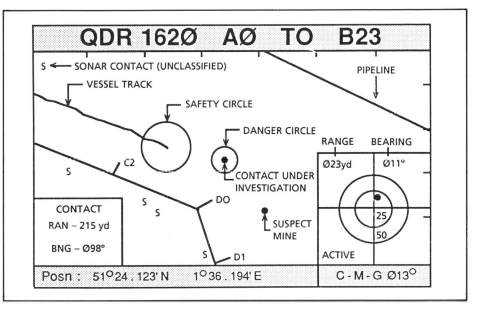

► At any time, the MHD can obtain an overview from the Tactical Display. The example shows a previous track, with waypoints and (at 'S') unclassified contacts. Current track and position of ship and contact are shown, each ringed by a safe approach limit. The inset shows the status of the ship's ROV, investigating the contact. (Racal Marine Systems Ltd)

be swept by steel-built craft which operate beyond the mines' sensing radius.

British practice is to construct simple and inexpensive ships (*River* class) for the task. Their design is a derivative of North Sea supply vessels, with wide after decks and well-suited to the deployment of the Extra-Deep Armed Team Sweep (EDATS). In contrast, the French have adopted a more complex alternative in the BAMO (Bâtiment Anti-Mines Océanique), the first of a planned class of ten of which is due to enter service in 1992. Where the Royal Navy ships have basic dimensions of 47.6 × 10.5 metres, the French, with catamaran construction, have a largely similar length of 46 metres but an extraordinary beam of 15 metres. They are, therefore, spacious on deck and, for their size, very steady. They will work out to 300 metres depth but, as they are designed also to supplement the effort of more conventional MCMVs, they are constructed of GRP (Glass Reinforced Plastic) and to full signature-suppression standards.[9] This is reflected in their price, the reported 1,900 million francs for the first six equating roughly to £30m apiece, or nearly as expensive as an MCMV. Their function will be to maintain safe routes from the ballistic missile submarine bases to the edge of the continental shelf.

Despite the advantages of a catamaran hull, only one other fleet has adopted it in the context of MCMVs. On a tight budget, the Australians are building their *Bay-*

class minehunters to a length of only 31 metres. Inherent stability allows all machinery to be carried above the waterline. This reduces radiated noise, the level of which is already low through the choice of Schottel rudder-propellers, vertically driven by hydraulic motors. Their full 360-degree directional characteristics are ideal for navigation, hovering or tight-manoeuvring.[10] An interesting feature is the 'bolt-on' modular control room, interchangeable for fault rectification or change of role. A tight specification, built around purely coastal operation, has allowed for a small crew of 13–14. (Even their victuals are all pre-prepared!) As unit cost increases remorselessly, precisely prescribed types of warship such as this will become increasingly common, their major drawback being an inflexibility with regard to later modification.

Traditional fishing industries such as that of the United Kingdom, have always provided an invaluable pool of craft suitable for rapid conversion for emergency mine countermeasures and, more importantly, experienced seafarers to man them. High operating costs, loss of traditional trades and lack of government support have combined to result in a wholesale flight of merchant shipping to flags of convenience (common to all Western maritime powers) and a drastic rundown of fishing fleets.

Trawlers (viewed officially as 'Craft of Opportunity' (COOP) have the deck machinery, fittings, power and control for low-speed towage, and such as remain would be converted with stockpiled deepwater sweep gear, deep and shallow water sonar, navigational equipment and, where required, mine disposal vehicles. To counter deep-laid mines, floating on short scopes close to an irregular seabed, the sweep gear 'flies' at a predetermined height above the bottom, terrain-following by the fitting of sensors to the sweep ends and referring their outputs to the control system of the high-speed winches aboard the ship.[11] A later development, the British Aerospace 'Towtaxi', can deploy a sonar at a given height above the seabed, the parent ship deploying also a modified sweep that obviates the need for team-sweeping.[12] The Pilotfish vehicle can perform a similar role, but, being agile, can be used also as a manoeuvrable decoy.

The problem of the pressure-sensitive mine remains. In simplified terms – as a hull moves through shallow water, its proximity to the seabed restricts the surrounding waterflow, which thus experiences increased velocity and reduced pressure.[13] A rudimentary safeguard is to proceed at low speed in suspected areas, but this is a defence, not a cure. Only a ship-sized object can currently simulate a correct pressure field, so only this and individual minehunting procedures are at present effective.

In this era of depressed merchant ship resale values, it would appear to make sense to experiment with a specialist, explosion-resistant 'mine-bumper', based, perhaps, on a 5–10,000 dwt tanker. This type of ship,

particularly a 'parcels tanker', has close compartmentation and, in a gas-free condition, is exceedingly difficult to sink. Extra inherent buoyancy could be guaranteed by sealing wing spaces, creating in effect a double-skinned hull, and filling the voids with sealed oil-drums. Tank plating would be removed top and bottom; the lower plating would be replaced with flexible diaphragms in way of each tank, the tanks being partly filled with water and left open at the top, giving the effect of a giant milk crate. The explosion effects from detonated mines would pass largely upwards through the structure, venting their energy and water ballast to atmosphere. As the remaining forward and after ends would still be heavily stressed by explosions, the finely toleranced and comparatively rigid engine and transmission should be removed in favour of self-contained and resiliently mounted propulsors such as Schottels. If accommodation and control positions are necessary, these should be sited in shock-mounted deckhouses, but remote control of the ship would not be difficult. Such a conversion would cost a fraction of an MCMV's price tag and, easily capable of being fitted with variable and enhanced acoustic and magnetic signatures, could be run back and forth through a minefield to cut a swathe. It would be viewed as expendable but would certainly be repairable.

It was the misfortune of the Hovercraft, or Surface-Effect Vehicle, to demonstrate its virtues in MCM during a calm period when budgets were unlikely to be

◀
Out of its element, the PAP Mk 5 remotely controlled mine disposal vehicle is shown under test. Visible are the relocation sonar in the 'chin' position, side nacelle with horizontal and vertical thrusters, the bottom-mounted 100kg countermining charge and the drag weight for maintaining height over seabed. (Société ECA)

stretched to investigate radical new concepts. As early as 1983 the 55-ton BH-7 demonstrated its ability to deploy the required equipment, but, more significantly, showed that the combination of light alloy construction and an air cushion reduced signatures to levels lower than those of dedicated MCMVs.[14] The effects of explosions close aboard were so attenuated by the air cushion that the vehicle survived, with minor damage, shocks that would have disabled a displacement ship. Hovercraft can work 'over the beach' in undeveloped areas, and deploy at five times the speed of an MCMV. A fair measure of local support needs to

be deployed with them, however, and their endurance is comparatively low. In trials the US Navy found the hovercraft superior to the helicopter in forward MCM and used the principle in its 200-ton MSH design. Unfortunately it combined one unfamiliar technology with another (GRP construction) and (much like the worthy DASH system before it) it failed through being ahead of available technology. In its place, the navy adopted a modified version of the Lerici MCMV where, in a textbook example of technology transfer, the Italian Intermarine company was invited to set up a joint-owned production facility in the United States.

▶
So discerning is the modern magnetic mine that ships need to be monitored regularly and their degaussing arrangements adjusted to minimize their signatures. The Thorn EMI MS90 transportable degaussing range enables a facility to be established at short notice. Its output, in the form of a 3D display, simplifies analysis and adjustment. (Thorn EMI, Naval Systems Division)

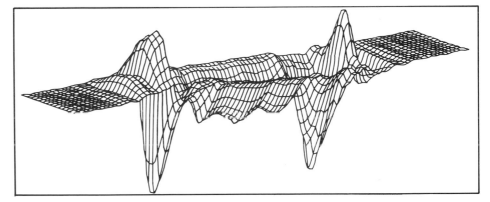

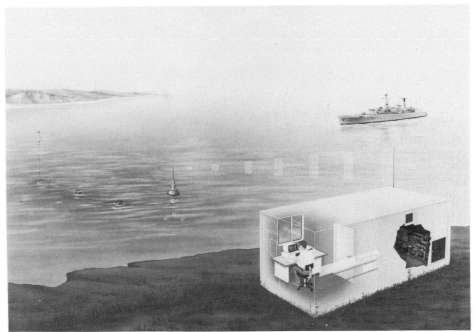

Sweeping buoyant mines moored close to the seabed involves 'flying' the cutters at a fixed height above the bottom to avoid damage. At a fixed ship speed through the water, wire tension for a given length is proportional to sweep depth. BAJ's strain-gauged tensionmeter link constantly monitors the tension, enabling depth to be continuously modified. (BAJ Ltd)

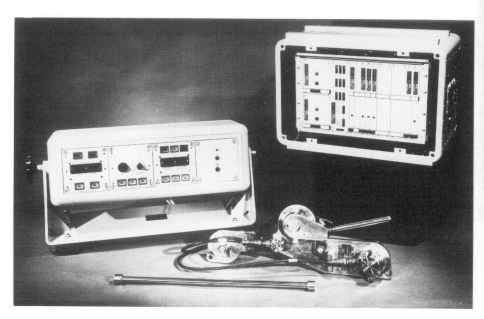

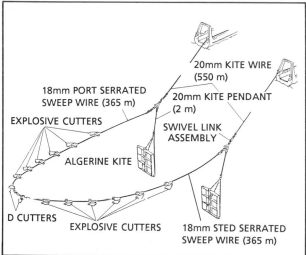

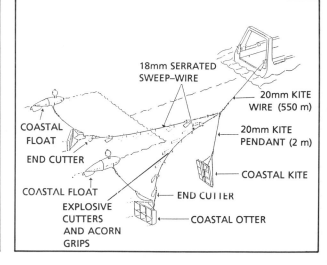

Nevertheless, the US Navy still views its newer air-cushion landing craft (LCAC) as having a useful MCM role in support of an amphibious task force.[15] Hostilities could see the MCM hovercraft concept resurrected for keeping open coastal 'safe routes'. Although MCMVs would be stationed at intervals along them, there would inevitably be isolated stretches, the speedy clearance of which could owe much to a hovercraft's rate of deployment.

Helicopters in a MCM role, as mentioned above, remain a peculiarly American concept. Their advantage lay in their ability to be quickly deployed worldwide. The recent introduction of the powerful MH-53E Sea Dragon helicopter allows for 20-knot towage of a minesweeping sled to within a five-metre tolerance of the desired system track.[16] These EDO-built hydrofoil sleds are configured for mechanical (Mk 103), acoustic (Mk 104), magnetic (Mk 105), or magnetic/acoustic (Mk 106) sweeping. Haiphong and Suez demonstrated system mobility, and its potential for sweeping mines.

▲
Trial laying of Dornier SM G2 ground mines from a tender of the West German Navy. (Dornier GmbH)

▶
Recovery of an experimental German G2 mine. The joint between the instrumentation and charge sections is obvious. This measure facilitates separate storage and maintenance, or the combining of alternative types of sub-unit to meet differing requirements. (Dornier GmbH)

◀
Moored buoyant mines are still common, especially in deep water, as an anti-submarine weapon, when they are on very short scopes. The Algerine Team Sweep is designed for use against such mines and can be deployed by such as the Royal Navy's *River-* class sweepers or a suitably modified commercial vessel. (BAJ Ltd)

◀◀
Buoyant mines for use against surface ships are laid in comparatively shallow water for which the single or three-wire Oropesa sweep is a suitable counter. The single wire version is simpler to stream while the three-wire sweep reduces tensile force in the Kite Wire. Craft with limited facilities can deploy a half-assembly, or single Oropesa. (BAJ Ltd)

However, there appears little guarantee that *every* mine has been detonated, while pressure-sensitive weapons remain immune. If the system is deployed by LPD rather than by air lift, the ship's dock can accommodate MSBs (minesweeping boats) to follow-up, check and clear any strays. At a time when rapid improvement in mine intelligence threatened to render such methods unreliable, a new breakthrough was reported during 1988 when a helicopter-borne scanning laser radar (or 'ladar') bathymeter successfully detected mines moored down to 30 metres in the Persian Gulf.[17]

While hull cost is not the greatest expense in MCMV construction, controversy still exists regarding the correct material to use. As a compromise between cost, signature reduction and shock resistance, the British-pioneered glass-reinforced plastic (GRP) has emerged favourite. British construction methods favour quite conventional framing while the majority (the French, Swedes, Danes and Australians) prefer the more easily worked foam-filled GRP sandwich. The successful Italian Lerici design, adopted in basis by the Americans for their MHC-51 ('Osprey') class, adopts a frameless monocoque approach, dependent upon its bulkheads and decks for stiffness. It is noteworthy that the sandwich type has produced widely varying results when subjected to shock-testing and fire.[18] Wood also exhibits shortcomings in these areas, besides being increasingly unobtainable in required qualities and being worked by fewer yards. Despite this, the current American Avenger MCM programme is of wood.

Alone in preferring amagnetic steels are the Germans, who have gained much experience in their fabrication and welding from their submarine programmes. It emerged clear favourite in a design competition held for the Germany Navy.[19] Steel, like aluminium (favoured by the Soviets) is electrically conductive, with potentials being induced by ship motion alone. The Germans claim that, as the steel is much the stronger, it can be used in thinner (4-6mm) sheets, leading to smaller current flows being developed. They claim further that its properties are so well documented that full neutralization is not difficult.

While GRP repair facilities are becoming more common world-wide, the skills of working in amagnetic steels is not, which is a prime reason for the materials' use currently being restricted to Germany's Types 332 and 343 hunters and sweepers. Steel ships can be 'de-permed' for temporary reduction in magnetic signature, or fitted with permanent generators

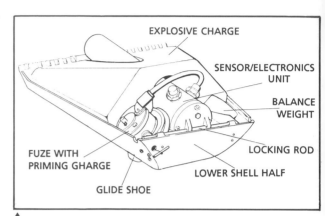

By judicious choice of shape and material the mine designer can greatly complicate the work of the minehunter. The 190kg Bofors ROCKAN is coloured to render it inconspicuous to television search; made largely of plastic to minimize signature and of unobtrusive shape, it glides a considerable distance from the point of laying. (AB Bofors)

and coils for full degaussing. Total protection becomes more complex as mines improve their discrimination, while the ship's signature is complicated further by transient effects due to her own motion and the combination of machinery and equipment in use at any particular time. It has become practice, therefore, to 'range' ships periodically over seabed detectors, establishing those characteristics which require to be neutralized. Indeed, the British firm of Thorn EMI has developed a transportable range which, with just two underwater sensors in place of the earlier eighteen, will produce a ranged ship's signature together with required remedial action in the space of 90 minutes.[20] Expensive and high-risk ships, such as the MCMVs themselves, may well need to move in the direction of embodying degaussing coils in several planes in their structure. Once ranged, the ship condition will be known for any machinery combination so that a microprocessor will be able continuously to monitor the ship's status and control the energization of each coil to achieve a correct combination.

An interesting recent innovation is the Variable Moment Magnet (VMM) device. Each comprises an assembly of eighteen individual magnetic cores and an electronics package, housed in a buoyant GRP body.[21 and 22] The cores have low coercivity but high remanence and can be driven on demand by solenoid into positive or negative saturation. Each body, therefore, can be set to nineteen different conditions, and a string of these, towed by an auxiliary craft, can be simply energized to simulate a full-sized ship signature. Not only is this a highly effective sweep device, but, due to the qualities of the VMM, it requires power only when its state is being changed. It is possible also to outsmart an intelligent mine by attaching VMM bodies to a ship and not attempt to mask her magnetic signature, which is difficult, but modify it to convince the mine that the ship is only a sweep and, therefore, to be ignored. The duel between intelligent mine and intelligent counter-measures will develop keenly over the next few years. The standard British acoustic sweep, the Osborn, is typical of current practice. It is a closed-loop system in which the Towed Acoustic Generator (TAG) is streamed at a safe distance astern of the sweeper, producing broad-band noise through the forced oscillation of several diaphragms.[23] On a second line, the sweeper streams a Towed Acoustic Monitor (TAM), whose hydrophone array is set at the expected height of mines above the seabed. Thus the TAG's output can be continuously adjusted to generate the correct noise spectrum *as seen by the mine*. While the basic system is sound and needs no replacement, it may well be necessary to develop the TAG to produce more finely tuned spectra in order to deceive tomorrow's mines.

Minehunting is a different matter, carried out in shallow water against weapons too dangerous or impossible to sweep. This painstaking occupation involves the location and charting of suspicious objects, their investigation and classification, then their disposal by recovery or countermining. The use of a remotely operated vehicle (ROV) both speeds up the operation and reduces the risk. Most widely used in the West is the French-built PAP Mk 5, a highly manoeuvrable miniature submarine which is controlled by its parent via an electrical or fibre-optic umbilical cable. Alternative payloads of close-range sonar, or lights and closed-circuit television (CCTV), enable it to define the object under scrutiny. The vehicle can then be equipped with manipulators (for cutting mooring lines or attaching a recovery line) or a 100kg countermining charge. The PAP can work down to 300 metres and, typically, perform five 20-minute missions on a single battery charge.[24] Its quoted range is 600 metres and here lies its current weakness. If new types of intelligent mobile mine, targeted specifically at MCMVs, can identify them at a greater range than this 600 metres, the ship is still at risk. It may not be necessary for the weapon to 'hear'

the MCMV sufficiently well to detect its 'footprint'; its erratic and slow movements, and even its *absence* of signature may well be sufficient to identify it.

Longer-range ROVs can allow the ship to lay further back and, if suitably equipped, even allow her to be built to lower standards of signature reduction, reducing considerably her unit procurement cost. Typical of these new vehicles is the German MBB Pinguin, designed around a variable payload of 450kg. An 8–10 hour endurance is claimed by virtue of the vehicle towing its power source on a surface catamaran.[25] The presence of the latter also allows for control by radio link.

Buoyant mines, surfaced after their cables have been cut, have traditionally been destroyed by small-calibre fire. This method often does not detonate the weapon, which sinks to the seabed, where it can remain a hazard. Specifically aimed at operations in the Persian Gulf, the British Admiralty Research Establishment developed the radio-controlled Scarab surface vehicle, which can be manoeuvred by CCTV to attach a towline or a charge.[26]

The cost of MCMV procurement is such as to limit numbers to the point where they need to be deployed to the utmost advantage. Essential routes are, therefore, precisely surveyed in peacetime, each item of seabed debris being logged, plotted or disposed of. Widely used for exact surveys are the Racal Hyper-Fix or Micro-Fix systems, a high-frequency shipboard receiver being used to triangulate on slave stations ashore. Hyper-Fix can range to 250km or better, while the higher precision Micro-Fix is accurate to 80km. Accuracy is claimed to be within one metre, probably better than the positions of the shore stations can be fixed, and of a degree where ship motion itself can significantly affect a reading.[27] With the complete survey contained in her databank, an MCMV now needs only to compare it with subsequent passes to detect any newly arrived objects. To this end, the Racal Tactical Display presents the stored data in real time, with ship's track, actual or desired, superimposed. Continuous comparison with the data bank will pick out any new object, which is displayed on the monitor and precisely logged. The ship completes her pass and can then print hard copy to assist in sweeping or for issue to essential shipping that cannot be delayed.

Charged with disposal, an MCMV can use the system to define a 'safety circle', establishing the closest point of approach. This, together with the chosen range and bearing, and inputs defining wind and tide, are used to control the ship's dynamic positioning system as she operates her ROV. Any deviation from the chosen spot or heading is detected by Micro-Fix and compass, and amplified as error signals which are fed back into the thrusters to reposition the ship. Superimposed on the Mine Hunt Director's monitor is an enlarged window showing the object and the ROV's continuous relationship to it.

For normal propulsion, a typical 50-metre, 15-knot MCMV may dispose of 1200kW (1,600hp), but requires also a silent, low-power system for 'hovering' in conditions of wind and tide. Voith-Schneider cycloidal propellers, long considered too noisy, have now been accepted as a means of combining both requirements. These devices can exert from a small thrust to full power in almost any direction and can be powered by diesels for long passages or by electric motors for silent manoeuvring. The generator for the latter function is housed high in the ship to minimize radiation. Cycloidal propellers are being installed in two new types, the American *Osprey* and the British *Sandown*. More common are various combinations of non-magnetic propulsion diesels, active rudders and bow thrusters. Electric drive for the latter units is complicated by GRP ships being, magnetically-speaking, nearly transparent. A useful alternative is, therefore, hydraulic drive. At a time when low-signature machinery and the rafts on which it is resiliently mounted (to de-couple its vibration from the hull) threaten to become prohibitively expensive, the high-endurance ROV may well allow for the MCMV's specification to be relaxed.

A significant development over recent years has been the use of minehunting drones. The German Troika project has seen six MCMVs modified, each to be parent to three 25-metre satellite craft. Built into these is a sectioned 15-metre solenoid-operated VMM, which produces a field claimed more realistically to portray a valid target than that produced by a sweep.[28] Each also carries a powerful acoustic generator. All machinery is thoroughly shock-mounted to survive explosions close aboard. They operate unmanned but take a passage crew of three. They can also deploy Oropesa-type mechanical minesweeping gear though this is unlikely while unmanned.[29] The Finns and Swedes, also threatened by shallow-water mining, have adopted largely similar systems, though the latter's drones are of a different pattern. Rather like a semi-submersible drilling rig in principle, they have two tubular GRP

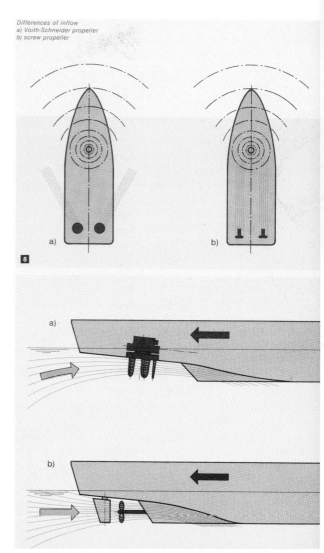

Differences of inflow
a) Voith-Schneider propeller
b) screw propeller

8

hulls spanned, at a height, by a working deck. Much of the shock of an explosion would actually pass through the vehicle to dissipate itself harmlessly in space.

Trends, at least in coastal channels, must be toward totally unmanned operation. Regular checks will be undertaken by a craft under control either through a radio link, using such as Micro-Fix to monitor her course, or at a greater range, by seabed transponders establishing essential waypoints. A seabed cable in the latter case could be used to mark the median line of the channel and transmit data to and from the craft. Digitized data from the latter's sidescan sonar would be continuously and automatically compared with the data-bank. The coordinates of any new feature would be radioed ashore. An unmanned follow-up craft could be used to mark the position and even put over an ROV, the CCTV signals from which would then be telemetered ashore for assessment and decision regarding appropriate action.

It should be noted that mines need not look like aforementioned mines. For instance the Swedish GMI 100 Rockan, in being designed to glide from the surface launch position, also has a shape which gives a reduced sonar return (assisted by being made of GRP) and which is not so obvious on a TV scan.[30] Partial burial by natural scour will further decrease the sonar cross-section. It can be coated with energy-absorbent material, defeating sonar to the point where new detectors, based on laser technology, are reported under active development.[31] It would, in addition, be perfectly feasible to equip a mine with a vibrating mechanism which would enable it to be self-burying in a sandy bottom. To counter this development, Britain is collaborating with France and the Netherlands in the Experimental Parametric Mine Detection System (EPDMS) using a highly stable towed 'fish'.[32] Further developments include discrete frequency selection to gauge the hardness of the bottom and to match correct wavelength with bottom particle size for maximum penetration.

Minefields will acquire a 'self-protect' capability. MCMVs and their associated devices may be targeted or ignored because their signatures and behaviour do not match those of 'legitimate' targets. Several mines may be interconnected to pool their sensor data to generate a more complete picture before discharging warheads akin to guided projectiles. These may be aimed, not to hit, but to detonate beneath the target's keel, like a torpedo, to inflict damage through a rapidly expanding gas bubble.[33]

◄
With its ability to produce nearly maximum thrust in any direction, together with the elimination of shafts, appendages and rudders, or the need for a separate 'creep' propulsion system, the Voith-Schneider is ideal for MCMV applications. Its new silent version is specified for British, American and Swedish minehunter classes. (J.M. Voith GmbH)

▶
Variable-moment magnets (VMM) are bundles of special steel rods whose magnetic characteristics can be altered at will by a surrounding solenoid. Each VMM buoyant body contains 18 such bundles and a considerable number of these can be towed by a minehunter or craft of opportunity (COOP) to sweep through simulation of a typical ship. (Vosper Thornycroft/Marconi)

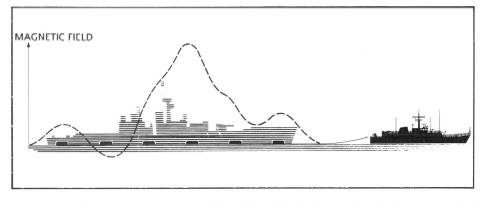

MAGNETIC FIELD

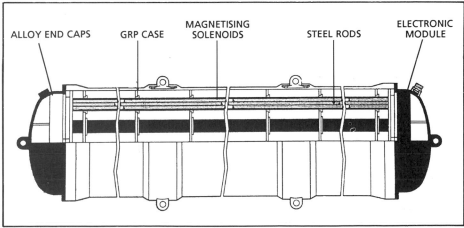

ALLOY END CAPS   GRP CASE   MAGNETISING SOLENOIDS   STEEL RODS   ELECTRONIC MODULE

◄ The Australian inshore mine-hunter *Rushcutter* deploys a PAP mine destructor vehicle. With the inherent stability of the cata-maran hull, all machinery is sited above the waterline, to reduce signatures. Propulsion and manoeuvring is vested in two 360-degree hydraulic units while the operations centre is sited in the topside container for simple removal and maintenance. (Carrington Slipways Pty Ltd)

References and Notes

1. De Stefano. 'The 27-ship Navy', in *US Naval Institute Proceedings*, February, 1988, p.37.
2. Leitenberg. 'Soviet submarine opera-tions in Swedish waters, 1980–6', in *The Washington Papers*, No.128.
3. Vincken. 'Seeminentechnik 1983 am Beispiel der Seegrundmine 80', in *Jahrbuch der Wehrtechnik* 14/84, p.178.
4. *Combat Fleets*, p.695.
5. Royal Navy Equipment Exhibition report, in *IDR*, November, 1987, p.1543.
6. e.g., *see*, Ronarch. 'The Naval Mine', in *IDR*, September, 1984, p.1247.
7. *Combat Fleets*, p.694.
8. Ibid., p.695.
9. Turbe. 'BAMO. The French MCMV', in *IDR*, October, 1987, p.1361.
10. 'The Carrington Minehunter. The RAN's cost effective solution to mine warfare', Publication by Carrington Slipways Pty Limited, Tomago, NSW.
11. Wettern. 'Trawler Minesweepers make a Comeback', in *Defence*, February, 1980, p.70.
12. Pengelley. 'New MCM vehicles for the Royal Navy', in *IDR*, July, 1988, p.824.
13. e.g., *see*, Gillmer. *Modern Ship Design*, p.111.
14. Blunden. 'Mine Countermeasures Hover-craft', in *IDR*, June, 1983, p.840.
15. McLeavy. 'Minesweeping Hovercraft; faster disposal, fewer risks', in *Jane's Defence Weekly*, 27 October 1984, p.742.
16. 'Minesweeping Systems', in *Navy Inter-national*, December, 1986, p.754.
17. 'Gulf test success for Optech airborne laser radar', in *Jane's Defence Weekly*, 27 October 1984, p.742.
18. Dawson and Hewish. 'Mine Warfare – new ship designs', in *IDR*, August, 1988, p.979.
19. Schutz and Fochs. 'Non-magnetic materials in the design of MCMVs', in *MaK Defense Journal*, January, 1984.
20. 'Thorn claims Mine Warfare first', in *Jane's Defence Weekly*, 29 October 1988, p.1088.
21. Cotton. 'The use of Controllable Magnets in Mine Countermeasures', in Issue 1, October, 1988, Marconi Command and Control Systems.
22. Royal Naval Equipment Exhibition report, 'The Vosper Thornycroft Sea Serpent', in *IDR*, November, 1987, p.1542.
23. 'Osborn Acoustic Minesweeping System', British Aerospace Dynamics Group Pub-lication No. NW58/1/84.
24. 'PAP Mark 5 Mine Disposal System', Société ECA Publication.
25. Dicker. 'Mine Warfare now and in the 1990s', in *IDR*, March, 1986, p.293.
26. Pengelley. 'New MCM Vehicles for the Royal Navy', in *IDR*, July, 1988, p.824.
27. 'System 880 for Mine Countermeasures', Racal Marine Systems Publication.
28. 'Minesweeping Systems', in *Navy Inter-national*, December, 1986.
29. *Combat Fleets*, p.181.
30. 'Bofors Coastal Defence Weapons. In-fluence Sea Mines', AB Bofors Publica-tion, PB-07-0149E.
31. Bangen. 'Der Einfluss moderner Tech-nologie auf die Leistung der Seemine', in *Marine Rundschau*, March, 1985, p.164.
32. Hewish, 'High Tech. sweeps in', in *IDR*, November, 1988, p.1474.
33. Bangen. op. cit., p.164.

MERCHANT SHIPPING

*T*oo often overlooked in consideration of the mechanics of seapower is the 'other' service, the Merchant Marine. The major contender for hostilities with the West remains the Warsaw Pact bloc which, it must be emphasized, is a near self-sufficient land power. If, at a stroke, it were to lose its regular and merchant fleets, the loss would probably make little difference to the outcome of a war in which it was engaged. West European economies remain founded on free trade – importing commodities, exporting finished goods. Their main defensive pact is the NATO link with the United States, upon which they are reliant for supplies in any protracted conflict. Merchant shipping is a vital factor, therefore, both in basic existence and in waging war. Its availability and protection should be paramount government considerations, but the hard fact is that, in times of extended peace, lessons learned in the past with the expenditure of so much blood and treasure are ignored for the purely economic impetus of 'market forces'.

Highly pertinent is the manner in which shipping has changed. Still the world's pre-eminent maritime power, Great Britain went to war in 1939 with about 4,000 merchant ships grossing some 21 million tons.[1] By 1948, with the majority of war losses replaced, the total stood at 6,294 vessels of more than 18 million gross registered tons (grt).[2] Booming trading conditions boosted the figures for the late seventies to

3,549 ships of nearly 33 million tons, i.e., fewer ships but of more than three times the average unit size.[3] Just ten years later, this had been reduced to 2,256 ships of about 11.5 million tons;[4] average individual hull size was again at pre-war level, but only half the number were available.

While these figures are for only one flag and may have been calculated using marginally different criteria, they demonstrate two significant trends. First of these was the post-war appreciation of the economics of scale, which resulted in explosive growth in the size of individual hulls. For instance, a typical pre-war tanker was the Anglo-Saxon Petroleum (now Shell) 'Three Twelves', one of whose parameters was a deadweight of 12,000 tons. By the sixties and seventies, the 250,000-tonner had become the 'workhorse' size, with many larger tankers (VLCC) of between 300,000 and 400,000 dwt, and a handful exceeding the prestigious 'half-million tons' capacity, built for long-haul trading. The largest of these, at 553,000 dwt, had the carrying power of no less than 46 of the 'Three Twelves', while employing a crew of less than one of them. It will be apparent that the loss of just one such ship would equate to the total destruction of two large tanker convoys of the Second World War.

Another example is the container ship, the concept of which was not new but 'marinized' only in post-war years. A large vessel serving trunk routes may stow

▶
The towed body of the EDO Model 780 VDS in the process of being streamed. A small sonar, developed originally for the 250-ton SAAR 2s of the Israeli Navy, which lacked ASW ships, this compact sonar system would lend itself admirably to service with craft of opportunity in an emergency. (EDO Corporation)

3,500 or more TEU (twenty-foot equivalent units). If each unit were stuffed with only half its rated capacity, such a ship would be carrying upwards of 55,000 dwt, equivalent to six cargo liners of the immediate post-war era. In peacetime, such a ship is highly efficient, but in war her dependence upon specialist container terminals and complex feeder/distribution networks makes her vulnerable. 'Second generation' container ships were both large and fast, speed being its own protection, but the escalating cost of bunkers stimulated the development of the larger, but slower, 'third generation' which would be more difficult to protect. The second trend illustrated by the figures is that, while Great Britain for a time operated a significant number of super-large ships, the average size has again decreased, as dramatically as the size of the fleet itself. Enormous hikes in the price of crude following the Middle East wars depressed the tanker trades before the wider spectrum of shipping and many VLCCs (Very Large Crude Carrier) found their way to the breakers, many virtually new, rapidly reducing the average unit size of the remaining fleet.

Exposed by the situation was the inordinate level of over-tonnaging in 'good times'. It is reported that, at one stage, of the 566 VLCCs in the world fleet, no less than 304 were surplus to requirements, a situation which depressed freight rates and left many vulnerable before the war upset the trading market.[5] Ship owners, hit by a fast-intensifying depression, looked urgently to savings. Of the rapidly diminishing order book, most went to the cheapest builders, mainly in the Far East. Traditional west European yards, even with the most modern of facilities and realistic working practices, could not compete and went, for the most part, out of business. With them went the invaluable infrastructure of the industry, particularly component supply. A plethora of new ship designs featured much technological innovation, some gimmicky and short-lived, some of lasting value. Slow steaming reduced fuel costs and kept many a ship in breadline employment, but the next obvious saving was in the costs of crewing. Numbers aboard could be reduced by automation, unmanned machinery spaces, 'ship-of-the-future' bridge layouts or by multi-function personnel, but there began an ominous drift from the registers of established flags to those which had rarely seen anything larger than a dhow. Associated financial advantages in taxation, classification fees and, particularly, in the employment of cheaper Third World crews and officers were such that competitors had to match them in order to stay in business. The drift became a stampede, and tonnages under the colours of the traditional maritime powers began to plummet, a slump which shows little sign of abating. There also seems little confidence that shipping under flags of convenience could be recalled to the flags of their owners in the event of emergency.

Traditional maritime powers, as reliant as ever upon their shipping, boast fewer but larger ships, many of which (e.g., chemical carriers, LPG/LNG tankers) are

too specialized to be easily switched to other cargoes if
their designated trade ceased with hostilities. Others,
such as the great, slab-sided Pure Car Carriers (PCC),
with a large number of low-height decks for the cheap
transport of thousands of Nissans and Datsuns, would
make excellent troop-ships, if nothing else. Without the
many yards of earlier times, replacement and repair in
war will be more difficult while, with so many ships
having originated in foreign yards, spares will be near
impossible to obtain.

There are three classes of merchantmen to be
considered: 1, Those that would require convoying and
full defence by an escort; 2, Those that could be
equipped with a measure of self-defence, enabling
them to proceed unescorted in lower-risk areas or add
to the total defence of an escorted convoy; 3, Those that
could be converted to capable auxiliary warships.
War's very unpredictability makes it unwise to state
that convoy networks as elaborate as those developed
in two world wars would never again be required.
Opinions still surface occasionally to the effect that the
convoy concept is outdated and routing of shipping
along patrolled lanes would be more efficient. This
reasoning was, and remains, specious in as much as
predators then know precisely where to find their
targets. The simple beauty of even the largest of
convoys is that, on the broad face of the ocean, it is
virtually as difficult to find as a single ship.

Equally important is the fact that the larger the
convoy the smaller, proportionately, is the number of
escorts required. This apparent paradox is because in
a circular grouping, the number of convoyed ships
increases as the square of the radius, while the
periphery and, hence, the number of escorts, increases
only linearly with the radius. Finally, predators have to
approach the convoy in order to attack it. In ASW
particularly, this saves effort expended in largely
fruitless sweeps. Free-ranging AS groups were effective
during the Second World War only once a sufficient
number of AS ships were available and when the
enemy's codes were being broken to the extent that
futile search was largely eliminated. The old argument
was that large assemblages of ships were easier to spot
and, once located, vulnerable to mass destruction. As
mentioned already, the first assumption is untrue
while, thus far, so has been the second. While a few
convoys took a fearful beating, the principle kept
mercantile losses to within replaceable limits and,
eventually, obliged the enemy himself either to accept
the unacceptable, in an impossible loss rate, or desist.
He desisted.

Today's ships are the more valuable through being
both larger and fewer. Unconvoyed, they would be
subjected to exactly the same type of waylaying as
those of earlier wars. To quote one George Santayana:
'Those who cannot remember the past are condemned
to repeat it.'[6] While some sort of protected convoy
system would be required, however, it would be
dangerous to under-estimate the hazards that each
group would face. Satellite observation is potentially

133

alarming, but, in practice, not easy to undertake in terms of 100 per cent coverage. A typical radar satellite is quoted as being in polar orbit at a height of 800km, with a period of about 100 minutes.[7] As the earth rotates 15 degrees in an hour, it will have turned through 25 degrees between one satellite pass and the next. In the latitude of the vital North Atlantic, this represents about 1,100 miles (1,760km). The Atlantic here is about 45 degrees in width, so the satellite will make only two passes over it per earth revolution. As the device's observable track from the height quoted is only some 62.5 miles (100km) wide, these two passes will cover only 16 per cent of the ocean. More than one satellite is, therefore, required. While low orbits are necessary for acceptable sensor definition, these mean short satellite life and increased vulnerability to anti-satellite (ASAT) systems.

The North Atlantic is plagued also by an endless series of depressions which, while making life uncomfortable for the seafarer, also give cloud cover thick enough to defeat many satellite-borne sensors. Finally, the platform itself has to take what data it has acquired, encrypt it and transmit it so that the enemy can receive and decrypt it in a form sufficiently uncorrupted and fast enough for it to be acted upon. On balance, a convoy still has as much to fear from the marauding long-range maritime patrol aircraft (MPA). Whether this attacks with stand-off weapons or acts just as a beacon to vector other forms of attack is immaterial – it has to be countered. For this purpose, area-defence SAMs can be discounted as the MPA can both observe and attack from beyond their range, besides which SAM-armed escorts will be in short supply and almost certainly in other company. There is, in fact, still an excellent case to be made for the auxiliary carrier, deploying V/STOL fighters for combat air patrol (CAP), Tiltrotor aircraft such as the SV-22 for rapid response to long-range submarine contacts and AS helicopters for the follow-up.

Conventional, fixed-wing aircraft find small carriers' lack of speed a limiting factor, but it is of little consequence to the types of aircraft mentioned. Tankers should make ideal candidates for conversion to auxiliary carriers. The recent Gulf War demonstrated that, even loaded and burning, tankers were difficult to sink; in a water-ballasted and gas-free condition, their sub-division makes them well-nigh indestructable. With the foredeck cleared of its usual

◄
SCADS (Shipborne Containerized Air Defence System) would use equipment supplied by three major manufacturers to convert a 2000 TEU container ship to an auxiliary carrier. Typically, she could deploy six Sea Harriers and two AEW Sea Kings. For defence, she would have all-round Seawolf and decoy coverage, together with surveillance radar and a command centre. (British Aerospace (Dynamics Division))

►
An interesting artist's impression which combines the split-funnel and take-off ramp concept of HMS *Campania* in 1916 with the boom and aircraft idea proposed by the Russian *Shishkov* in 1913! The Skyhook system, equally applicable to a mercantile conversion, is fully up to date, but demonstrates that most good ideas have already been floated. (British Aerospace (Dynamics Division))

►
Skyhook is a proposal that would permit a ship as small as 5500 tonnes and a length of 120 metres to operate a flight of Sea Harriers. The crane head is stabilized to take account of ship motion, leaving the aircraft pilot the task of hovering briefly in the 'capture window' so that the lock-on jack can locate with an airframe strongpoint. (British Aerospace (Dynamics Division))

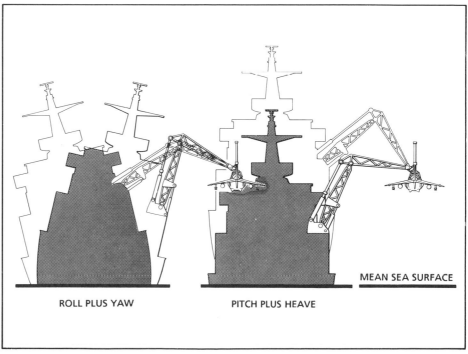

ROLL PLUS YAW   PITCH PLUS HEAVE   MEAN SEA SURFACE

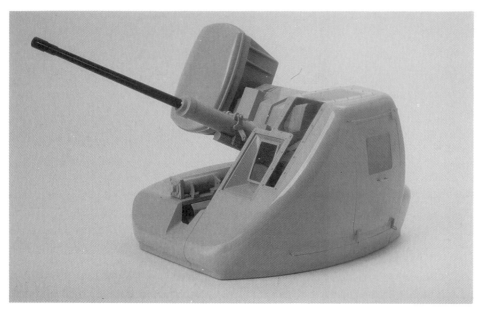

◄

With autonomous sensors, the latest version of the famous Bofors 40mm weighs 4.4 tonnes and can be added to any ship with a minimum of structural alteration. A unique feature is that each round of the so-called Trinity 3P ammunition is programmed in any of six modes, automatically, as the sensor sees its mission function. (AB Bofors)

maze of pipes and manifolds or simply decked-over with a light spar deck, an unobstructed 600 × 140-foot (183 × 43-metre) flying area should not be difficult to achieve on a VLCC, sufficient to give a V/STOL fighter a performance-boosting, rolling take-off. As covered stowage for embarked aircraft would not be simple to improvise, Arapaho-style modular construction should be stockpiled in the period of heightened tension likely to precede hostilities. An interesting possibility would be the fitting of the tanker with a bow sonar; carried deep and steady, it could prove surprisingly effective on ships fitted with bulbs for optimized flow conditions.

If tankers could be transformed into acceptible 15-knot convoy escorts, flight-deck conversions of container ships, with their extra speed, could co-operate more closely with fleet units (a rough analogy is the mercantile-hulled CVEs and the cruiser-hulled CVLs of the Second World War). The American Arapaho system is not new, employing a container ship's same modular ISO dimensions for the prefabrication of lightweight flightdeck panels which can be laid over a tier of topside 'boxes' or directly on to the hatch covers. Aircraft and personnel accommodation, power supplies, fuel, ordnance and maintenance facilities are all 'ISO-friendly' and, theoretically, could be exchanged between one ship, leaving the combat zone, and another about to enter it. The effort, involved, however, remains considerable and further refinement is necessary. Unfortunately the Americans, having evaluated the concept, demonstrated their characteristic distaste for inexpensive expedients and shelved it. Hired by the British Government during the South Atlantic campaign of 1982, Arapaho was put aboard a chartered container ship, but the modification took too long to enable combat evaluation to be achieved. Although cheaply available during depressed peacetime trading conditions, none of these ships could easily be spared from cargo-carrying in war though, in theory, much of their capacity would still be usable, the ships operating in an auxiliary role, like the MACs of the Second World War.

An interesting variation, guaranteeing availability for a specific function, has been suggested by the German builder Bremer Vulkan.[8] Its Seaborne Universal Logistic Scheme (SUNLOG) proposes to exchange the fleet's present force of ten obsolete tenders with an unspecified number of the firm's BV300 multi-purpose hulls. The '300' refers to the TEU capacity,

which containers could be used purely for freight carriage or fitted out for the specific needs of various types of tender. RoRo cargo can be carried up to the weight of a main battle tank (MBT) and the ship's after end is laid out for helicopter operation, though no hangar is provided. The attraction of SUNLOG to tight naval budget-minders is the provision of a force of new ships which would be 12-year chartered from a management company, who would also provide the 18-man mercantile crew. Bonn has yet (early 1989) to decide on the proposal, but BV's estimate of a 20 per cent saving in costs would not appear to be over-attractive and, indeed, seems remarkably slender when it is remembered that each of the present tenders has a 120-strong naval crew and, being 20 or more years of age, is increasingly expensive to maintain. How the SUNLOG layout accords with housing the repair facilities so vital to a tender is also not clear.

A third type of ship suitable for conversion to higher-quality auxiliary carrier is the large RoRo though, here

◀
While classified officially as an Aviation Training Ship, the RFA *Argus* is an extremely useful auxiliary carrier. Her conversion from a medium-sized container ship was more thorough than could be undertaken in time of emergency, and her ability to ship a dozen Harriers is offset by the presence of the massive superstructure that inhibits their use. (Harland & Wolff plc)

again, availability would be at a premium. Of particular value would be those examples whose weather deck was connected to the vehicle deck by large elevator rather than by the more usual ramps. As long as her freeboard deck is kept above the waterline, the large RoRo can absorb action damage, as evidenced by the Atlantic Conveyor which, disabled by two SSMs in the South Atlantic in 1982, succumbed eventually to the fire and explosion of her cargo rather than to foundering. The danger would be that official use would see them loaded more deeply than normal while, to provide an easier motion for aircraft operation, they would be selectively ballasted, which could only be at the expense of their stability reserve.

Merchantmen have traditionally embarked armament and associated personnel in times of war. Indeed the concept of the Defensively-Equipped Merchant Ship enabled the Germans to argue effectively during the First World War that unrestricted submarine warfare was the only possible option because such armament prevented a submarine from surfacing, searching and destroying a ship in accordance with internationally accepted Prize Rules. It had already been pointed out by Fisher, however, that to a sub-

◄
The Offshore Support Vessel (OSV) is very seaworthy, well powered, manoeuvrable and capacious. It is also available in numbers that, in emergency, would see it employed in a wide variety of roles. Here it is seen fitted with the Babcock-Lockheed high-volume mine delivery system which, it is proposed, would be stockpiled in peacetime. (Babcock Energy Ltd)

Very considerable addition to defensive firepower can now be made by man-portable anti-air weapons, which can be deployed by any ship under threat. A Royal Marine squad is seen launching a Javelin missile which, employing line-of-sight tracking, is useful particularly against targets with low IR signatures. Deck letters indicate HMS *Phoebe*, and the intrusive nature of the Type 2031 towed array adjacent to the helicopter deck is noteworthy. (Short Brothers Ltd)

marine, sinking was the only option because her limited crew could not stretch to the provision of prize crews aboard captures.

As future conflicts are hardly likely even to be concerned with the niceties of justification, defensive armament will be vital to survival. The minimum outfit required will be passive/active decoy measures, complete with associated sensors. For the most valuable ships in the highest-risk areas, modularized point-defence missiles will need to be shipped. In this context, it is noteworthy that the *Fort Victoria* AORs, currently under construction, will be the first British fleet auxiliaries to have a permanently assigned armament which may possibly affect their mercantile status. The missile element of this armament is the vertical-launched Seawolf, but British Aerospace are able to supply also a fully modularized, lightweight version for use by merchantmen. An area for peacetime research would appear to be how such sophisticated weaponry can be integrated between escort and escorted to avoid its becoming as great a threat to friend as to foe.

A potentially valuable type of craft is the Offshore Supply Vessel (OSV). Rugged in construction, they have power, manoeuvrability, endurance, capacity and seaworthiness. Many could stand in for the salvage

tugs that have been greatly thinned-out by the depression, notwithstanding the high-risk prizes to be won during the recent Gulf War. OSVs spend much time idling on station so their machinery would appear to complement their layout in suitability for service as specialized towed-array ships, after the manner of the first group of American T-AGOS craft. This would release a frigate's space and time to pursue the business of ASW rather than barrier warfare. Currently, the price of oil is low again and, as the level of new undersea oil exploration has dropped as a result, OSVs are cheaply available. The purchase of a few would be timely.

Merchant shipping, or the lack of it, was the means by which Britain was made to contemplate capitulation in both world wars. Merchant shipping, and profligacy in its employment, was responsible more surely than the dawn of nuclear warfare for the surrender of Japan in 1945. For need of it, Britain would now be more vulnerable in an extended conflict than she has ever been, a situation exacerbated through being tied by treaty to an equally improvident Europe. Co-ordinated policies toward shipping as a national asset, by both Britain and NATO governments, is long, long overdue.

References and Notes
1. Roskill. *'The War at Sea'*, vol.1, HMSO, 1954, p.42.
2. Lloyd's figure as of 1 July 1948. Quoted in *Jane's Fighting Ships*, 1949–50, p.1.
3. Lloyd's figure as of 1 July 1976. Quoted in *Jane's Fighting Ships*, 1977–8, p.481.
4. Quoted in *Combat Fleets*, p.199.
5. Davis. 'A plea for sanity in good times', in *Lloyds Ship Manager*, January, 1989, p.64.
6. Himself quoted by Davis, op. cit.
7. Stefanick. *Strategic Anti-submarine Warfare and Naval Strategy*. Institute for Defense and Disarmament Studies, Lexington, 1987, p.23.
8. Sauerwein. 'SUNLOG. A promising concept for belt-tightening navies', in *IDR*, January, 1989, p.91.

It has been stated that conventional, monohull warship construction represents a mature technology, whose possibilities are well understood and which is unlikely to produce any major surprises in the future.[1] For particular applications, such as to meet requirements for high speed, sea-keeping, low signatures, etc., the unconventional may be a promising alternative. Success is likely to be at the expense of some other quality, however, as warships are a compromise of interactive elements where, to gain on the swings, a designer will surely lose on the roundabout.

An excellent example is the Hovercraft, or Surface Effect Ship. Despite the French Agnes 200, and the associated aim to produce a 1400-ton SES escort by the year 2000, it would seem unlikely to mark the way ahead for mainstream development. Nevertheless, the concept has qualities which, if not applicable to the requirements of every ASW ship, can prove useful in other directions. We have seen, for instance, how its low signatures can be turned to advantage in mine countermeasures (MCM), although the considerable costs would likely be supportable only in war. We have seen, too, how the Air Cushion Vehicle's (ACV) true amphibious nature has been utilized in the highly effective LCAC. To gauge the likelihood of a particular 'exotic' having a practical future, therefore, one has to forecast a real need for its

peculiar qualities. By this yardstick one can, unexpectedly, see a future for the ACV in anti-submarine warfare (ASW). Earlier chapters have discussed the growing significance of the Arctic ice cap to submarine operations, forming a roofed basin within the bounds of which a submarine is currently proof against the majority of methods of detection and attack from the air. As surface ASW operations are ruled out, other submarines are the only feasible ASW platforms, and it will be apparent that these could be assisted considerably by activities carried out 'on the roof'.

During 1985, the American Naval Sea Systems Command (Nav Sea) commenced a study aimed at the definition of an ACV capable of working over the ice cap by the year 2000, ostensibly for 'logistics' and general search and rescue (SAR) missions.[2] Beneath the ice, however, are SSBNs seeking to remain covert and SSNs trying to find them, while the whereabouts of the latter are sought by SSNs supporting the SSBNs . . . It requires little imagination to envisage a network of sensors, suspended through the ice after the fashion of the cartoon fishing Eskimo, continuously monitoring sub-ice activities. Most of the Arctic ice cap lies beyond national boundaries. Not being 'terra firma', this is truly neutral territory – at once an unsinkable aircraft carrier and a surveillance platform accessible to all. In any major

◄
Gas turbine power. The *Mandau* is a 54-metre guided missile patrol boat built by the Korean subsidiary of Tacoma Boat. Her LM-2500 can propel her at 41 knots, but she presents the typical logistics problem of a developing economy. These include Swedish guns, Dutch fire control, French anti-ship missiles, German cruising diesels and an American gas turbine built under licence in Italy. (General Electric Marine and Industrial Engines)

UNCONVENTIONALS, SMALLER WARSHIPS AND FUTURE TRENDS

East-West struggle, the northern ice cap could well become a major issue, yet it has received remarkably little attention.

A world away, literally, is the Antarctic, differing in being an ice-bound continent whose fringes merge near imperceptibly with an extensive skirting of fast sea ice. The land enjoys a precarious neutrality which would be unlikely to survive prolonged activity by any state bent on establishing permanent rights in the teeth of any UN resolution. While territory itself can be a major lure, the growing evidence of yet-unexploited natural wealth could prove irresistible as minerals become scarcer or unobtainable through political embargo.

With even strengthened surface ships able to probe only the outer edges of an ice cap, ACVs have an enormous advantage in being able to travel 'over', rather than 'through'. By ACV is meant the fully-flexible-skirted craft, rather than the rigid side-walled SES, better able to lift over the discontinuities of rafted ice and pressure ridges. The American Arctic ACVs (AACV) were based largely on LCAC technology, but with double-depth skirts. Attempts were made to formulate the relationship between skirt depth, mean obstruction height and distance 'made good', analogous to performance of wheeled vehicles in rough terrain. Useful results included the finding that a 12-foot (3.66-metre) deep skirt was the

minimum practicable. To achieve acceptable stability, this required in turn a minimum inflated cushion beam of about 70 feet (21.33) metres and a consequent unloaded weight of approaching 150 tonnes. Preferred propulsion machinery was the gas turbine, being much lighter than a diesel of similar power, a significant point in a craft which absorbs 86 per cent of its power in lift and less than 12 per cent in forward thrust at 40 knots. A further useful bonus offered by the ACV, at least in thinner ice conditions, is its ability to function as an icebreaker. Traditional monohull ice-breakers have often been fitted with a bow propeller, not for the purposes of manoeuvring but to create a suction beneath the ice ahead, subjecting it to sagging stresses which facilitate its break by the additional weight of the ship.[3] The action of the ACV in continuous breaking appears to be the removal of the lamina of water immediately supporting the ice, causing it to sag, whereupon it is shattered by the cushion pressure of the vehicle. By such means, a small 50-foot (15.2-metre), ten-tonne ACV is quoted as breaking twelve inches (0.3m) of ice at a continuous 14 knot speed.[4]

Far older than the Hovercraft, the Hydrofoil's patents stretch back over a century, so its technology is mature. Like aircraft, hydrofoils rely on lifting surfaces, so are weight-critical. Weight, however, in-

▶
Despite a 2-metre sea, with a wavelength approximating to that of her hull, the American hydrofoil *Pegasus* (PHM-1) rides smoothly at speed where a displacement craft of the same size would have had to slow considerably. The single LM2500 gas turbine drives a water jet propulsor to obviate the need for complex transmission to a conventional propeller. While a mature technology, hydrofoils have yet to find a real role. (General Electric Marine and Industrial Engines)

creases as the cube of a craft's dimensions, whereas lift increases only as the square, which militates against significant growth in size.[5] Indeed, for a similar maximum speed of 35 knots, a 3,000-ton conventional monohull would require only about 90 per cent of the installed power of a hypothetical 3,000-ton hydrofoil. As only FAC-sized craft can be built efficiently as hydrofoils, the genre has limited application because the majority of 'blue-water' fleets simply have no peacetime role for them.

A major drawback is poor endurance. For example, an Italian Sparviero can manage only 400 miles (640km) foilborne at 45 knots, sufficient for the specific aim of contesting a chokepoint as close as the Sicily Channel but too little to allow the craft to be switched flexibly to other missions, a limitation exacerbated by its light armament.[6] Even the flotilla of larger PHMs operated by the US Navy have yet to establish a true role, offering little that more versatile conventional FACs could not offer far more cheaply. Operators of significant inshore fleets, created to counter amphibious assualt, both the Soviets and Chinese have large numbers of hydrofoils and semi-hydrofoils, the latter having foil-supported bows and flat, planing after runs. It is in such specialist applications that hydrofoil interest is likely to remain concentrated.

Mention has already been made of the Small Waterplane Area Twin Hull (SWATH) in connection with both towed array surveillance duties and as an aviation-capable ASW vessel. Both roles exploit the SWATH's main virtues of steadiness and generous deck space. As with all warship compromise, SWATH's qualities have been bought at a·price, so that the concept should be restricted to those areas where its advantages outweigh its drawbacks. Demerits include larger wetted area (increasing skin friction losses),

deeper draught (complicating shallow-water navigation and increasing the hazard from mines) and a tendency to assume large angles of trim and heel on flooding or shifting heavy loads.[7] While highly responsive in the pitch mode, a SWATH can be controlled in this plane by active stabilizers, not possible with conventional monohulls. The necessary wide separation of propulsors confers excellent manoeuvrability. Finally, SWATH's constricted layout encourages the installation of machinery for silent running. An effective arrangement is to site diesel- or gas-turbine-driven alternators in the upper hull, well above the waterline, feeding suitably conditioned electric power by cable down through the slender vertical pylons to compact, reversible and gearbox-free motors sited in the after confines of the restricted lower hulls. Exhaust gases would be vented between the hulls, reducing IR signature, space demands for up- and downtakes and the weight of funnels.

Future propulsion motors will decrease in size with rapid advances in higher-temperature superconducting material technology. A considerable amount of cryogenic engineering is required, but, even now, it is possible to run cooled by comparatively inexpensive liquid nitrogen.

Monohulls still have the capacity for improvements. Pressures to minimize cost through keeping ships small are balanced by others seeking to increase size for the improvement of seakeeping, versatility, etc. Development tends, in any case, to be cyclic, a type increasing in size through succeeding classes until a point is reached where a radical re-assessment is undertaken and a new start made. No class seems immune to this phenomenon.

Few fleets can afford sophisticated frigates in the 3,500-4,000-ton range, considered currently to be the optimum size. There is, therefore, a useful market for

◄

Tailormade. Charged with NATO control of the Baltic exits, the West Germans operate several groups of FACs equipped with anti-ship missiles. The older MM38 Exocet is obviously equal to the engagement ranges while distances involved mean that exotic hull forms are unnecessary. The PUMA (P6122) has received also the long-delayed RAM missile. (German Navy)

▶

The ex-Norwegian minelayer *Gor* (N48) following a hit by an air-launched Mk 2 Penguin, whose warhead size is similar to that of the new Mk 3. It is interesting that the target has been hit right aft; as the ship was, presumably, 'dead', no part was significantly hotter than the remainder to attract the terminal IR homer. FACs carry up to six Penguins. (Norsk Forsvarsteknologi sa)

▶

Warships may, in some areas, become more specialized: to tow arrays for extended periods at low speed, to be exceptionally steady for optimum helicopter operation, to have maximum deck space for a variety of reasons. Both SWATH and catamarans have their merits, the latter being exemplified by the spacious decks of HMAS *Rushcutter*. (Carrington Slipways Pty Ltd)

corvettes which, with a modern range of sensors and weapons, are quite capable warships. The corvette also occupies the useful middle ground between the low-end of the frigate scale and the upper end of the FAC range. Larger FACs, exceeding 60 metres in length, are designed for seakeeping and endurance rather than sheer speed, though can commonly better 36 knots. While carrying a surface armament that could disable several frigates, however, FACs are, in general, vulnerable to air attack, carry few command and control facilities (despite working in flotillas), have no ASW equipment and are still much hostage to weather conditions. Their longer-range SSMs require OTH targeting, so even a single small helicopter can be of great value to a flotilla, and for use also in ESM. Monohulls of this size represent the bottom end of helicopter capability, being unable to operate them in even moderate conditions, but the first so fitted, the 61.7-metre Israeli *Aliyah* type, carry also two types of anti-surface ship missile (SSM) and a 20mm Vulcan-Phalanx CIWS. Probably more practical is the proposed French *Combattante VI*, the latest in a long series of evolving designs and carrying a more general-purpose outfit. Her generous 73-metre hull has a proportionately greater beam than that of the Israeli and, together with the smaller-than-usual SSM battery, yields margins for a Dauphine-2 helicopter, a six-cell Sadral point-defence missile-launcher and, unusually,

six AS torpedoes and a VDS.[8] The *Combattante VI* continues a trend to twin diesel, twin-shaft arrangement. Such corvette-sized craft are powered only for 30 plus knots and, given their extra draught, can absorb the necessary power with only two propellers, thereby saving valuable space.

In many respects, however, vessels of this size, complexity and form have many of the drawbacks of FACs while possessing none of the advantages of full displacement corvettes. The already superior sea-keeping of the latter could well be improved further by the so-called Deep Vee Hull Form, developed recently by Hydro Research Systems.[9] It features a bow section whose keel profile, for about 20 per cent of the waterline length, slopes downward below the normal baseline, achieving maximum draught just abaft the forefoot. A sharp deadrise increases in angle right aft, meeting the ship's sides in a hard knuckle. At the after end are long, fixed skegs.

Although different from the average displacement hull, the 'Deep Vee' is an inexpensive, low-risk modification which improves seakeeping without resort to less-versatile, 'high-tech' exotics. Compared to a similarly sized, conventionally hulled corvette, a Deep Vee ship would experience reduced slamming in head sea conditions, enabling her to maintain speed in worse sea states. Accelerations would, in general, be reduced while more generous waterplanes would enhance

The simply engineered MATRA Mistral point-defence missile can be employed in any of several systems. All-up weight of a round including launch motor is about 24kg so it is easily man-portable. Its maximum speed of Mach 2.5 enables it to intercept aerial targets, between 500 and 5,300 metres. In the event of the IR seeker not functioning, the weapon self-destructs after 15 seconds. (MATRA)

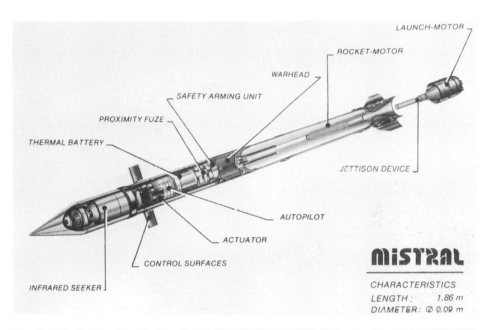

LAUNCH-MOTOR
ROCKET-MOTOR
WARHEAD
SAFETY ARMING UNIT
PROXIMITY FUZE
THERMAL BATTERY
JETTISON DEVICE
AUTOPILOT
ACTUATOR
CONTROL SURFACES
INFRARED SEEKER

MISTRAL

CHARACTERISTICS
LENGTH :   1.86 m
DIAMETER: Ø 0.09 m

Guns, usually drawn from super-annuated stock, would be wholly inadequate for the rapid arming of high-value merchantmen and auxiliaries in future emergencies. Light-weight 'bolt-on' point-defence systems such as the French Sinbad, firing standard Mistral rounds, with one operator and, if required, visually guided would be urgently required. (MATRA)

◄
West Germany's considerable force of Fast Attack Craft (*Bussard*/P.G. 114 shown) poses a considerable threat to any fleet contesting the Baltic exits. Except for the DP qualities of the 76mm guns, however, the armament is conspicuously anti-surface ship. Data links facilitate co-ordinated attack by a flotilla. (Foto-Marincamt)

The Swedish corvette *Stockholm* typifies the highly adaptable solution to naval requirements in restricted waters such as the Baltic. Small and nimble, with low signature levels, she can easily interchange armament between large or ASW torpedoes, anti-surface ship missiles or mines. (AB Bofors)

◄
The *Puma*/P-6122 belongs to a later group of FACs than the *Bussard*. It will be noted that the torpedo tubes and after 76mm gun have been landed in favour of mine rail and the 21-shot Rolling Airframe Missile (RAM). (Foto-Marineamt)

▶
West German technology favours construction in non-magnetic steels rather than composites. This FAC concept is based on an obvious extrapolation of the highly seaworthy SAR-33 hull, and is driven by water jet. (Abeking & Rasmussen)

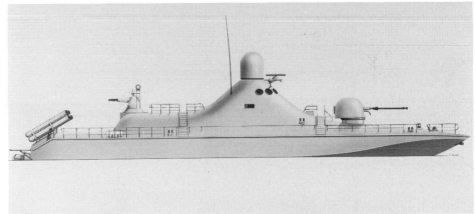

▶
Largest in Lurssen's extensive range of FACs is the 62-metre corvette. It is available in three different configurations, two of them with a helicopter, the third as a surface combatant. Note-worthy is the wide range of optronic control devices and ESM/ECM outfit. The twin-screw propulsion will give a sprint speed of 34.7 knots. (Fr. Lärssen Werft)

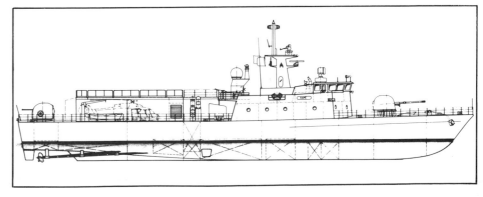

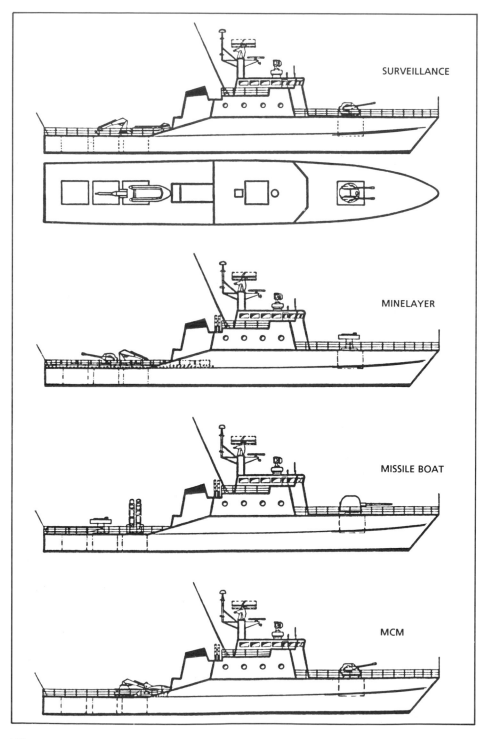

SURVEILLANCE

MINELAYER

MISSILE BOAT

MCM

◀
The Danish Standard Flex 300 design accommodates interchangeable weapons and sensors, configured in standard-sized modules. By this means a 300-ton CODAG craft can be fitted for one of a variety of roles currently undertaken by vessels of several classes, all due for replacement. Such standardization effects considerable savings. (Naval Material Command Denmark)

stability. An earlier design study indicated that an 'aviation configured' 3,500-ton Deep Vee frigate could accommodate 4–6 ASW helicopters, as opposed to only a pair on a conventional, round-bilged form of the same dimensions.[10] This alternative is possible due to the extra buoyancy of the fuller afterbody and a reduction of the L/B ratio from a typical nine to less than eight. It will be no surprise that the author of the design study is one of the 'short-fat' warship lobby, the concept of which has been rejected by the Royal Navy, whose leaner designs are more easily driven, are able to maintain speed in poorer conditions and permit weapon and sensor layouts with a lesser degree of mutual interference. Hydrodynamically, the 'short-fat' proposal would need to plane in order to achieve its claimed performance, requiring unrealistic power in a frigate that has, in any case, little use for high speed. Although the proposal aroused much public debate in the United Kingdom, it was based on flawed assumptions. In the words of one American defence analyst, the concept was not so much scorned as 'having been accorded more respect than it merits'.[11]

As 200-mile exclusive economic zones (EEZ) become more commercially developed worldwide, so will the demand for well-designed weatherly corvettes that, with reduced armament, would double in the Offshore Patrol Vessel (OPV)/Coastguard role. Some states will have claim to vast expanses of ocean, often exposed and, possibly disputed with neighbours. The United Kingdom's annexation of the isolated islet of Rockall extends her offshore zone considerably, but causes dissent with the Republic of Ireland. Where this is unlikely to lead to hostilities, it is a different matter with the likes of the Spratly and Paracel groups in the South China Sea, which are situated over proven natural resources but whose ownership is hotly disputed.

It may be difficult to comprehend Argentina and Chile endlessly rattling sabres over remote islands at their mutual border in the far south of their continent, but a situation such as Egypt controlling the Strait of Tiran and preventing lawful Israeli traffic from using its own port of Aqaba is immediately understandable. Over the period considered by this book, it is far more likely that widespread hostilities be triggered over such flashpoints than by disputes between major power blocs.

As a symbol and tool of political will, the warship is common to both firebrand and peacekeeper alike, but the cost is now so startling that the new phenomenon of leasing has appeared. India's high-profile hire of a Soviet Charlie I SSN has already been mentioned but Denmark, with a firmly pegged defence budget, has been able to uprate her over-aged submarine squadron by the purchase of two refitted German-built, ex-Norwegian boats. Others of the type will become available but Denmark may well need to lease the three more that she needs.

The provision of a common class of frigate to meet the needs of both Australia and New Zealand has prompted extended and pungent debate. Current practice is to acquire only the first-of-class from the country of origin then, through 'technology transfer', to build the remainder in home yards with such technical assistance as has been contracted. Both states have bargained hard for a fair level of participation, but a tightly budgeted New Zealand has, reportedly, been driven to discussing an option whereby Australia funds the twelve-ship programme, with the RNZN leasing four of the completed vessels.[12]

By mid-1989, Pakistan will have taken over, on generous lease terms, eight older American steam frigates, four *Brookes* and four *Garcias*.[13] Labour intensive, they would not have been modernized, but all offer ASROC and four the Standard MR in addition. The transfer is a clear message to India from the USA that naval dominance of the Indian Ocean will be acquired only at considerable cost, while acquisition of a nuclear submarine and a further carrier has been, to some extent, offset. Further units of the classes may go to Turkey and Brazil, the latter again probably to offset recent modern Argentinian naval acquisitions. Proposed transfers to Turkey have already promoted heated protest from fellow NATO member Greece, which sees the move as 'destabilizing'.

The US Navy is itself nearing the end of a far-reaching series of studies, initiated in 1987 by the outgoing Deputy CNO. Known as the 'Revolution at Sea', or 'Navy 21', it seeks to define both the navy and its requirements beyond the turn of the century.[14] The studies embrace three major areas. The Surface Combatant Force Requirements group used analyses of hypthetical engagements and force interaction to determine the number of modern units required to defeat a Soviet threat projected to the year 2010. A Ship Operational Characteristics group defined individual ships and prioritized their systems, while the enigmatically labelled 'Group Mike' set out to identify the technologies that would be required to achieve designated characteristics and to examine how they could best be utilized by ship designers. Having launched these eminently relevant lines of investigation, the Deputy CNO then provocatively stated his belief that a warship should initially be designed completely full of missile-launchers; for any system subsequently added, there should be total justification made as to why that system was more important than those missile-launchers that it necessarily replaced! While tongue-in-cheek, the argument does underline the intentions of a return to heavier armaments. Such a trend is likely to be at the expense of habitation and, as creative comforts are considered important, this must lead to smaller crews, possible only through more extensive automation and labour-saving procedures.

With probably the most exacting task of the three, Group Mike is behind the others in presenting its findings, but one obvious area for scrutiny is the role of artificial intelligence in a naval context. During 1988, in the course of the Gulf War, the American Aegis cruiser *Vincennes* shot down an Iranian airliner. Following the massacre of Marines in Beirut, where the medium was an innocent-looking civilian truck, it is possible that the cruiser was taking no chances but, in the event that it was truly an accident, it shows that Aegis-type ships, soon to be the norm, produce data at such a rate that its presentation in an unambiguous manner, for assimilation by a crew working under the stress of combat conditions, becomes a matter of vital consequence if correct decisions are to be taken. Even as a fighter pilot is becoming something of a passenger in his own cockpit, and some shipboard defensive systems have had to go fully automatic in order to

function, so must non-human decision-making inexorably work upwards through higher levels of responsibility. Data will flow at such a rate that only a computer will be able to act on the efforts of others.

Within the next decade will appear a wider range of options in marine propulsion. Selection of a system depends as much on stealth as on efficiency although for evaluation of 'baseline' designs, uprated machinery or even slight reductions in sustained speeds can make a significant impact on dimensions and cost.[15]. One evaluation of those quoted above featured destroyers driven through under-hull pods, streamlined containments enclosing reduction/reversing gears driving a pair of fixed-pitch, contra-rotating propellers. The general concept is common enough already in such as azimuth thrusters or 'get-you-home' installations, such as the two 720hp propulsors fitted to the single-shaft FFG-7 frigates. What is different is that the propellers, at the forward end of the pods, 'pull' rather than 'push', giving an inflow to the propeller disc that is very clean compared with the confused wake condition usually experienced. How the propulsive power of the propellers is transferred to the hull through the medium of the slender struts supporting the pod is not too clear. Equally unclear is why the pod is powered through a vertical shaft with right-angled drives when, in these days of silent running, direct electrical drive is available, albeit at the expense of size. The proposal shows rafted LM2500 gas turbines, high in the ship, driving directly through shafts, the noise reduction on the one being offset by a gain on the other. If the LM2500s were to drive alternators, four (say) pods could be driven near-silently.

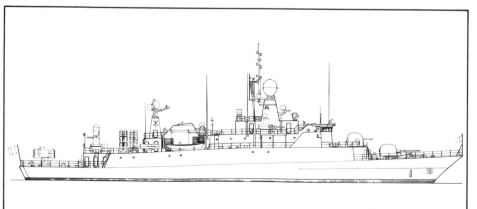

◄
Tacoma Boatbuilding is one of the few American yards building for the export market rather than for the US Navy. It specializes in stylish smaller combatants, such as the Thai *Rattanakosin* sisters. Scaled-up, diesel-driven versions of ACGs built for Saudi Arabia, they are noteworthy for their range of armaments. The Vulcan-Phalanx CIWS will be replaced by a Goalkeeper. (Tacoma Boatbuilding Co.)

▶
More powerful computers, expanding data bases and pain-free stress analysis will see a revolution in ship design. Computer simulation in some areas remains far from realistic and, for instance, the method for checking whether a ship meets shock criteria is still to 'suck it and see'. (Carrington Slipways Pty Ltd)

▼▼
Ultimately, whatever the paths of technology and warship developments, the quality of the crew will prove to be the deciding factor. Whether manning the intricate consoles of the CIC or handling ammunition, watch-keeping on the bridge or maintaining machinery, it is they that will determine the worth of a fleet on 'The Day'. (AB Bofors)

Projected up-rating of the LM2500 from 21,500 to 26,000hp means that only three need be fitted in place of an earlier four, the reduction in total power little affecting maximum speed yet still meeting the cruiser requirement of 5,000nm (9,200km) at 18 knots. Overall, a well-considered package of high-technology machinery can save about 1,750 tons on a DD-963 equivalent, with about 10 per cent on initial cost and, assuming it is reliable, about 12½ per cent on through-life cost. As defence budgets tighten further, such considerations will loom larger in warship design. Neglecting cost and armament, silent operation and endurance are the most important factors in AS frigate design. Submarines are becoming continually quieter

so ships that hunt them must follow suit. At the moment, silence is at a premium, to avoid being heard and to maximize the performance of on- and off-board sensors.

Submarine noise signature control will, however, produce boats either quieter than the ocean's ambient noise level, or emitting sound only at those frequencies that are most rapidly attenuated. Frigates will then probably need to resort to active sensing, reducing the significance of their own stealth and, perhaps, restoring endurance as the primary asset. While the so-called CODLAG propulsion of the British Type 23 (*Norfolk*) class is probably the quietest available, it is bought at a price, including extra weight and bulk.

◄
By virtue of its vectored-thrust engines, an airship can not only hover, but hover in the same place, irrespective of weather. It can thus simply lower and retrieve a boarding craft by winch. An airship destined for ASW in war can therefore be used for EEZ policing in peace. Note the French markings. (Airship Industries (UK) Ltd)

►
Competent instruction and effective 'after sales service' are as important to export sales as having a good product. Here, staff from Wallop Industries give field training in the intricacies of the lightweight Barricade decoy launcher to the crew of a patrol boat of a Middle-Eastern navy. (Wallop Industries)

►►
The 900-tonne capacity gantry crane at Newport News Shipbuilding lifts the complete superstructure block of the nuclear carrier *Theodore Roosevelt*. Such construction techniques owe much to those developed for the rapid building of commercial vessels, an area which has still more to offer. This shipyard is the sole source of the US Navy's nuclear carriers, which must be a strategic headache. (Newport News Shipbuilding)

These features are not likely to be reduced in the near future by even a combination of cryogenics and new superconductors, nor such as segmented-magnet motors.[16] Efficiencies could, however, be improved by using AC, rather than DC propulsion systems.

Gas turbines are being gradually adapted to be more in accord with a warship's operational profile. If running at optimum efficiency is possible, machinery life and mission endurance will be increased. None the less, the same source quotes the statistic that, for 90 per cent of her time at sea, the average ship utilizes less than 20 per cent of her installed propulsive power.[17] As this pattern is little likely to change, and silence may prove to be less golden than before, the diesel, which is efficient over a wide range of power, stands an excellent chance of becoming the standard prime mover for medium-sized ships. Such choice would also be linked to national preference, for instance the Italian *Maestrale* (CODOG) and the Dutch *Karel Doorman* (CODAG) frigates feature licence-built or imported gas turbines teamed with indigenous diesels in 'or' and 'and' combinations.

In the near future, the machinery scene is likely to be dominated by refinements and variations on existing technologies, despite exotic research such as that being pursued by the Japanese in superconducting electro-magnetic propulsion. Ultimately, they predict, this will produce the 100-knot ship by building, in effect, a linear stator into the ship's hull and accelerating water past it in place of a conventional arma-

ture. Should such speeds prove feasible, hulls and surface finishes will need to change. In this context, it is reported that British Maritime Technology in co-operation with the Admiralty Research Establishment, has experimented successfully with a vehicle, known as Moby-D, that has a skin corrugated 'with microscopic parallel grooves called 'riblets'.[18] Borrowed from sharkskin, the idea is to reduce turbulent flow and, thus, energy expended in overcoming drag. A significant 3 per cent improvement was demonstrated, though the difficulties of extrapolating the technique to the scale of a warship's hull would be considerable.

Electro-magnetic propulsion would eliminate propellers, shafts and associated appendages, but would still require rudders or other means of steering. It is

tempting to speculate on the possibilities of water jet propulsion which, even with current technology, eliminates propellers and steering surfaces altogether. Most efficient at high speeds, water jets are currently confined to such as hydrofoils, where their operation obviates the need for complex drive shafting.[19] Such units are noisy, but have not had the benefit of several generations of refinements in noise reduction. Not long ago, the Voith Schneider cycloidal propeller was also labelled 'noisy' and not considered by warship designers. Once its unique qualities were recognized for use in such as the British Sandown class of single-role minehunter, however, it was soon quietened sufficiently to meet a demanding specification. One feels that, to a great extent, only prejudice stands between

A feature of developing NATO capabilities is the creation of homogeneous task groups, able to deploy anywhere as required. The Netherlands fleet has completed two *Kortenaer*s as air defence escorts/flagships, enabling the formation of four groups. Here, the *Witte de With* (F813) is seen leading the frigates *Kortenaer* (F807) and *Jan van Brakel* (F825), and the replenishment ship *Zuiderkruis*. (Netherlands Navy)

the water jet and a future in larger specialist warships.

Measures designed to defeat the anti-ship missiles are subtly changing the appearance of warships. Eyes accustomed to the squared-off styles of recent years will become attuned to increasingly rakish looks with rounded and sloping surfaces. Finish may be less attractive as areas are built from, or clad with, radar absorbent and/or protective composites. Funnels may disappear as exhausts are directed to below the water-line to reduce heat emission.

By the turn of the century a frigate may well be sporting a profile more akin to that of a sheikh's motor yacht than a warship, but the shape of her armament is less predictable. Much will, of course, be concealed below in vertical-launch missile farms, but ancillary weaponry is a different matter. Laser mountings, covering the full 360 degrees, will likely be the unobtrusive means of ranging accurately. While not capable of directing energy sufficient to cause material destruction, they should be quite capable, if stabilized to an adequate degree, of also damaging or destroying an opponent's optical sensors, including the eyes of unwary observers.

New research in the areas of electrical generation and storage, as well as superconductivity, is making possible the construction of electro-magnetic weapons such as the Rail Gun. During the period under consideration such a device will almost certainly be evaluated ashore, its transition afloat being then a matter of time. Briefly, when a circular electric coil is energized, the resultant magnetic field exerts a powerful component force axially through the coil's centre. A suitable projectile would be accelerated by such a force and, if a series of coils were to be set up on a common axis, and energized sequentially as the projectile passed, the latter's velocity would be boosted to levels far greater than those obtainable with a conventional gun.[20] The weapon's name is derived from the projectile needing to be guided only by a rail rather than a barrel. Special impulse generators provide current surges of millions of amperes in research aimed initially at producing firing velocities of 2,000 metres/second and, ultimately, double this figure (cf. the muzzle velocity of a typical conventional gun, say, 1,300metres/second). Such velocities confer enormous energy to a projectile, whose mass could be considerably reduced, while the reduced time of flight would greatly improve accuracy.

Beyond the Rail Gun are more esoteric forms of electro-magnetic weapon, whose practicality and form can only be surmised. Research work, for instance, is being conducted on high-power, microwave pulse devices which could prove destructive both to sensors and human tissue.[21]

Conventional medium-calibre guns will, however, be still fitted to our hypothetical future frigate, having earned their keep through adaptability and cost-effectiveness. Guided projectiles will become general. Martin-Marietta's continued development of the laser-guided Copperhead supports the military 155mm (6-inch) gun, a calibre all but extinct at sea. The technology gained should, however, be eventually applicable to the naval 5-inch projectile, the difference in whose bulk is rather greater than the straight comparison of calibres would suggest. Copperhead is currently being tested with a more effective tandem warhead while, under development, is a combined IR/laser seeker.[22]

▶
Copperhead is designed to be fired from Army 155mm howitzers, homing on to a target designated by laser energy from a forward platform such as a helicopter or RPV. Though the American Navy Guided Projectile programme was cancelled in 1988, continuing development of Copperhead is technologically relevant to a smaller-calibre naval round. (Martin Marietta)

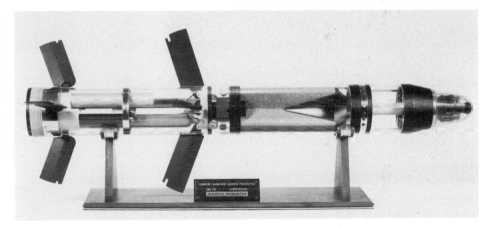

▶
A Copperhead guided projectile in terminal dive on a military target. It takes an average of 300 conventional rounds to destroy a similar target. Laser designation would remove much of the difficulty of laying a naval gun situated on a moving platform. The projectile is being currently improved through the addition of an IR seeker. (Martin Marietta)

▲
The medium-calibre gun will remain a standard weapon; the 5-inch/127mm being likely to become more popular as the first to benefit from laser-guided ammunition. Guns are versatile and cost-effective, and can engage targets unsuitable for missiles. The weapon being fitted here is a 127mm, 54 calibre OTO MELARA. (Blohm & Voss)

Such American ammunition is apparently best suited to precision shore bombardment, but European manufacturers are seeking to 'correct' (as opposed to 'guide') 76mm rounds of the rapid-fire OTO-Melara for the purpose of extending close-in AA fire from the effective limits of a CIWS (say 800 metres) out to about 3,000 metres. British Aerospace and the Dutch HSA company are working on the problem, with the Dutch apparently in the lead at the moment with their Correctable Ammunition System (CORAS). This is 'viffed' in flight by vectored puffs of pressurized gas, stored within the projectile.[23] Control depends on a simple radio link, but, while jammable, is claimed to cost less than a quarter of a point-defence missile system.

Fleet composition will change continuously as a result of evolving strategies. As already noted, the Japanese Navy is once again growing rapidly as it shoulders greater responsibility for home defence. Shortfalls in NATO, due to emergency deployments elsewhere, have seen a German naval squadron deploy for the first time in the Mediterranean. At the time of writing the Bundesmarine was reported to be designing its projected Type 212 submarines around Atlantic operations from the mid-1990s.[24]

Politics and budgets, technological developments and perceived threats steadily mould a fleet as climate does the landscape. Only outright war disturbs this steady trend to any marked degree and, short of this, seapower at the threshhold of a new millenium will comprise much that is familiar today.

References and Notes

1. Gates. *Surface Warships*. Brassey, London, 1987, p.174.
2. Kolescr and Lavis. 'Air Cushion Vehicles for Arctic Operation', in (US) *Naval Engineers' Journal*, November, 1988, p.59.
3. e.g., *see* Crenshaw. *Naval Shiphandling*. US Naval Institute Press, Annapolis, 1963, p.306.
4. Lavis. 'Air Cushion Craft', 'Modern Ships and Craft', reprint by (US) *Naval Engineers' Journal*, February, 1985, p.288.
5. e.g., *see* Gillmer. *Modern Ship Design*. US Naval Institute Press, Annapolis, 1981, p.299.
6. *Combat Fleets*, p.310.
7. McClure and Gaul. 'Let "SWATH be SWATH"', in *US Naval Institute Proceedings*, April, 1987, p.106.
8. Details from Lenton. 'Fast Attack Craft', in *Navy International*, March, 1989, p.106.
9. Kehoe, Brower and Serter. 'Deep-vee hulls; Improved seakeeping for small, fast warships', in *IDR*, November, 1986, p.1649.
10. Serter. 'An Air-Capable Frigate for NATO', in *IDR*, August, 1984, p.1114.
11. Norman Friedman. 'S90; a US viewpoint', in *Jane's Defence Weekly*, 11 October 1986, p.813.
12. 'New Zealand may lease ANZAC frigates', in *Jane's Defence Weekly*, 29 April 1989, p.723.
13. 'Pakistan Navy Frigate Deliveries', in *Navy International*, March, 1989, p.142.
14. Pariseau and Gunn. 'Increasing Ordnance on Target in the Revolution at Sea', in (US) *Armed Forces Journal International*, April, 1989, p.59.
15. Rains. 'Design Trade offs for Destroyers', in (US) *Naval Engineers' Journal*, May, 1983, p.234.
16. 'Electric cruise drive for frigates', in *Marine Propulsion*, November, 1983, p.27. Article derived from paper 'Frigate Electric Cruise Propulsion and Ship's Service Power from a Common Distri-bution Network' by Kastner, Davidson and Hills. SNAME, New York.
17. Kastner, Davidson and Hills. ibid.
18. Highfield. 'Shark technology found to reduce drag on aircraft', in London *Daily Telegraph*, 14 January 1989.
19. e.g., *see* Gillmer. *Modern Ship Design*. US Naval Institute Press, Annapolis, 1981, pp.128–9.
20. Witt and Loffler. 'The Electro-Magnetic Gun – Closer to Weapon System Status', in *Military Technology*, May, 1988, p.80.
21. Liebig. 'Radio Frequency Weapons: Strategic Context and Implications', EIR Special Report. Wiesbaden, 1988, p.43.
22. 'Improved warhead, new seeker for Copperhead', in *Jane's Defence Weekly*, 24 December 1988, p.1601.
23. 'CORAS uprates shipgun hit capability', in *Jane's Defence Weekly*, 6 May 1989, p.822.
24. Elliott. 'W(est) German submarines for Atlantic?' in *Jane's Defence Weekly*, 6 May 1989, p.783.

INDEX